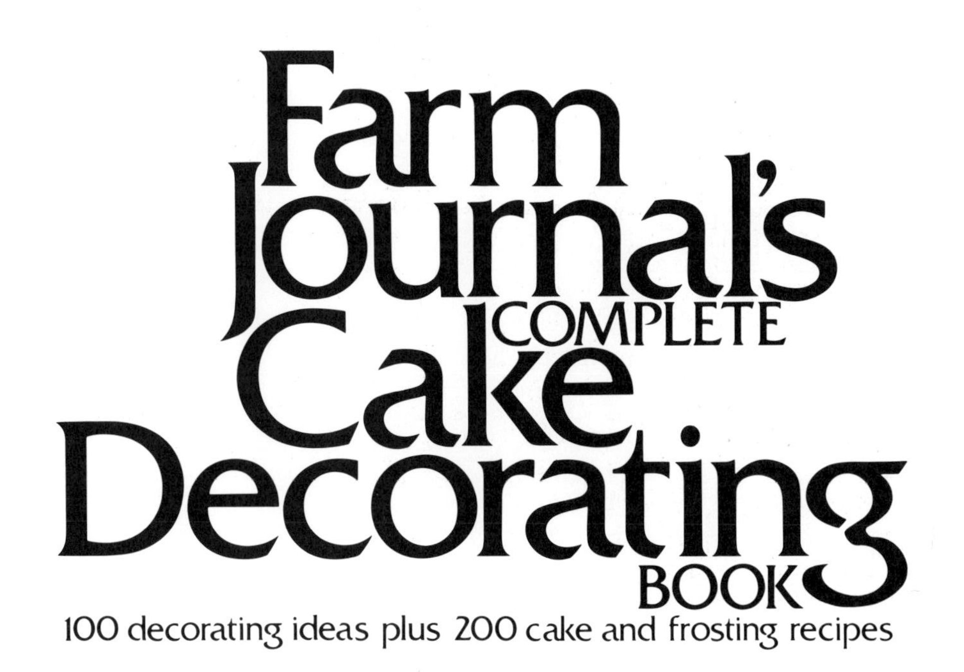

100 decorating ideas plus 200 cake and frosting recipes

By the Food Editors of Farm Journal

Patricia A. Ward, Editor
Ronnie J. Fulvi, Associate Editor
Joanne G. Fullan, Assistant Editor

Farm Journal, Inc.
Philadelphia, Pennsylvania

Distributed to the trade by
Doubleday & Company, Inc.
Garden City, New York

OTHER FARM JOURNAL COOKBOOKS

Farm Journal's Country Cookbook

Homemade Bread

America's Best Vegetable Recipes

Homemade Ice Cream and Cake

Country Fair Cookbook

Farm Journal's Homemade Snacks

Farm Journal's Best-Ever Recipes

Farm Journal's Great Dishes from the Oven

Farm Journal's Freezing and Canning Cookbook

Farm Journal's Friendly Food Gifts from your Kitchen

Farm Journal's Choice Chocolate Recipes

Farm Journal's Cook It Your Way

Farm Journal's Complete Home Baking Book

Farm Journal's Meal & Menu Planner Cookbook

Farm Journal's Speedy Skillet Meals

Farm Journal's Best-Ever Cookies

Farm Journal's Best-Ever Pies

Farm Journal's Picnic & Barbecue Cookbook

Book design: Michael P. Durning

Photography: William Hazzard/Hazzard
Studios, pp. 29-30; 31 (top); 32; 81-84;
101-104; 137-140
Michael P. Durning p.31 (bottom)

Illustrations: Len Epstein

Library of Congress Cataloging in Publication Data

Farm journal's complete cake decorating book.

Includes index.
1. Cake decorating.
2. Icings, Cake.
I. Farm journal (Philadelphia, Pa.: 1956)

TX771.F28 1983 641.8'653 83-5528
ISBN 0-385-18376-3

Printed in the United States of America

Contents

1 First the Cake

A lovingly made and beautifully decorated cake is a work of art—one that anyone can create and everyone will enjoy. A homemade fudge cake swirled with chocolate butter cream frosting or a feather-light sponge cake simply decorated with fruit or flowers can make any day a special occasion, and a cake designed to celebrate a birthday or recognize an achievement can create memories that last a lifetime.

With a little imagination and a lot of willingness to experiment, you'll discover that you can make cakes you like better than any you'll see on a bakery shelf. When you bake a cake yourself, you know that the ingredients are fresh and pure, the choice of flavors is yours, and you can add a special ingredient that can't be purchased at any price—your own personality.

Every cake and frosting recipe in this book has been double-checked and tasted in Farm Journal's own Test Kitchens. If you follow these recipes to the letter, choosing your favorite flavors and decorating the cakes in the colors you like best, you'll be rewarded with marvelous desserts and the sense of satisfaction that comes from creating something that's truly yours.

GUIDELINES FOR CAKE BAKING

Any cake can look special if you add a little something extra to decorate it, and the choice of cakes is wide. In this chapter you'll find recipes for butter cakes—white cakes, yellow cakes, chocolate cakes, spice cakes, pound cakes, and dark fruitcakes heavy with nuts and raisins; foam cakes—angel food, sponge and chiffon cakes; and cakes that can be microwaved.

Most of the cakes in this book are baked in standard-size pans in five basic shapes: round, square, rectangular, tube or loaf.

Any cake may be baked up to three months in advance of decorating day and frozen in aluminum foil; just be sure to thaw the cake completely before decorating. If you keep in mind the baking tips that follow, you'll have a perfect foundation for decorating.

Ten basic baking tips

*PREHEAT THE OVEN: Do this before you begin to mix your cake to be sure it will be the right temperature when the batter is ready. Most ovens need 10 to 15 minutes to preheat.

*USE THE CORRECT INGREDIENTS: You'll notice that some of these recipes call for "flour," and others specify "cake flour." When the recipe simply specifies "flour," all-purpose flour will do the job. All-purpose flour is a blend of soft and hard wheats; cake flour is made only from soft wheat and produces a more delicate texture. Most of our angel food and chiffon cakes are made with cake flour.

Several kinds of shortening are used in these recipes, including butter and margarine. Do use the one specified; but don't use whipped butter or the soft and spreadable margarine sold in tubs. The choice between sweet and lightly salted butter is yours.

*ASSEMBLE THE INGREDIENTS IN ADVANCE AND MEASURE CAREFULLY: A little too much of this or that will upset the delicate balance of ingredients that's needed. Shortening, eggs and milk should be at room temperature in order for the cake to reach its maximum volume.

*USE THE RIGHT BAKING PANS: If the pan is too small, the finished cake may have a lip around the edge; too large a pan will reduce the volume of the cake.

Shiny metal pans produce the prettiest cakes because they reflect heat away from the cake and result in a light brown crust. Dark metal pans absorb more heat and produce darker, harder crusts.

*PREPARE THE BAKING PANS: Most cakes are baked in pans greased with shortening. (The exceptions are angel food cakes, chiffon cakes and some sponge cakes—ones that are baked in tube pans. These cakes need to be baked in pans that are spotlessly clean and free of any oil or grease so that the cakes can rise high in the pans.)

Layer cakes are easier to remove from baking pans if the pans have been greased, then lined with waxed paper.

*FOLLOW THE RECIPE: It goes without saying that shortcuts in baking can change the final result. When a recipe specifies "cream together butter and sugar," the sugar should be added gradually while beating continually; this will produce a mixture that's light and fluffy. Our angel food cake recipes ask that you sift the flour and sugar three or four times, and it really does make a difference in the lightness of the cake.

*SPREAD THE BATTER EVENLY: Using a rubber or metal spatula, spread the batter from the center of the pan to the edges. If you're making a layer cake, be sure to divide the batter equally so that the layers will bake evenly. (If you want to be precise, use a scale.) Then tap the bottoms of the pans lightly on a countertop to break large air bubbles in the batter.

*ARRANGE THE PANS PROPERLY: Use the middle rack for most cakes, and the lower rack for angel food cakes. When you bake a layer cake, arrange the pans on the rack diagonally and be sure they don't touch each other or the sides of the oven.

*DON'T PEEK! Once you've put a cake in the oven to bake, don't interrupt it; if you open the oven door, the cake may sink. Wait until just five minutes before the end of the time specified in the recipe and then test for doneness as directed. If the cake tests done, immediately remove it from the oven.

*COOL CAKES AS DIRECTED: A warm cake is very delicate, so most of our recipes suggest cooling the cake in the pan on a rack for 10 minutes. After standing for about 10 minutes, a cake becomes firm enough to remove from the pan, but if you wait longer, the cake may stick when you try to remove it from the pan.

Before removing, loosen the edges with a spatula; then turn the cake onto a rack, remove the waxed paper, and invert on a second rack so that the cake is right side up.

Angel food cakes and chiffon cakes, as well as sponge cakes baked in tube pans, should be cooled in their pans while placed upside down on a funnel or bottle.

Never frost a cake until it's completely cool; a warm cake will melt frosting, and most cakes take at least an hour to cool. If you freeze a cake before decorating it, let it thaw thoroughly before you begin to decorate.

Equipment you'll need

*BAKING PANS

Most of the cakes in this book are baked in these standard-size baking pans; 8 or 9″ round; 8 or 9″ square; 13x9x2″; a 15½x10½x1″ jelly-roll pan; a 9x5x3″ loaf pan; or a 10″ tube pan.

*CARDBOARD

Bases of heavy corrugated cardboard make it easy to transfer cakes from the decorating surface to serving plates, and you'll also find cardboard bases especially handy if you need to refrigerate a cake because they take up less space than most plates. You can cut your own bases from cardboard boxes. Just cut a base about an inch larger than your cake; for example, a 10″ round is suitable for either an 8″ or 9″ round cake.

*COOLING RACKS

Any cake except a foam cake should be cooled on a rack so that air can circulate around it. Two sizes of wire cooling racks are handy—a 10″ square and a 14x10″ rectangle—but you can substitute oven racks or the removable burners from your range.

*ELECTRIC MIXER

A heavy-duty mixer makes quick work of beating cake batter and icings. We use mixers on stands in Farm Journal's Test Kitchens, but a portable model will do.

*FLOUR SIFTER OR SIEVE

A sifter or large sieve is needed to sift dry ingredients before measuring and to mix baking soda or baking powder with other dry ingredients. A small sieve is handy for sprinkling confectioners' sugar or cocoa over a cake to create a simple decoration.

*KNIFE

A long, sharp kitchen knife with a serrated edge is needed to split cake layers, to level cake layers and to cut cakes for serving. If you use a back-and-forth sawing motion when cutting a cake, you'll get more even slices.

*MEASURING CUPS

For accurate measurement, you'll need two types of measuring cups to measure dry and liquid ingredients. Never use one type of measuring cup for another.

Sets of nested metal or plastic cups are used to measure dry ingredients. They're usually sold in sets of four: ¼ cup, ⅓ cup, ½ cup and 1 cup.

Liquids are measured in glass or plastic cups with cup measurements marked on the side. These cups are available in 1-cup, 1-pint and 1-quart sizes.

*MEASURING SPOONS

A basic set of four is essential to measure the ingredients in these cake and frosting recipes: ¼ teaspoon, ½ teaspoon, 1 teaspoon and 1 tablespoon.

*MIXING BOWLS

Large mixing bowls for beating cake batter and icings are essential: one 1½-quart bowl and one 4-quart or larger bowl. We like stainless steel or glass mixing bowls because they're easier to keep free of grease.

*OVEN THERMOMETER

The temperature of most ovens will vary, so it's best to double-check the temperature before baking. Place the thermometer in the oven and preheat your oven; then check the thermometer before putting your cake into the oven and adjust the setting as needed.

*SPATULAS

A flexible rubber or plastic spatula is handy for folding in egg whites and for scraping cake batter from the sides of the mixing bowl.

You'll also need at least one flexible metal spatula to frost cakes, smooth the icing, and fill decorating bags with frosting. A spatula about 8 or 10″ long is best for filling decorating bags. Most people prefer a longer spatula, about 12″ long, to frost cakes and smooth icing, but some decorators prefer the smaller ones.

*TIMER

For best results, you'll need a timer. Always set it for five minutes *less* than the baking time given in the recipe and then test for doneness. When using microwave recipes, test for doneness one minute before the total time specified, or when a range is given, check the cake after the *minimum* time given.

Storing and freezing cakes

A cake is at its best the same day it's made, but most cakes can be stored at room temperature for one or two days if they're placed under a cake cover or under a large inverted bowl. Cut surfaces should be covered with aluminum foil or plastic wrap.

Cakes frosted with boiled or 7-minute frostings are best stored at room temperature because these frostings toughen when chilled, but on very hot or humid days it's better to refrigerate frosted cakes to prevent the frosting from softening. Of course, any cake made with whipped cream or a cream filling should be refrigerated.

Both frosted and unfrosted cakes can be frozen for several months. To freeze an unfrosted cake, wrap the cake in aluminum foil or plastic wrap or place it in a plastic bag and freeze for up to four months. Let the cake thaw at room temperature about an hour before frosting or serving.

To freeze a frosted cake, place the cake on a baking sheet or a sheet of cardboard and freeze until firm. Then wrap in aluminum foil, plastic wrap or place in a large plastic bag and freeze up to three months. To serve, let thaw at room temperature about an hour before serving.

Cutting the cake

It's easy to cut a cake if you use the right knife: a sharp, long-bladed knife with a serrated edge. To cut any cake, use a sawing motion. After each cut, wipe the crumbs from the blade with a damp cloth or rinse the knife in warm water.

Normally, we estimate that an 8″ round layer cake or a 9″ angel food cake will serve ten persons, and that you'll get a dozen servings from an 8″ square layer cake, a 9″ round layer cake, or a cake baked in a 10″ tube pan. Plan on 16 standard-size servings from a 9″ square layer cake, a 13x9x2″ cake or any cake baked in a jelly roll pan.

How to get more servings from your cake

When you're serving a cake that's extra-rich or accommodating a few extra guests, you can divide your cake into a much larger number of equal portions by cutting it creatively.

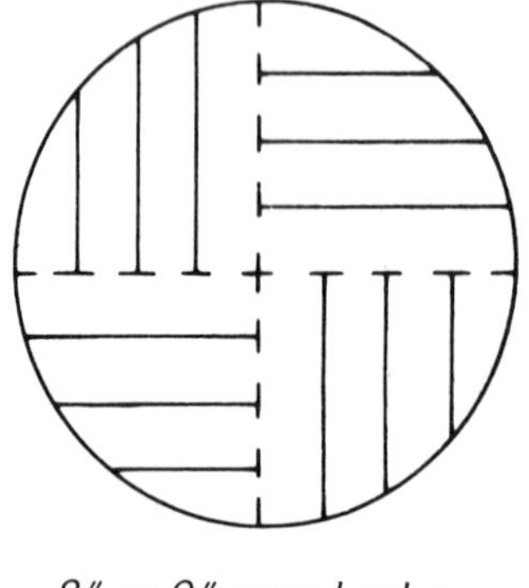

8″ or 9″ round cake serves 16

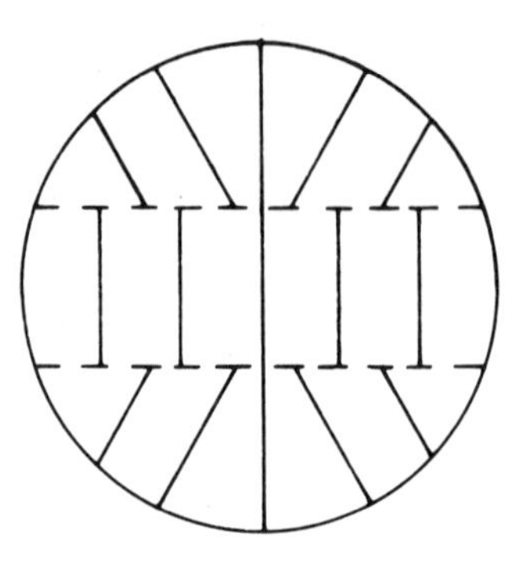

8″ or 9″ round cake serves 18

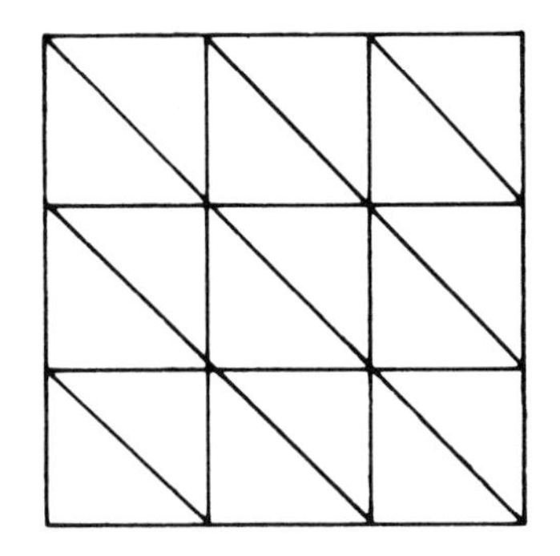

8″ or 9″ square cake serves 18

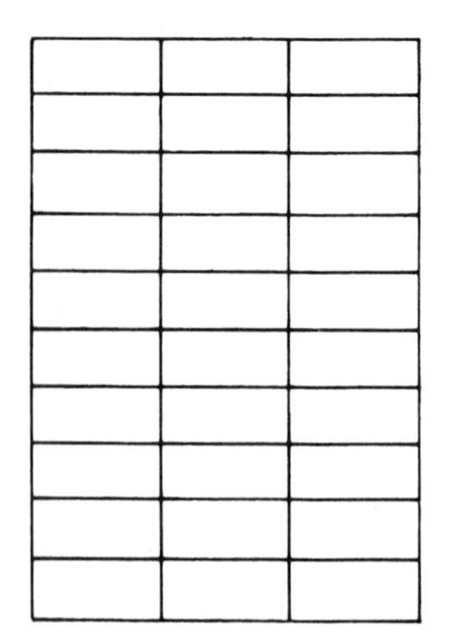

13x9x2″ or 15½x10½x1″ cake serves 30

RECIPES

There are two big categories of cakes, each with its own tempting array of delicious variations: butter cakes, or cakes made with butter, margarine or shortening of some kind, and foam cakes—angel food, sponge and chiffon.

Butter cakes include a vast array of white cakes, yellow cakes, spice cakes and cakes flavored with such diverse ingredients as chocolate, pumpkin, applesauce, lemon and carrots. Pound cakes and fruitcakes are butter cakes, too. Foam cakes are the lightest cakes of all, and each one differs from the other.

To help distinguish between all the choices available in this chapter, we've organized our recipes into these categories: basic butter cakes; fruitcakes; pound cakes; angel food cakes; sponge cakes; chiffon cakes; and cakes that can be microwaved.

Basic butter cakes

Originally these cakes were always made with pure creamery butter, but several kinds of shortening, including margarine, are now used in these recipes. The ingredients for these cakes are combined in several different ways, and each recipe tells which method to use.

The fastest method is the one bowl method, used for quick and easy recipes such as our Hurry-Up Cake and Feather-light Yellow Cake. In these recipes, the flour and shortening are beaten together with other ingredients. In the conventional method, the shortening and the sugar are creamed together before the dry ingredients are added alternately with the liquids. This method does take a little longer, but it results in a cake with a more fine-grained texture.

Basic White Layer Cake

(12 servings)

2⅔ c. sifted cake flour
2¼ tsp. baking powder
½ tsp. salt
1 c. butter or regular margarine
1¼ c. sugar
4 egg whites
1 tsp. vanilla
⅔ c. cold water
7-Minute Penuche Frosting (recipe follows)

Sift together cake flour, baking powder and salt. Set aside.

Cream together butter and sugar in bowl until light and fluffy, using an electric mixer at medium speed. Add egg whites, one at a time, beating well after each addition. Blend in vanilla.

Gradually add dry ingredients alternately with cold water to creamed mixture, beating well after each addition, using low speed. Pour batter into 2 greased and waxed paper-lined 9″ round baking pans.

Bake in 325° oven 25 to 30 minutes, or until a cake tester or toothpick inserted in center comes out clean. Cool in pans on racks 10 minutes. Remove from pans. Cool on racks.

Fill and frost sides and top of cake with 7-Minute Penuche Frosting.

7-Minute Penuche Frosting

2 egg whites
¾ c. sugar
¾ c. packed brown sugar
⅓ c. water
¼ tsp. cream of tartar
1 tsp. vanilla

Combine all ingredients except vanilla in top of double boiler. Beat 1 minute, using an electric mixer at high speed.

Place over simmering water. Cook 7 minutes, beating constantly at high speed, until soft glossy peaks form.

Remove from hot water. Blend in vanilla.

Silver White Cake

(12 servings)

2¼ c. sifted cake flour
1½ c. sugar
3½ tsp. baking powder
1 tsp. salt
½ c. shortening
1 c. milk
1 tsp. vanilla
4 egg whites
Clear Lemon Filling (recipe follows)
White Mountain Frosting (see page 62)
1½ c. flaked coconut

Sift together cake flour, sugar, baking powder and salt into bowl. Add shortening, ½ c. of the milk and vanilla. Beat 2 minutes, using an electric mixer at medium speed.

Add remaining milk and egg whites; beat 2 minutes more. Pour batter into 2 greased and floured 9" round baking pans.

Bake in 350° oven 30 minutes, or until a cake tester or toothpick inserted in center comes out clean. Cool in pans on racks 10 minutes. Remove from pans. Cool on racks.

Fill cake layers with Clear Lemon Filling. Frost sides and top of cake with White Mountain Frosting. Sprinkle sides and top with coconut.

Clear Lemon Filling

¾ c. sugar
3 tblsp. cornstarch
¼ tsp. salt
¾ c. water
1 tblsp. butter or regular margarine
2 tblsp. lemon juice
2 tblsp. grated lemon rind

Combine sugar, cornstarch and salt in small saucepan; mix well. Stir in water. Cook over medium heat, stirring constantly, or until mixture comes to a boil. Boil 1 minute.

Remove from heat. Stir in butter, lemon juice and lemon rind. Cool. Makes 1 c.

Never-Fail White Cake

(16 servings)

4 egg whites
1½ c. sugar
2½ c. sifted cake flour
3 tsp. baking powder
½ tsp. salt
½ c. shortening
1 c. milk
2 tsp. vanilla
Creamy Pineapple Frosting (see page 60)

Beat egg whites in bowl until foamy, using an electric mixer at high speed. Gradually add ½ c. of the sugar, beating until stiff peaks form. Set aside.

Sift together cake flour, baking powder, salt and remaining sugar into another bowl.

Add shortening and ½ c. of the milk. Beat 2 minutes, using an electric mixer at medium speed. Add remaining milk and vanilla and beat 2 minutes more. Fold in egg white mixture. Pour batter into greased and waxed paper-lined 13x9x2" baking pan.

Bake in 350° oven 30 minutes, or until a cake tester or toothpick inserted in center comes out clean. Cool in pan on rack.

Frost top of cake in pan with Creamy Pineapple Frosting.

Blue Ribbon Yellow Cake

(12 servings)

2¼ c. sifted cake flour
2½ tsp. baking powder
½ tsp. salt
½ c. shortening
1½ c. sugar
2 eggs
1 tsp. vanilla
1 c. plus 2 tblsp. milk
Chocolate 7-Minute Frosting (recipe follows)

Sift together cake flour, baking powder and salt. Set aside.

Cream together shortening and sugar in bowl until light and fluffy, using an electric mixer at medium speed. Add eggs, one at a time, beating well after each addition. Blend in vanilla.

Gradually add dry ingredients alternately with milk to creamed mixture, beating well after each addition, using low speed. Pour batter into 2 greased and waxed paper-lined 9″ round baking pans.

Bake in 375° oven 20 minutes, or until a cake tester or toothpick inserted in center comes out clean. Cool in pans on racks 10 minutes. Remove from pans. Cool on racks.

Fill and frost sides and top of cake with Chocolate 7-Minute Frosting.

Chocolate 7-Minute Frosting

2 egg whites
1½ c. sugar
⅓ c. water
¼ tsp. cream of tartar
1 tsp. vanilla
2 (1-oz.) squares unsweetened chocolate, melted and cooled

Combine egg whites, sugar, water and cream of tartar in top of double boiler. Beat 1 minute, using an electric mixer at high speed.

Place over simmering water. Cook 7 minutes, beating constantly at high speed, until soft glossy peaks form.

Remove from hot water. Blend in vanilla. Gently fold in chocolate. Makes 4 c.

Hurry-Up Cake

(16 servings)

3 c. sifted cake flour
1¾ c. sugar
3 tsp. baking powder
1 tsp. salt
1¼ c. milk
¾ c. shortening
3 eggs
2 tsp. vanilla

Sift together cake flour, sugar, baking powder and salt into bowl. Add milk and shortening. Beat 2 minutes, using an electric mixer at medium speed.

Add eggs and vanilla. Beat 1 minute more. Pour batter into greased and waxed paper-lined 13x9x2″ baking pan.

Bake in 350° oven 30 minutes, or until a cake tester or toothpick inserted in center comes out clean. Cool in pan on rack 10 minutes. Remove from pan. Cool on rack.

Frost sides and top of cake as you wish.

Yellow Cake Ring

(8 servings)

1 c. sifted cake flour
1½ tsp. baking powder
¼ tsp. salt
¼ c. butter or regular margarine
½ c. sugar
1 egg
½ tsp. vanilla
⅓ c. milk
1¼ c. butter cream frosting (see Index)

Sift together cake flour, baking powder and salt. Set aside.

Cream together butter and sugar in bowl until light and fluffy, using an electric mixer at medium speed. Add egg and beat well. Blend in vanilla.

Gradually add dry ingredients alternately with milk to creamed mixture, beating well after each addition, using low speed. Pour batter into greased 8″ ring mold.

Bake in 350° oven 20 minutes, or until a cake tester or toothpick inserted in center comes out clean. Cool in pan on rack 10 minutes. Remove from pan. Cool on rack.

Frost sides and top of cake with butter cream frosting.

Feather-light Yellow Cake

(8 servings)

1½ c. sifted cake flour
¾ c. sugar
1½ tsp. baking powder
½ c. milk
¼ c. butter or regular margarine, melted
1 egg
1 tsp. vanilla

Sift together cake flour, sugar and baking powder into bowl. Add milk, melted butter, egg and vanilla. Beat ½ minute, using an electric mixer at low speed. Beat 2 minutes more at medium speed. Pour batter into a greased and waxed paper-lined 8″ square baking pan.

Bake in 350° oven 40 minutes, or until a cake tester or toothpick inserted in center comes out clean. Cool in pan on rack 10 minutes. Remove from pan. Cool on rack.

Frost sides and top of cake as you wish.

Italian Cream Cake

(12 servings)

2 c. sifted flour
1 tsp. baking soda
5 eggs, separated
½ c. butter or regular margarine
½ c. shortening
2 c. sugar
1 tsp. vanilla
1 c. buttermilk
¾ c. flaked coconut
½ c. finely chopped walnuts
Apricot Filling (recipe follows)
Sweetened Whipped Cream II (see page 63)
sliced almonds

Sift together flour and baking soda. Set aside.

Beat egg whites in bowl until very stiff peaks form, using an electric mixer at high speed. Set aside.

Cream together butter, shortening and sugar in another bowl until light and fluffy, using an electric mixer at medium speed. Add egg yolks, one at a time, beating well after each addition. Blend in vanilla.

Gradually add dry ingredients alternately with buttermilk to creamed mixture, beating well after each addition, using low speed. Stir in coconut and walnuts.

Gradually pour batter over egg whites, folding just until blended. Pour batter into 3 greased and waxed paper-lined 9″ round baking pans.

Bake in 350° oven 30 minutes, or until a cake tester or toothpick inserted in center comes out clean. Cool in pans on racks 10 minutes. Remove from pans. Cool on racks.

Fill cake layers with Apricot Filling. Frost sides and top of cake with Sweetened Whipped Cream II. Sprinkle top with sliced almonds.

Apricot Filling

1 c. dried apricots
boiling water
3 tblsp. packed brown sugar
¼ tsp. ground mace

Place apricots in bowl; cover with boiling water. Let stand until completely cool. Drain apricots, reserving ⅓ c. liquid.

Combine apricots, reserved ⅓ c. liquid and brown sugar in small saucepan. Cook over low heat, stirring constantly, until mixture thickens, about 10 minutes. Remove from heat. Stir in mace. Cool completely.

Place mixture in blender container or food processor bowl and process until smooth.

Fluffy Gold Cake

(16 servings)

2½ c. sifted cake flour
1⅔ c. sugar
4 tsp. baking powder
1 tsp. salt
½ c. shortening
1¼ c. milk
1 tsp. grated lemon rind
1 tsp. vanilla
5 egg yolks
7-Minute Frosting (see page 62)

Sift together cake flour, sugar, baking powder and salt into bowl. Add shortening and ¾ c. of the milk. Beat 2 minutes, using an electric mixer at medium speed.

Add remaining milk, lemon rind, vanilla and egg yolks. Beat 2 minutes more. Pour batter into greased and waxed paper-lined 13x9x2″ baking pan.

Bake in 350° oven 45 minutes, or until a cake tester or toothpick inserted in center comes out clean. Cool in pan on rack 5 minutes. Remove from pan. Cool on rack.

Frost sides and top of cake with 7-Minute Frosting.

Boston Cream Pie

(12 servings)

2 c. sifted cake flour
1¼ c. sugar
2½ tsp. baking powder
1 tsp. salt
⅓ c. shortening
1 c. milk
1 tsp. vanilla
3 drops yellow food coloring
1 egg
Creamy Custard Filling (recipe follows)
Chocolate Glaze I (recipe follows)

Sift together cake flour, sugar, baking powder and salt into bowl. Add shortening, milk, vanilla and food coloring. Beat 2 minutes, using an electric mixer at medium speed.

Add egg; beat 2 minutes more. Pour batter into 2 greased and waxed paper-lined 9″ round baking pans.

Bake in 350° oven 25 to 30 minutes, or until a cake tester or toothpick inserted in center comes out clean. Cool in pans on racks 10 minutes. Remove from pans. Cool on racks.

Fill cake layers with Creamy Custard Filling. Prepare Chocolate Glaze and quickly spread over top of cake. Refrigerate until serving time.

Creamy Custard Filling

⅓ c. sugar
4 tblsp. flour
⅛ tsp. salt
1½ c. milk
3 drops yellow food coloring
4 egg yolks
2 tsp. vanilla

Combine sugar, flour and salt in 2-qt. saucepan. Gradually stir in milk and food coloring.

Cook over medium heat, stirring constantly, until mixture comes to a boil. Cook 2 minutes, stirring constantly. Remove from heat.

Beat egg yolks in small bowl. Stir a small amount of hot mixture into egg yolks; blend well. Stir egg yolk mixture back into hot mixture, blending well.

Cook over low heat, stirring constantly, 2 minutes. Remove from heat. Stir in vanilla. Cool completely.

Chocolate Glaze I

1 (1-oz.) square unsweetened chocolate
½ c. sifted confectioners' sugar
½ tsp. vanilla
4 tsp. hot water

Melt chocolate in saucepan over low heat. Remove from heat.

Stir in confectioners' sugar and vanilla. Add hot water, 1 tsp. at a time, blending well after each addition, using a spoon. Mixture should be smooth and satiny.

Bourbon Cake

(12 servings)

1 (18½-oz.) box yellow cake mix
½ c. cornstarch
½ c. sugar
1 c. water
4 eggs
½ c. cooking oil
1 tsp. vanilla
Bourbon Glaze (recipe follows)

Sift together cake mix, cornstarch and sugar into bowl. Add water, eggs, oil and vanilla. Beat ½ minute, using an electric mixer at low speed. Beat 3 minutes more at medium speed. Pour batter into greased 10″ tube pan.

Bake in 350° oven 50 minutes, or until a cake tester or toothpick inserted in center comes out clean. Cool in pan on rack 10 minutes.

Meanwhile, prepare Bourbon Glaze.

Remove cake from pan and thoroughly pierce surface of cake with a fork.

Immediately pour half of the glaze over surface of warm cake. Let stand 1 hour. Pierce cake again. Pour on remaining glaze.

To store: Place cake in tightly covered container.

Bourbon Glaze

1 c. corn syrup
¼ c. butter or regular margarine
¼ c. sugar
½ c. bourbon or orange juice

Combine corn syrup, butter and sugar in small saucepan.

Cook over medium heat, stirring constantly, until sugar is dissolved. Remove from heat. Stir in bourbon. Makes 2 c.

Poppy Seed Cake

(12 servings)

1 tblsp. white vinegar
2½ oz. poppy seed
1 c. milk
2½ c. sifted flour
2 tsp. baking powder
1 tsp. baking soda
½ tsp. salt
1 c. butter or regular margarine
1½ c. sugar
4 eggs
1 tsp. vanilla
1 tsp. ground cinnamon
2 tblsp. sugar
Thin Glaze (see page 63)

Stir white vinegar and poppy seed into milk. Cover and refrigerate overnight.

Sift together flour, baking powder, baking soda and salt. Set aside.

Cream together butter and 1½ c. sugar until light and fluffy, using an electric mixer at medium speed. Add eggs, one at a time, beating well after each addition. Blend in vanilla.

Gradually add dry ingredients alternately with poppy seed mixture to creamed mixture, beating well after each addition, using medium speed. Spoon half of the batter into greased and floured 10″ fluted tube pan.

Combine cinnamon and 2 tblsp. sugar. Sprinkle over batter. Top with remaining batter.

Bake in 350° oven 55 minutes, or until a cake tester or toothpick inserted in center comes out clean. Cool in pan on rack 10 minutes. Remove from pan. Cool on rack.

Pour Thin Glaze over top of cake, letting some of the glaze run down sides of cake.

Lime Cake

(10 servings)

2¼ c. sifted cake flour
1½ c. sugar
1 tsp. baking powder
1 tsp. baking soda
1 tsp. salt
¼ c. butter or regular margarine
¼ c. shortening
¾ c. buttermilk
1½ tsp. grated lime rind
¼ c. lime juice
⅔ c. egg whites (about 4 large)
Lime Butter Cream (recipe follows)

Sift together cake flour, sugar, baking powder, baking soda and salt into bowl. Add butter, shortening and half of the buttermilk. Beat 2 minutes, using an electric mixer at medium speed.

Add remaining buttermilk, lime rind, lime juice and egg whites. Beat 2 minutes more. Pour batter into 2 greased and waxed paper-lined 8″ round baking pans.

Bake in 350° oven 30 minutes, or until a cake tester or toothpick inserted in center comes out clean. Cool in pans on racks 10 minutes. Remove from pans. Cool on racks.

Fill and frost sides and top of cake with Lime Butter Cream.

Lime Butter Cream

⅓ c. butter or regular margarine
3 c. sifted confectioners' sugar
1 to 2 tblsp. milk
1 tblsp. lime juice
2 tsp. grated lime rind

Combine butter and 1 c. of the sifted confectioners' sugar in bowl; beat until light and fluffy, using an electric mixer at medium speed.

Add remaining confectioners' sugar alternately with milk and lime juice, beating until smooth and of spreading consistency. Stir in lime rind. Makes 1⅓ c.

Festive Layer Cake

(12 servings)

1 (3-oz.) pkg. vanilla pudding and pie filling mix
2 c. milk
1 tsp. vanilla
⅔ c. flaked coconut
1 c. sifted flour
4½ tsp. cornstarch
1½ tsp. baking powder
½ tsp. salt
4 eggs, separated
1 c. sugar
3 tblsp. cold water
1 tsp. vanilla
⅔ c. raspberry jam
1 c. heavy cream
¼ c. sifted confectioners' sugar
½ tsp. vanilla
fresh strawberries (optional)

Prepare vanilla pudding mix according to package directions, using 2 c. milk. Mix in 1 tsp. vanilla and coconut. Cover and refrigerate.

Sift together flour, cornstarch, baking powder and salt. Set aside.

Beat egg whites in bowl until stiff peaks form, using an electric mixer at high speed. Set aside. Combine egg yolks, sugar and water in bowl. Beat 5 minutes, using an electric mixer at high speed. Blend in 1 tsp. vanilla. Add dry ingredients and beat 1 minute at low speed.

Gradually fold batter into beaten egg whites. Pour batter into 2 greased and waxed paper-lined 9″ round baking pans.

Bake in 375° oven 15 minutes, or until top springs back when touched. Remove from pans. Cool on racks.

Cut each cake layer horizontally into 2 equal layers. Spread half of the chilled pudding on 1 layer; top with second layer. Spread with raspberry jam; top with third layer. Spread with remaining pudding and top with final layer.

Whip cream, confectioners' sugar and ½ tsp. vanilla in chilled bowl until soft peaks form, using an electric mixer at high speed.

Frost sides and top of cake with whipped cream. Refrigerate at least 1 hour before serving. If you wish, decorate with fresh whole strawberries.

Lemon-Coconut Cake

(24 servings)

3¾ c. sifted cake flour
2 tsp. baking powder
1½ tsp. baking soda
½ tsp. salt
1 c. shortening
2 c. sugar
4 eggs
1¼ tsp. vanilla
1½ tsp. grated lemon rind
2 c. buttermilk
Lemon Filling (recipe follows)
Lemony Frosting (recipe follows)
2 c. flaked coconut

Sift together cake flour, baking powder, baking soda and salt into bowl.

Add shortening, sugar, eggs, vanilla, lemon rind and buttermilk. Beat until moistened, using an electric mixer at low speed. Beat 3 minutes more at medium speed. Pour batter into 2 greased and waxed paper-lined 13x9x2″ baking pans.

Bake in 350° oven 25 minutes, or until a cake tester or toothpick inserted in center comes out clean. Cool in pans on racks 10 minutes. Remove from pans. Cool on racks.

Fill layers with Lemon Filling. Frost sides and top of cake with Lemony Frosting. Sprinkle cake with coconut.

Lemon Filling

¾ c. sugar
3 tblsp. cornstarch
¾ c. water
3 egg yolks
1 tblsp. butter or regular margarine
¾ tsp. grated lemon rind
3 tblsp. lemon juice

Mix together sugar and cornstarch in 2-qt. saucepan. Stir in water. Cook over medium heat, stirring constantly, until mixture comes to a boil. Boil 1 minute; reduce heat to low.

Beat egg yolks with fork. Stir some of the hot mixture into egg yolks. Stir egg yolk mixture back into hot mixture. Cook, stirring constantly, over low heat 2 minutes.

Remove from heat. Stir in butter, lemon rind and lemon juice. Cool to room temperature. Makes 1 c.

Lemony Frosting

6 tblsp. butter or regular margarine
1 (1-lb.) box confectioners' sugar, sifted
2 tblsp. lemon juice
½ tsp. grated lemon rind
2 egg whites

Combine all ingredients in bowl. Beat until smooth and creamy, using an electric mixer at medium speed. Makes 2¼ c.

Coconut-Pecan Cake

(12 servings)

2 c. sifted flour
1 tsp. baking soda
½ tsp. salt
1 c. butter or regular margarine
2 c. sugar
5 eggs, separated
1 tsp. vanilla
1 c. buttermilk
½ c. finely chopped pecans
3 c. coconut
Cream Cheese Frosting III
(see page 62)

Sift together flour, baking soda and salt. Set aside.

Cream together butter and sugar in bowl until light and fluffy, using an electric mixer at medium speed. Add egg yolks, one at a time, beating well after each addition. Blend in vanilla.

Gradually add dry ingredients alternately with buttermilk to creamed mixture, beating well after each addition, using low speed. Fold in pecans and 1 c. of the coconut.

Beat egg whites until stiff peaks form, using an electric mixer at high speed. Fold into batter. Pour batter into 3 greased and waxed paper-lined 9" round baking pans.

Bake in 350° oven 30 minutes, or until a cake tester or toothpick inserted in center comes out clean. Cool in pans on racks 10 minutes. Remove from pans. Cool on racks.

Fill and frost sides and top of cake with Cream Cheese Frosting III. Sprinkle remaining coconut on sides and top of cake.

Walnut Cake

(12 servings)

2 c. sifted flour
2 tsp. baking powder
½ tsp. ground nutmeg
¼ tsp. salt
½ c. butter or regular margarine
1½ c. sugar
3 eggs, separated
1 c. milk
1 c. finely chopped walnuts
1 tsp. vanilla
Caramel Frosting (see page 25)
coarsely chopped walnuts

Sift together flour, baking powder, nutmeg and salt. Set aside.

Cream together butter and sugar in bowl until light and fluffy, using an electric mixer at medium speed. Beat in egg yolks.

Gradually add dry ingredients alternately with milk to creamed mixture, beating well after each addition, using low speed. Stir in 1 c. walnuts and vanilla.

Beat egg whites in another bowl until stiff peaks form, using an electric mixer at high speed. Fold egg whites into batter. Pour batter into 2 greased and waxed paper-lined 9" round baking pans.

Bake in 350° oven 25 minutes, or until a cake tester or toothpick inserted in center comes out clean. Cool in pans on racks 10 minutes. Remove from pans. Cool on racks.

Fill and frost sides and top of cake with Caramel Frosting. Sprinkle with walnuts.

Praline Cake

(16 servings)

1 c. packed brown sugar
½ c. dairy sour cream
2 tblsp. butter
2 tsp. cornstarch
½ tsp. vanilla
1½ c. sifted flour
⅔ c. sugar
1 c. graham cracker crumbs
3 tsp. baking powder
½ c. butter
1 pt. vanilla ice cream, softened
2 eggs, beaten
½ c. chopped pecans

Combine brown sugar, sour cream, 2 tblsp. butter and cornstarch in 2-qt. saucepan. Cook over medium heat, stirring constantly, until thick and bubbly. Remove from heat. Stir in vanilla. Set aside.

Stir together flour, sugar, graham cracker crumbs and baking powder in bowl. Set aside.

Melt ½ c. butter in 3-qt. saucepan over medium heat. Remove from heat. Stir in ice cream until well blended.

Add dry ingredients and eggs to ice cream mixture; stir until well blended. Spread batter in greased 13x9x2″ baking pan.

Spoon ½ c. of the brown sugar topping over batter. Bake in 350° oven 30 minutes, or until a cake tester or toothpick inserted in center comes out clean.

Stir pecans into remaining topping and carefully spread over hot cake.

Cool in pan on rack.

Peanut Butter Layer Cake

(10 servings)

1 c. peanut butter-flavored pieces
1 c. milk
¼ c. butter or regular margarine
1 c. sifted flour
3 tsp. baking powder
¼ tsp. salt
2 eggs
1 c. sugar
1 tsp. vanilla
Best Butter Cream Decorating Icing
(see page 60)

Combine peanut butter pieces, milk and butter in small saucepan. Heat over medium heat, stirring constantly, until smooth. Remove from heat; cool slightly.

Sift together flour, baking powder and salt. Set aside.

Combine eggs and sugar in mixing bowl. Beat 3 minutes, using an electric mixer at medium speed. Blend in vanilla.

Gradually add dry ingredients alternately with peanut butter mixture to egg mixture, beating well after each addition, using low speed. Pour batter into 2 greased and floured 8″ round baking pans.

Bake in 350° oven 30 minutes, or until a cake tester or toothpick inserted in center comes out clean. Cool in pans on racks 10 minutes. Remove from pans. Cool on racks.

Fill and frost sides and top of cake with Best Butter Cream Decorating Icing.

Peanut Butter Cake Squares

(16 servings)

2 ¼ c. sifted cake flour
3 tsp. baking powder
¾ tsp. salt
¾ c. butter or regular margarine
2 ¼ c. packed brown sugar
¾ c. smooth peanut butter
3 eggs
½ tsp. vanilla
1 c. milk
Broiled Peanut Butter Frosting I
(recipe follows)

Sift together cake flour, baking powder and salt. Set aside.

Cream together butter, brown sugar and peanut butter in bowl until light and fluffy, using an electric mixer at medium speed. Add eggs, one at a time, beating well after each addition. Blend in vanilla.

Gradually add dry ingredients alternately with milk to creamed mixture, beating well after each addition, using low speed. Pour batter into greased 13x9x2″ baking pan.

Bake in 350° oven 45 minutes, or until a cake tester or toothpick inserted in center comes out clean. Cool in pan on rack 20 minutes.

Frost warm cake with Broiled Peanut Butter Frosting I and broil as directed. Cool in pan on rack.

Broiled Peanut Butter Frosting I

1 c. packed brown sugar
⅓ c. butter or regular margarine
⅔ c. smooth peanut butter
¼ c. milk
⅔ c. chopped peanuts

Combine brown sugar, butter, peanut butter and milk in 2-qt. saucepan.

Cook over medium heat, stirring constantly, until butter melts and mixture is warm. Remove from heat. Stir in peanuts.

Spread frosting over top of cake in pan. Broil 3″ from source of heat 1 minute or until golden brown and bubbly.

Peanut Butter-Chocolate Chip Cake

(16 servings)

2 ¼ c. sifted cake flour
2 c. packed brown sugar
1 c. smooth peanut butter
½ c. butter or regular margarine
1 tsp. baking powder
½ tsp. baking soda
1 c. milk
1 tsp. vanilla
3 eggs
1 (6-oz.) pkg. semisweet chocolate pieces

Combine cake flour, brown sugar, peanut butter and butter in bowl. Beat until crumbly, using an electric mixer at low speed. Remove 1 c. crumb mixture and set aside.

Add baking powder, baking soda, milk, vanilla and eggs to remaining crumb mixture. Beat at low speed until blended. Beat 3 minutes more at medium speed. Pour batter into greased 13x9x2″ baking pan. Sprinkle with reserved crumb mixture and chocolate pieces.

Bake in 350° oven 40 minutes, or until a cake tester or toothpick inserted in center comes out clean. Cool in pan on rack.

Meringue Cradle Cake

(12 servings)

2 c. sifted flour
3 tsp. baking powder
1 tsp. salt
4 eggs, separated
2 c. sugar
1 c. finely chopped pecans
1 (1-oz.) square semisweet chocolate, grated
½ c. butter or regular margarine
1 tsp. vanilla
¾ c. milk

Sift together flour, baking powder and salt. Set aside.

Beat egg whites in bowl until foamy, using an electric mixer at high speed. Gradually add 1 c. of the sugar, 2 tblsp. at a time, beating until stiff glossy peaks form. Fold in pecans and chocolate.

Spread meringue mixture over bottom and 2¾″ up sides of 10″ tube pan,* greased and lined with waxed paper. Set aside.

Cream together butter and remaining sugar in another bowl until light and fluffy, using an electric mixer at medium speed. Add egg yolks, one at a time, beating well after each addition. Blend in vanilla.

Gradually add dry ingredients alternately with milk, beating well after each addition, using low speed. Pour batter into meringue-lined pan.

Bake in 325° oven 65 minutes, or until a cake tester or toothpick inserted in center comes out clean. Cool in pan on rack 25 minutes. Remove from pan. Cool on rack.

**Note:* To bake this cake in a 9″ tube pan, increase baking time to 1 hour 20 minutes.

Marble Squares à la Mode

(9 servings)

⅔ c. sifted flour
½ tsp. baking powder
¼ tsp. salt
½ c. butter or regular margarine
¾ c. sugar
2 eggs
1½ tsp. vanilla
1 (1-oz.) square unsweetened chocolate, melted and cooled
vanilla ice cream
Fudge Sauce (recipe follows)

Sift together flour, baking powder and salt. Set aside.

Cream together butter and sugar in bowl until light and fluffy, using an electric mixer at medium speed. Add eggs, one at a time, beating well after each addition. Blend in vanilla.

Gradually add dry ingredients to creamed mixture, beating well after each addition, using low speed.

Spoon half of the cake batter into another

bowl. Stir in cooled chocolate. Drop chocolate batter and vanilla batter alternately (like a checkerboard) into greased 8″ square baking pan. Swirl batters with metal spatula.

Bake in 350° oven 25 to 30 minutes, or until a cake tester or toothpick inserted in center comes out clean. Cool in pan on rack.

To serve, cut into squares. Top each square with a scoop of ice cream. Spoon Fudge Sauce over top.

Fudge Sauce

¾ c. sugar
3 tblsp. baking cocoa
dash of salt
2 tblsp. water
⅔ c. evaporated milk
2 tblsp. butter or regular margarine
1 tsp. vanilla

Combine sugar, cocoa and salt in 2-qt. saucepan. Add water, stirring until cocoa is dissolved. Stir in evaporated milk.

Cook over medium heat, stirring constantly, until mixture comes to a boil. Reduce heat to low and cook, stirring constantly, 3 to 4 minutes, or until mixture thickens. Remove from heat.

Stir in butter and vanilla. Cool to lukewarm. Makes 1 c.

Devil's Food Cake

(12 servings)

2¼ c. sifted cake flour
1¾ c. plus 2 tblsp. sugar
¾ c. baking cocoa
2 tsp. baking soda
1 tsp. salt
½ tsp. cream of tartar
1½ c. milk
1 c. shortening
1½ tsp. vanilla
3 eggs
Super-smooth Chocolate Frosting
(recipe follows)

Sift together cake flour, sugar, cocoa, baking soda, salt and cream of tartar into bowl. Add 1 c. of the milk, shortening and vanilla. Beat 2 minutes, using an electric mixer at medium speed. Add remaining milk and eggs. Beat 2 minutes more. Pour batter into 2 waxed paper-lined 8″ square baking pans.

Bake in 350° oven 40 minutes, or until a cake tester or toothpick inserted in center comes out clean. Cool in pans on racks 10 minutes. Remove from pans. Cool on racks.

Fill and frost sides and top of cake with Super-smooth Chocolate Frosting.

Super-smooth Chocolate Frosting

½ c. butter or regular margarine
½ c. baking cocoa
1 (1-lb.) box confectioners' sugar, sifted
1 tsp. vanilla
⅓ c. hot milk

Cream together butter, cocoa and half of the confectioners' sugar in bowl, using an electric mixer at low speed. Blend in vanilla and hot milk.

Beat in remaining confectioners' sugar. Continue beating until smooth and creamy, using medium speed.

Chocolate Velvet Cake

(12 servings)

3 (1-oz.) squares unsweetened chocolate
1 c. water
2½ c. sifted cake flour
1½ tsp. baking soda
½ c. butter or regular margarine
2 c. sugar
3 eggs
1 tsp. vanilla
1 c. buttermilk
Creamy Coffee Frosting (recipe follows)
1(1-oz.) square unsweetened chocolate
1 tsp. butter or regular margarine

Combine 3 squares chocolate and water in saucepan. Cook over medium heat until mixture comes to a boil and chocolate melts. Remove from heat and cool.

Sift together cake flour and baking soda. Set aside.

Cream together ½ c. butter and sugar in

bowl until light and fluffy, using an electric mixer at medium speed. Add eggs, one at a time, beating well after each addition. Blend in vanilla.

Gradually add dry ingredients alternately with buttermilk to creamed mixture, beating well after each addition, using low speed. Blend in chocolate mixture. Pour batter into 2 greased and waxed paper-lined 9″ round baking pans.

Bake in 350° oven 35 minutes, or until top springs back when touched. Cool in pans on racks 10 minutes. Remove from pans. Cool on racks.

Fill and frost sides and top of cake with Creamy Coffee Frosting.

Melt 1 square chocolate and 1 tsp. butter in small saucepan over low heat. Cool slightly. Spoon chocolate mixture along edge of cake, allowing it to drip down sides.

Creamy Coffee Frosting

2 tsp. instant coffee powder
2 tblsp. hot water
¾ c. butter or regular margarine
6 c. sifted confectioners' sugar
4 tblsp. milk
1 tsp. vanilla

Dissolve coffee powder in hot water.

Combine coffee mixture and remaining ingredients in bowl. Beat until smooth and creamy, using an electric mixer at medium speed.

Fudge Cake

(12 servings)

3 c. sifted cake flour
1½ tsp. baking soda
¾ tsp. salt
¾ c. butter or regular margarine
2¼ c. sugar
3 eggs
3 (1-oz.) squares unsweetened chocolate, melted and cooled
1½ tsp. vanilla
1½ c. iced water
Date Cream Filling (recipe follows)
Fudge Frosting (recipe follows)

Sift together cake flour, baking soda and salt. Set aside. Cream together butter and sugar in bowl until light and fluffy, using an electric mixer at medium speed. Add eggs, one at a time, beating well after each addition. Blend in chocolate and vanilla.

Gradually add dry ingredients alternately with iced water to creamed mixture, beating well after each addition, using low speed. Pour batter into 3 greased and waxed paper-lined 8″ round baking pans.

Bake in 350° oven 30 to 35 minutes, or until top springs back when touched. Cool in pans on racks 10 minutes. Remove from pans. Cool on racks.

Fill layers with Date Cream Filling. Frost sides and top of cake with Fudge Frosting.

Date Cream Filling

1 c. milk
½ c. chopped, pitted dates
1 tblsp. flour
¼ c. sugar
1 egg, beaten
½ c. chopped walnuts
1 tsp. vanilla

Combine milk and dates in top of a double boiler. Heat over simmering water.

Combine flour and sugar in small bowl. Add egg; beat until smooth. Stir flour mixture into hot date mixture. Cook, stirring constantly, until mixture is thick. Remove from hot water and cool completely.

Stir walnuts and vanilla into cooled mixture.

Fudge Frosting

2 c. sugar
¼ tsp. salt
1 c. light cream
2 tblsp. light corn syrup
2 (1-oz.) squares unsweetened chocolate, cut up

Combine all ingredients in 2-qt. saucepan. Cook over low heat, stirring constantly, until sugar dissolves. Cover saucepan and cook 2 minutes.

Remove cover and cook until temperature reaches 234° (soft ball) on candy thermometer. Remove from heat.

Beat until frosting is thick enough to spread,

using a wooden spoon. If frosting becomes too stiff, add a little hot water; if it is too thin, add a little confectioners' sugar.

Anna Marie's Chocolate Cake

(12 servings)

2 tsp. baking soda
2 c. hot coffee
2¼ c. sifted flour
2 c. sugar
1 c. baking cocoa
1 tsp. salt
2 eggs
1 c. cooking oil
1½ tsp. vanilla

Dissolve baking soda in hot coffee. Set aside.

Sift together flour, sugar, cocoa and salt into bowl. Add eggs, oil and vanilla. Beat ½ minute, using an electric mixer at medium speed. Add coffee mixture and beat 2 minutes more. Pour batter into 2 waxed paper-lined 9″ round baking pans.

Bake in 350° oven 30 minutes, or until a cake tester or toothpick inserted in center comes out clean. Cool in pans on racks 10 minutes. Remove from pans. Cool on racks. Fill and frost sides and top of cake as you wish.

Foolproof Chocolate Cake

(16 servings)

½ c. baking cocoa
1 tsp. baking soda
½ c. boiling water
½ c. butter or regular margarine
2 c. sugar
2 eggs
1 tsp. vanilla
2½ c. sifted flour
1 c. buttermilk
Broiled Icing (recipe follows)

Combine cocoa, baking soda and boiling water in bowl; stir until blended. Set aside.

Cream together butter and sugar in bowl until light and fluffy, using an electric mixer at medium speed. Add eggs, one at a time, beating well after each addition. Blend in vanilla.

Gradually add flour alternately with buttermilk to creamed mixture, beating well after each addition, using low speed. Blend in cocoa mixture. Pour batter into greased 13x9x2″ baking pan.

Bake in 350° oven 35 minutes, or until top springs back when touched.

Frost warm cake with Broiled Icing and broil as directed. Cool in pan on rack.

Broiled Icing

⅔ c. packed brown sugar
⅓ c. butter or regular margarine, melted
¼ c. half-and-half
1 c. flaked coconut

Combine all ingredients in bowl; mix well.

Spread frosting over top of cake in pan. Broil 3″ from source of heat 1 minute or until golden brown and bubbly.

Grandma's Chocolate Cake

(12 servings)

3 c. sifted flour
¼ c. baking cocoa
1 tsp. baking soda
1 tsp. salt
1 c. butter or regular margarine
2 c. sugar
3 eggs
½ c. warm water
1 tsp. vanilla
1 c. buttermilk
Coconut-Pecan Frosting (recipe follows)

Sift together flour, cocoa, baking soda and salt. Set aside.

Cream together butter and sugar in bowl until light and fluffy, using an electric mixer at medium speed. Add eggs, one at a time, beating well after each addition. Blend in water and vanilla.

Gradually add dry ingredients alternately with buttermilk to creamed mixture, beating well after each addition, using low speed. Pour batter into 2 greased and waxed paper-lined 9″ round baking pans.

Bake in 350° oven 30 minutes, or until a cake tester or toothpick inserted in center comes out clean. Cool in pans on racks 10 minutes. Remove from pans. Cool on racks.

Fill and frost sides and top of cake with Coconut-Pecan Frosting.

Coconut-Pecan Frosting

⅔ c. evaporated milk
⅔ c. sugar
⅓ c. butter or regular margarine
2 egg yolks
1 tsp. vanilla
1 c. flaked coconut
⅔ c. chopped pecans

Combine evaporated milk, sugar, butter and egg yolks in small saucepan. Cook over low heat, stirring constantly, until mixture thickens, about 12 minutes. Remove from heat.

Stir in vanilla, coconut and pecans. Cool until thick enough to spread, stirring occasionally.

Sweepstakes Chocolate Cake

(16 servings)

¾ c. hot water
½ c. baking cocoa
3 c. sifted cake flour
1 tsp. baking soda
¼ tsp. salt
½ c. butter or regular margarine
2 c. sugar
2 eggs
1 tsp. vanilla
1 c. sour milk*
Chocolate Cream Cheese Frosting (see page 61)

Pour hot water over cocoa in small saucepan. Cook over low heat until mixture thickens. Cool to room temperature.

Sift together cake flour, baking soda and salt. Set aside.

Cream together butter and sugar in bowl until light and fluffy, using an electric mixer at medium speed. Add eggs, one at a time, beating well after each addition. Blend in vanilla. Add dry ingredients alternately with sour milk to creamed mixture, beating well after each addition, using low speed. Blend in cocoa mixture. Pour batter into 3 greased and waxed paper-lined 9″ round baking pans.

Bake in 350° oven 25 minutes, or until top springs back when touched. Cool in pans on racks 10 minutes. Remove from pans. Cool on racks.

Fill and frost sides and top of cake with Chocolate Cream Cheese Frosting.

**Note:* To sour milk, place 1 tblsp. vinegar in measuring cup. Add enough milk to make 1 c.

Hot Water Chocolate Cake

(10 servings)

2 c. sifted flour
½ c. baking cocoa
2 tsp. baking soda
½ tsp. salt
½ c. butter or regular margarine
1½ c. sugar
2 eggs
½ c. milk
1 tsp. vanilla
1 c. boiling water
Creamy Chocolate Frosting (recipe follows)

Sift together flour, cocoa, baking soda and salt. Set aside.

Cream together butter and sugar in bowl until light and fluffy, using an electric mixer at medium speed. Add eggs, one at a time, beating well after each addition. Blend in milk and vanilla.

Stir dry ingredients into creamed mixture. Add boiling water and stir until smooth. Pour batter into 2 greased and waxed paper-lined 8″ round baking pans.

Bake in 325° oven 30 minutes, or until a cake tester or toothpick inserted in center comes out clean. Cool in pans on racks 10 minutes. Remove from pans. Cool on racks.

Fill and frost sides and top of cake with Creamy Chocolate Frosting.

Creamy Chocolate Frosting

3 c. sifted confectioners' sugar
⅓ c. butter or regular margarine
2 (1-oz.) squares unsweetened chocolate, melted and cooled
3 to 4 tblsp. milk
1 tsp. vanilla

Combine all ingredients in bowl. Beat until smooth and creamy, using an electric mixer at medium speed.

Gram's Chocolate Cake

(16 servings)

2½ c. sifted flour
¼ c. baking cocoa
2 tsp. baking soda
1 tsp. salt
½ c. shortening
2 c. sugar
2 eggs
1 egg yolk
1 tsp. vanilla
½ c. buttermilk
1 c. boiling water
Butterfly Frosting (recipe follows)

Sift together flour, cocoa, baking soda and salt. Set aside.

Cream together shortening and sugar in bowl until light and fluffy, using an electric mixer at medium speed. Add eggs and egg yolk, one at a time, beating well after each addition. Blend in vanilla.

Gradually add dry ingredients alternately with buttermilk to creamed mixture, beating well after each addition, using low speed. Blend in boiling water. Pour batter into greased 13x9x2" baking pan.

Bake in 350° oven 40 minutes, or until a cake tester or toothpick inserted in center comes out clean. Cool in pan on rack.

Frost in pan with Butterfly Frosting.

Butterfly Frosting

1 c. sifted confectioners' sugar
1 egg white
¼ tsp. cream of tartar
¼ c. boiling water
1 tsp. vanilla

Combine confectioners' sugar, egg white and cream of tartar in bowl. Beat until blended, using an electric mixer at low speed.

Add boiling water. Beat at high speed 4 minutes, or until stiff glossy peaks form. Beat in vanilla.

Mahogany Cake

(12 servings)

3 c. sifted cake flour
¼ c. baking cocoa
1 tsp. baking powder
½ tsp. baking soda
½ tsp. salt
1 c. shortening
2 c. packed brown sugar
4 eggs
1 tsp. vanilla
1½ c. sour milk*
Light Chocolate Frosting (recipe follows)

Sift together cake flour, cocoa, baking powder, baking soda and salt. Set aside.

Cream together shortening and brown sugar in bowl until light and fluffy, using an electric mixer at medium speed. Add eggs, one at a time, beating well after each addition. Blend in vanilla.

Gradually add dry ingredients alternately with sour milk to creamed mixture, beating well after each addition, using low speed. Pour batter into 2 greased and waxed paper-lined 9" round baking pans.

Bake in 350° oven 30 minutes, or until a cake tester or toothpick inserted in center comes out clean. Cool in pans on racks 10 minutes. Remove from pans. Cool on racks.

Fill and frost sides and top of cake with Light Chocolate Frosting.

**Note:* To sour milk, place 4½ tsp. vinegar in measuring cup. Add enough milk to make 1½ c.

Light Chocolate Frosting

⅓ c. butter or regular margarine
2 (1-oz.) squares unsweetened chocolate, melted and cooled
1½ tsp. vanilla
4 c. sifted confectioners' sugar
¼ c. milk

Combine butter and chocolate in bowl. Beat until smooth, using an electric mixer at medium speed. Blend in vanilla.

Gradually add confectioners' sugar alternately with milk, beating well after each addition. Continue beating until smooth and creamy.

One-Bowl Cocoa Cake

(16 servings)

2 c. sifted flour
1¾ c. sugar
½ c. baking cocoa
2 tsp. baking soda
½ tsp. salt
⅔ c. butter or regular margarine
3 eggs
1 c. milk
1 tsp. vanilla
Broiled Peanut Butter Frosting II
  (recipe follows)
mini-chips or colored sprinkles

Sift together flour, sugar, cocoa, baking soda and salt into bowl. Add butter, eggs, milk and vanilla. Beat ½ minute, using an electric mixer at low speed. Beat 3 minutes more or until smooth and well blended, using medium speed. Pour batter into greased and floured 13x9x2" baking pan.

Bake in 350° oven 40 minutes, or until a cake tester or toothpick inserted in center comes out clean. Cool in pan on rack.

Frost with Broiled Peanut Butter Frosting II and broil as directed. Cool in pan on rack. Sprinkle with mini-chips or colored sprinkles.

Broiled Peanut Butter Frosting II

⅔ c. packed brown sugar
⅓ c. peanut butter
¼ c. butter or regular margarine
¼ c. heavy cream
1 c. chopped peanuts

Combine all ingredients in bowl. Mix until well blended. Makes 1⅔ c.

Spread frosting over top of cake in pan. Broil 5" from source of heat 2 minutes or until golden brown and bubbly.

Original Chocolate Mayonnaise Cake

(9 servings)

1 c. cut-up pitted dates
1 tsp. baking soda
1 c. boiling water
1 c. mayonnaise
1 c. sugar
6 tblsp. grated unsweetened chocolate
1 tsp. vanilla
2 c. sifted cake flour
1 c. chopped walnuts
Chocolate Cream Frosting (recipe follows)

Combine dates and baking soda in small bowl. Pour boiling water over mixture and let stand until completely cool.

Cream together mayonnaise and sugar in another bowl until light and fluffy, using an electric mixer at medium speed. Blend in chocolate and vanilla.

Gradually add cake flour, beating well after each addition, using low speed. Stir in date mixture and walnuts. Spread batter in greased 9" square baking pan.

Bake in 350° oven 45 minutes, or until a cake tester or toothpick inserted in center comes out clean. Cool in pan on rack.

Frost cake in pan with Chocolate Cream Frosting.

Chocolate Cream Frosting

1 (6-oz.) pkg. semisweet chocolate pieces
4 oz. cream cheese, softened
¼ tsp. salt
½ tsp. vanilla
1½ c. sifted confectioners' sugar
1 to 2 tblsp. milk

Melt chocolate pieces over hot (not boiling) water in top of a double boiler. Remove from hot water.

Combine melted chocolate, cream cheese and salt in bowl. Beat until light and fluffy, using an electric mixer at medium speed. Blend in vanilla.

Add confectioners' sugar alternately with milk to creamed mixture, beating well after each addition. Continue beating until creamy.

Light Chocolate Brownie Cupcakes

(24 servings)

4 (1-oz.) squares semisweet chocolate
1 c. butter or regular margarine
1 c. chopped walnuts
1 tsp. vanilla
1 c. sifted flour
1¾ c. sugar
4 eggs

Melt chocolate and butter in 2-qt. saucepan over low heat. Remove from heat. Stir in walnuts and vanilla. Set aside.

Sift together flour and sugar into bowl. Add eggs, beating until well blended, using an electric mixer at medium speed. Stir in chocolate mixture. Pour batter into paper-lined 2½″ muffin-pan cups, filling half full.

Bake in 325° oven 35 minutes, or until a cake tester or toothpick inserted in center comes out clean. Remove from pans. Cool on racks.

Old-fashioned Peppermint Fudge Cake

(12 servings)

2 c. sifted flour
⅔ c. baking cocoa
1¼ tsp. baking soda
¼ tsp. baking powder
1 tsp. salt
⅔ c. butter or regular margarine
1⅔ c. sugar
3 eggs
½ tsp. vanilla
1⅓ c. water
½ c. crushed peppermint candy
Peppermint Cream Frosting (recipe follows)
crushed peppermint candy

Sift together flour, cocoa, baking soda, baking powder and salt. Set aside.

Cream together butter and sugar in bowl until light and fluffy, using an electric mixer at medium speed. Add eggs, one at a time, beating well after each addition. Blend in vanilla.

Gradually add dry ingredients alternately with water to creamed mixture, beating well after each addition, using low speed. Stir in ½ c. crushed peppermint candy. Grease 2 (9″) round baking pans and dust with cocoa. Pour batter into prepared pans.

Bake in 350° oven 35 minutes, or until a cake tester or toothpick inserted in center comes out clean. Cool in pans on racks 10 minutes. Remove from pans. Cool on racks.

Fill and frost sides and top of cake with Peppermint Cream Frosting. Sprinkle with crushed peppermint candy.

Peppermint Cream Frosting

⅓ c. butter or regular margarine
¾ c. baking cocoa
2½ c. sifted confectioners' sugar
3 to 4 tblsp. milk
½ tsp. peppermint extract

Cream together butter and cocoa in bowl until light and fluffy. Gradually add confectioners' sugar and milk, beating until smooth and of spreading consistency. Beat in peppermint extract. Makes 1⅔ c.

Chocolate Oatmeal Cake

(16 servings)

1 c. old-fashioned oats
1½ c. boiling water
1⅓ c. sifted flour
½ c. baking cocoa
1 tsp. baking soda
½ tsp. salt
½ c. shortening
1½ c. sugar
2 eggs
1 tsp. vanilla
½ c. chopped walnuts
1 (6-oz.) pkg. semisweet chocolate pieces

Combine oats and boiling water in bowl; stir well to blend. Let stand for 20 minutes.

Sift together flour, cocoa, baking soda and salt. Set aside.

Cream together shortening and sugar in bowl until light and fluffy, using an electric mixer at medium speed. Add eggs, one at a time, beating well after each addition. Blend in vanilla.

Gradually add dry ingredients alternately with oat mixture to creamed mixture, beating well after each addition, using low speed. Stir in walnuts. Pour into greased 13x9x2" baking pan.

Bake in 350° oven 35 minutes, or until a cake tester or toothpick inserted in center comes out clean. Place on rack.

Sprinkle top of warm cake with chocolate pieces and let cool for 5 minutes, or until chocolate pieces are softened. Spread chocolate over top of cake in pan. Cool in pan on rack.

Chocolate-Coconut Torte

(12 servings)

1 (12-oz.) pkg. semisweet chocolate pieces
2⅔ c. flaked coconut
2 c. chopped walnuts
½ c. plus 2 tblsp. shortening, melted
1 (10") tube cake (see Index)
2 c. heavy cream, whipped

In blender or food processor container, process ½ c. of the chocolate pieces at high speed into fine grains, about 10 seconds.

Combine ground chocolate, ¼ c. of the coconut, ¼ c. of the walnuts and 2 tblsp. of the shortening in small bowl. Mix well. Set aside.

Melt remaining chocolate pieces with remaining shortening in top of double boiler over simmering (not boiling) water. When chocolate is melted, remove from heat but keep over hot water. Stir in remaining coconut and walnuts. Cool slightly.

Cut cake horizontally into 3 equal layers. Spread 1 rounded cup of melted chocolate-coconut mixture on one layer. Spread one-third of the whipped cream on top. Repeat with the remaining two layers. Sprinkle top with reserved chocolate-coconut mixture.

German Birthday Torte

(12 servings)

1 (6-oz.) pkg. semisweet chocolate pieces
2 c. sifted flour
1 tsp. baking soda
1 tsp. salt
½ c. butter or regular margarine
1½ c. sugar
3 eggs
1¼ c. sour milk*
¾ c. graham cracker crumbs
½ c. chopped walnuts
½ c. flaked coconut
⅓ c. butter or regular margarine, melted
2 c. heavy cream, whipped

Melt ⅓ c. of the chocolate pieces in small saucepan over low heat. Remove from heat. Cool completely.

Sift together flour, baking soda and salt. Set aside.

Cream together ½ c. butter and sugar in bowl until light and fluffy, using an electric mixer at medium speed. Add eggs, one at a time, beating well after each addition, using low speed.

Gradually add dry ingredients alternately with sour milk to creamed mixture, beating well after each addition.

Beat in melted chocolate. Pour batter into 2 greased and floured 9" round baking pans.

Combine remaining chocolate pieces, graham cracker crumbs, walnuts, coconut and ⅓ c. melted butter. Mix well. Sprinkle over batter.

Bake in 375° oven 35 minutes, or until a cake tester or toothpick inserted in center comes out clean. Cool in pans on racks 10 minutes. Remove from pans. Cool on racks.

Fill and frost sides and top of cake with whipped cream.

**Note:* To sour milk, place 3¾ tsp. vinegar in measuring cup. Add enough milk to make 1¼ c.

Party Baked Alaska

(24 servings)

1 ½ c. sifted flour
1 tsp. baking powder
½ tsp. salt
4 eggs
1 c. sugar
1 c. packed brown sugar
1 ½ tsp. vanilla
4 (1-oz.) squares unsweetened chocolate, melted and cooled
⅔ c. cooking oil
3 tblsp. instant coffee powder
1 c. chopped walnuts
1 (½-gal.) block coffee ice cream
Meringue (recipe follows)

Sift together flour, baking powder and salt. Set aside.

Beat eggs, sugar, brown sugar and vanilla in bowl 2 minutes, using an electric mixer at high speed. Beat in chocolate, oil and coffee powder. Stir in dry ingredients and walnuts, mixing well. Spread in greased and waxed paper-lined 15½x10½x1″ jelly roll pan.

Bake in 350° oven 25 minutes, or until top springs back when touched. Cool in pan on rack 10 minutes. Remove from pan. Cool on rack.

Place cake on foil-lined baking sheet. Cut ice cream into 1″ slices. Arrange ice cream slices on cake, leaving ¾″ border. Freeze 2 hours or until firm.

Prepare Meringue.

Quickly spread Meringue over entire surface of ice cream and cake, right down to foil. Bake immediately or freeze up to 24 hours.

Bake in 500° oven 3 minutes, or until meringue is lightly browned. Serve immediately.

Meringue

8 egg whites
1 tsp. cream of tartar
1 tsp. vanilla
1 c. sugar

Combine egg whites, cream of tartar and vanilla in bowl. Beat until foamy, using an electric mixer at high speed. Gradually add sugar, beating until stiff glossy peaks form.

Black-Bottom Peanut Butter Chipcakes

(20 servings)

1 (8-oz.) pkg. cream cheese
2 eggs
1 ⅓ c. sugar
⅛ tsp. salt
1 c. peanut butter-flavored pieces
1 ¼ c. sifted flour
⅓ c. baking cocoa
¾ tsp. baking soda
½ tsp. salt
1 c. buttermilk or sour milk*
⅓ c. cooking oil
1 tsp. vanilla
Peanut Butter Frosting (recipe follows)

Beat cream cheese in bowl until creamy, using an electric mixer at medium speed. Add 1 egg, ⅓ c. of the sugar and ⅛ tsp. salt. Beat until well blended. Stir in ¾ c. of the peanut butter pieces. Set aside.

Sift together flour, remaining sugar, cocoa, baking soda and ½ tsp. salt into another bowl. Add buttermilk, oil, remaining egg and vanilla. Beat until well blended, using an electric mixer at medium speed. Spoon batter into 20 paper-lined 3″ muffin-pan cups, filling one-third full. Top each with a slightly rounded tblsp. of cheese mixture.

Bake in 350° oven 25 minutes, or until a cake tester or toothpick inserted in center comes out clean. Remove from pans. Cool on racks.

Frost cupcakes with Peanut Butter Frosting. Sprinkle cupcakes with remaining peanut butter pieces.

**Note:* To sour milk, place 1 tblsp. vinegar in measuring cup. Add enough milk to make 1 c.

Peanut Butter Frosting

⅓ c. sugar
¼ c. evaporated milk
2 tblsp. butter or regular margarine
1 c. peanut butter-flavored pieces
1 tsp. vanilla

Combine sugar, evaporated milk and butter in small saucepan. Cook over medium heat, stirring constantly, until mixture comes to a boil. Remove from heat.

Add peanut butter pieces, stirring constantly, until melted. Blend in vanilla. Makes 1 c.

Chocolate-Ricotta Torte

(10 servings)

¾ c. sifted flour
½ tsp. baking soda
⅓ c. butter or regular margarine
⅔ c. sugar
3 eggs
¾ c. chocolate-flavored syrup
½ tsp. vanilla
Chocolate-Ricotta Filling (recipe follows)
½ c. finely chopped walnuts
Chocolate Glaze II (recipe follows)

Sift together flour and baking soda. Set aside.

Cream together butter and sugar in bowl until light and fluffy, using an electric mixer at medium speed. Add eggs, one at a time, beating well after each addition. Blend in chocolate syrup and vanilla. Spread batter in greased and waxed paper-lined 15½x10½x1″ jelly roll pan.

Bake in 350° oven 16 minutes, or until top springs back when touched. Cool 5 minutes. Remove from pan. Cool on rack.

Cut cake crosswise into 4 layers, each measuring about10x3¾″.

Spread top of one cake layer with one-third of the Chocolate-Ricotta Filling. Sprinkle 2 tblsp. walnuts over filling. Place second cake layer on top. Repeat layers, ending with cake layer.

Frost top of cake with Chocolate Glaze II. Sprinkle with remaining walnuts.

Chocolate-Ricotta Filling

½ c. semisweet chocolate pieces
1 (15-oz.) container ricotta cheese
4 tsp. orange juice
1½ tsp. grated orange rind
1½ tsp. sugar

Melt chocolate pieces over hot water in top of double boiler. Remove from hot water.

Beat in remaining ingredients, using an electric mixer at low speed. Makes 2 c.

Chocolate Glaze II

½ c. semisweet chocolate pieces
2 tblsp. corn syrup
1½ tsp. water

Melt chocolate pieces over hot water in top of a double boiler. When chocolate is melted, slowly add corn syrup and water, stirring until smooth. Makes about ½ c.

Chocolate Apricot Torte

(16 servings)

6 eggs, separated
⅔ c. butter or regular margarine
1¼ c. sugar
4 (1-oz.) squares unsweetened chocolate, melted and cooled
½ c. finely grated almonds
1 c. sifted flour
1 (12-oz.) jar apricot preserves
⅓ c. light corn syrup
3 (1-oz.) squares unsweetened chocolate
2 tsp. hot water

Beat egg yolks in bowl until thick and lemon-colored, using an electric mixer at high speed. Set aside.

Cream together butter and 1 c. of the sugar in another bowl until light and fluffy, using an electric mixer at medium speed. Beat egg yolks into butter mixture. Stir in 4 squares chocolate and ½ c. almonds. Fold in flour.

Beat egg whites in another bowl until foamy, using an electric mixer at high speed. Gradually add remaining sugar, beating well after each addition. Continue beating until soft peaks form. Fold egg white mixture into chocolate mixture. Pour batter into greased and floured 9″ springform pan.

Bake in 300° oven 50 to 60 minutes, or until top springs back when touched. Cool in pan on rack overnight.

Remove from pan. Cut cake horizontally into 2 equal layers. Spread half of the preserves on top of one layer; place second layer on top. Spread remaining preserves on sides and top of cake.

Heat corn syrup in small saucepan over medium heat until it comes to a boil. Remove from heat and add 3 squares chocolate. Let stand until chocolate melts and mixture is lukewarm. Stir until smooth; blend in hot water. Quickly spread on top and sides of torte.

Waldorf Spice Cake

(12 servings)

3 c. sifted flour
2 tblsp. baking soda
½ tsp. salt
1½ tsp. ground cinnamon
½ tsp. ground nutmeg
¼ tsp. ground cloves
2 eggs
2 c. sugar
1 c. mayonnaise
⅓ c. milk
3 c. finely chopped, pared apples
1 c. raisins
1 c. finely chopped walnuts
Sweetened Whipped Cream II (see page 63)

Sift together flour, baking soda, salt, cinnamon, nutmeg and cloves. Set aside.

Beat eggs until thick and lemon-colored, using an electric mixer at high speed. Gradually add sugar, beating well after each addition. Continue beating until thick.

Beat in mayonnaise and milk, using low speed. Add dry ingredients; blend well.

Stir in apples, raisins and walnuts. Pour batter into 2 greased and waxed paper-lined 9″ round baking pans.

Bake in 350° oven 45 minutes, or until a cake tester or toothpick inserted in center comes out clean. Cool in pans on racks 10 minutes. Remove from pans. Cool on racks.

Fill and frost sides and top of cake with Sweetened Whipped Cream II.

Federal Cake

(12 servings)

2 c. sifted flour
1 tsp. baking soda
1¼ tsp. ground cinnamon
¼ tsp. ground nutmeg
⅛ tsp. ground cloves
½ c. shortening
2 c. packed brown sugar
2 eggs
1 egg white
1 c. sour milk*
1 c. chopped walnuts
Caramel Frosting (recipe follows)

Sift together flour, baking soda, cinnamon, nutmeg and cloves. Set aside.

Cream together shortening and brown sugar in bowl until light and fluffy, using an electric mixer at medium speed. Add eggs and egg white, one at a time, beating well after each addition.

Gradually add dry ingredients alternately with sour milk to creamed mixture, beating well after each addition, using low speed. Stir in walnuts. Pour batter into 2 greased and waxed paper-lined 8″ round baking pans.

Bake in 350° oven 30 minutes, or until a cake tester or toothpick inserted in center comes out clean. Cool in pans on racks 10 minutes. Remove from pans. Cool on racks.

Fill and frost sides and top of cake with Caramel Frosting.

**Note:* To sour milk, place 1 tblsp. vinegar in measuring cup; add enough milk to make 1 c.

Caramel Frosting

1 c. packed brown sugar
½ c. butter or regular margarine
¼ c. milk
2½ c. sifted confectioners' sugar

Combine brown sugar and butter in 2-qt. saucepan. Cook over medium heat, stirring constantly, until mixture comes to a boil.

Gradually stir in milk. Cook, stirring constantly, until mixture returns to a boil. Boil 1 minute. Remove from heat. Cool to room temperature.

Gradually add confectioners' sugar, beating well after each addition, using a wooden spoon. Beat until mixture is thick enough to spread.

Oatmeal Cake

(9 servings)

1 ⅓ c. boiling water
1 c. quick-cooking oats
1 ⅓ c. sifted flour
1 tsp. ground cinnamon
1 tsp. baking soda
½ tsp. salt
½ c. shortening
1 c. packed brown sugar
1 c. sugar
2 eggs
1 tsp. vanilla
Broiled Coconut Frosting (recipe follows)

Pour boiling water over oats. Let stand 10 minutes. Sift together flour, cinnamon, baking soda and salt. Set aside.

Cream together shortening, brown sugar and sugar in bowl until light and fluffy, using an electric mixer at medium speed. Add eggs, one at a time, beating well after each addition. Blend in vanilla.

Gradually add dry ingredients alternately with oat mixture to creamed mixture, beating well after each addition, using low speed. Spread batter in greased 9″ square baking pan.

Bake in 350° oven 35 minutes, or until a cake tester or toothpick inserted in center comes out clean.

Frost warm cake with Broiled Coconut Frosting and broil as directed. Cool in pan on rack.

Broiled Coconut Frosting

⅔ c. chopped walnuts
⅔ c. flaked coconut
¼ c. butter or regular margarine
1 tsp. vanilla
⅔ c. packed brown sugar
3 tblsp. evaporated milk

Combine all ingredients in small saucepan. Cook over medium heat, stirring constantly, until butter melts. Makes 2 c.

Spread frosting over top of cake in pan. Broil 3″ from source of heat 1 minute or until golden brown and bubbly.

Applesauce Cake

(12 servings)

1 c. boiling water
1 ½ c. raisins
3 c. sifted flour
⅛ tsp. salt
3 tsp. ground cinnamon
2 tsp. ground nutmeg
½ tsp. ground cloves
2 tsp. baking soda
1 c. chopped walnuts
½ c. butter or regular margarine
2 c. sugar
2 eggs
2 c. applesauce
2 tsp. vanilla
confectioners' sugar

Pour boiling water over raisins in bowl. Let stand 30 minutes. Drain. Set aside.

Sift together flour, salt, cinnamon, nutmeg, cloves and baking soda. Set aside. Toss raisins and walnuts with ¼ c. of the dry ingredients. Set aside.

Cream together butter and sugar in bowl until light and fluffy, using an electric mixer at medium speed. Add eggs, one at a time, beating well after each addition. Blend in applesauce and vanilla.

Gradually add remaining dry ingredients to creamed mixture, beating well after each addition, using low speed. Stir in raisin-walnut mixture. Pour batter into greased and floured 10″ tube pan.

Bake in 375° oven 10 minutes. Reduce temperature to 325°. Bake 55 minutes more, or until a cake tester or toothpick inserted in center comes out clean. Cool in pan on rack 10 minutes. Remove from pan. Cool on rack.

Sprinkle top of cake with confectioners' sugar.

Spicy Applesauce Cake

(16 servings)

2 c. sifted flour
2 tsp. baking soda
1/8 tsp. salt
1 tsp. ground cinnamon
1/2 tsp. ground nutmeg
1/4 tsp. ground cloves
1/4 tsp. ground ginger
1/2 c. butter or regular margarine
1 c. sugar
2 eggs
1 1/2 c. applesauce
1/4 c. water
1 c. raisins
1 c. chopped walnuts
Sweetened Whipped Cream I (see page 63)

Sift together flour, baking soda, salt, cinnamon, nutmeg, cloves and ginger. Set aside.

Cream together butter and sugar in bowl until light and fluffy, using an electric mixer at medium speed. Add eggs, one at a time, beating well after each addition. Blend in applesauce.

Gradually add dry ingredients alternately with water to creamed mixture, beating well after each addition, using low speed. Stir in raisins and walnuts. Pour batter into greased 13x9x2″ baking pan.

Bake in 375° oven 35 minutes, or until a cake tester or toothpick inserted in center comes out clean. Cool in pan on rack.

Serve topped with Sweetened Whipped Cream I.

Applesauce Layer Cake

(12 servings)

2 c. sifted flour
1 tsp. baking soda
1 tsp. baking powder
1 tsp. salt
1 tsp. ground cinnamon
1/4 tsp. ground cloves
2 eggs
1 1/2 c. sugar
1/2 c. cooking oil
1 c. applesauce
Butter Cream Filling (recipe follows)

Sift together flour, baking soda, baking powder, salt, cinnamon and cloves. Set aside.

Beat eggs and sugar in bowl 3 minutes, using an electric mixer at medium speed. Blend in oil.

Gradually add dry ingredients alternately with applesauce to egg mixture, beating well after each addition, using low speed. Pour batter into 2 greased and waxed paper-lined 9″ round baking pans.

Bake in 350° oven 30 minutes, or until a cake tester or toothpick inserted in center comes out clean. Cool in pans on racks 10 minutes. Remove from pans. Cool on racks.

Fill and frost top of cake with Butter Cream Filling.

Butter Cream Filling

2 c. sifted confectioners' sugar
3 tblsp. butter or regular margarine
1 1/2 tsp. vanilla
2 tblsp. milk

Combine all ingredients in bowl. Beat until smooth and creamy, using an electric mixer at medium speed.

Chocolate Applesauce Cake

(16 servings)

2 c. sifted flour
3 tblsp. baking cocoa
1 tblsp. cornstarch
2 tsp. baking soda
1 tsp. ground cinnamon
1/2 tsp. ground cloves
1/4 tsp. salt
1/2 c. cooking oil
1 c. sugar
1 1/2 c. applesauce
1 c. chopped walnuts
Glossy Chocolate Frosting (recipe follows)

Sift together flour, cocoa, cornstarch, baking soda, cinnamon, cloves and salt. Set aside.

Combine cooking oil and sugar in bowl. Beat 2 minutes, using an electric mixer at medium speed.

Add dry ingredients, applesauce and walnuts to oil mixture, stirring to blend well. Pour batter into greased 13x9x2″ baking pan.

Bake in 325° oven 35 minutes, or until a cake tester or toothpick inserted in center comes out clean. Cool in pan on rack.

Frost in pan with Glossy Chocolate Frosting.

Glossy Chocolate Frosting

¼ c. butter or regular margarine
¼ c. baking cocoa
dash salt
3 tblsp. strong coffee
½ tsp. vanilla
2¼ c. sifted confectioners' sugar

Cream together butter, cocoa and salt in bowl until smooth, using an electric mixer at medium speed. Blend in coffee and vanilla.

Gradually add confectioners' sugar, beating well after each addition, using low speed. Continue beating until smooth and creamy.

Fresh Apple Cake

(9 servings)

1½ c. sifted flour
2 tsp. baking soda
1 tsp. pumpkin pie spice
½ tsp. salt
½ c. butter or regular margarine
1 c. sugar
2 eggs
4 c. finely chopped, pared apples
1 c. morsels of wheat bran cereal
confectioners' sugar

Sift together flour, baking soda, pumpkin pie spice and salt. Set aside.

Cream together butter and sugar in bowl until light and fluffy, using an electric mixer at medium speed. Add eggs, one at a time, beating well after each addition.

Gradually add dry ingredients to creamed mixture, beating well after each addition, using low speed. Stir in apples and cereal. Spoon mixture into greased and floured 9″ square baking pan.

Bake in 350° oven 45 minutes, or until a cake tester or toothpick inserted in center comes out clean. Cool in pan on rack.

Sprinkle with confectioners' sugar.

Jewish Apple Cake

(12 servings)

3 tsp. ground cinnamon
2½ c. sugar
6 c. sliced, pared red delicious apples
(4 medium)
3 c. sifted flour
3 tsp. baking powder
1 c. cooking oil
4 eggs
¼ c. orange juice
2½ tsp. vanilla

Combine cinnamon and ½ c. of the sugar in bowl. Toss with apples. Set aside.

Sift together flour, remaining sugar and baking powder into another bowl. Add oil, eggs, orange juice and vanilla. Beat 2 minutes, using an electric mixer at medium speed. Pour half of batter into greased 10″ tube pan. Top with half of apple mixture. Repeat layers, ending with apple mixture.

Bake in 350° oven 1 hour 35 minutes, or until a cake tester or toothpick inserted in center comes out clean. Cool in pan on rack 20 minutes. Remove cake from pan. Cool cake right side up on rack.

Fresh Pear Cake

(12 servings)

3 c. sifted flour
1 tsp. salt
1 tsp. baking soda
¼ tsp. ground cinnamon
¼ tsp. ground nutmeg
2 c. sugar
1½ c. cooking oil
2 eggs
2 tsp. vanilla
2 c. chopped, pared pears
1⅓ c. flaked coconut
confectioners' sugar

Sift together flour, salt, baking soda, cinnamon and nutmeg. Set aside.

Beat sugar, oil, eggs and vanilla in bowl, using an electric mixer at medium speed.

Add dry ingredients, beating well at medium speed. Stir in pears and coconut. Pour batter

At a birthday party for a young child or as the centerpiece of a baby shower, a set of Alphabet Blocks (page 115) will bring smiles. For a shower, the letters could announce BABY. The blocks are cut from a square layer cake; the letters and borders are piped with a round decorating tube.

The blossoms for the Fruit-and-Nut Flower cake at left are made from slivered almonds and dried apricots (see page 99). To reverse the color scheme, substitute halves of pitted prunes for apricots, and golden raisins for dark.

Most of the decorating for the Pinwheel Quilt cake shown below is done in advance (see page 128). The pattern is created by piping Royal Icing into a dozen design blocks, then letting them harden before arranging them on top of the cake. Butter cream frosting in three different shades adds the finishing touches.

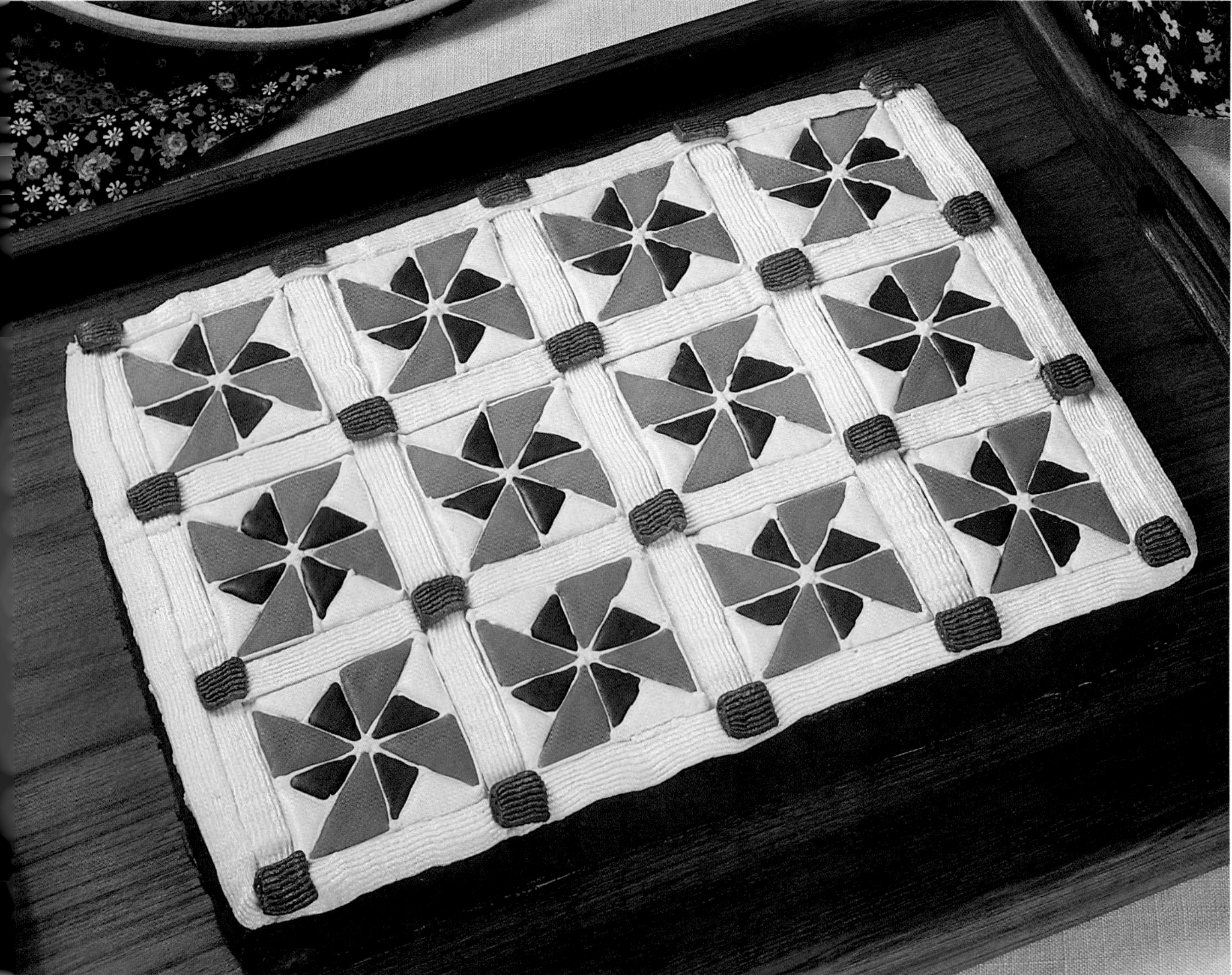

The easy, informal Summer Garden cake shown above is decorated with licorice and other store-bought candies (see page 96). Any 13x9″ cake is a good base for this sort of breezy design, and you can create your own floral varieties with other candies.

Brimming with make-ahead Royal Icing blossoms, the Spring Flower Basket at right was inspired by a Kansas woman's prize-winning design (see page 127). Just a few of these flowers can make any cake beautiful; step-by-step directions are in Chapter 2.

Dress up cupcakes with Royal Icing flowers—if you pipe two or three dozen of these posies and store them in a covered container, you'll be able to offer an elegant assortment of individual desserts like these (page 127) at a moment's notice. The cupcakes can be frozen and decorated as needed.

into greased 10″ fluted tube pan.
Bake in 300° oven 1 hour 20 minutes, or until a cake tester or toothpick inserted in center comes out clean. Cool in pan on rack 10 minutes. Remove from pan. Cool on rack.
Sprinkle with confectioners' sugar.

Heirloom Gingerbread

(16 servings)

2½ c. sifted flour
1½ tsp. baking soda
½ tsp. salt
1 tsp. ground cinnamon
1 tsp. ground ginger
¼ tsp. ground cloves
½ c. butter or regular margarine
½ c. sugar
1 egg
1 c. molasses
1 c. hot water

Sift together flour, baking soda, salt, cinnamon, ginger and cloves. Set aside.
Cream together butter and sugar in bowl until light and fluffy, using an electric mixer at medium speed. Add egg; beat well. Gradually beat in molasses.
Gradually add dry ingredients alternately with hot water to creamed mixture, beating well after each addition, using low speed. Pour batter into greased 13x9x2″ baking pan.
Bake in 350° oven 25 minutes, or until a cake tester or toothpick inserted in center comes out clean. Cool in pan on rack.

Old-fashioned Gingerbread

(Makes 16 servings)

2½ c. sifted flour
1½ tsp. baking soda
1 tsp. ground ginger
1 tsp. ground cinnamon
½ tsp. salt
½ c. shortening
½ c. sugar
1 egg
1 c. dark molasses
½ c. hot water

Sift together flour, baking soda, ginger, cinnamon and salt. Set aside.
Cream together shortening and sugar in bowl until light and fluffy, using an electric mixer at medium speed. Beat in egg and molasses.
Gradually add dry ingredients alternately with hot water to creamed mixture, beating well after each addition, using low speed. Pour batter into greased 9″ square baking pan.
Bake in 350° oven 45 minutes, or until a cake tester or toothpick inserted in center comes out clean. Cool in pan on rack.

Nutmeg Cake with Tangy Lemon Sauce

(9 servings)

2 c. sifted cake flour
2 c. packed brown sugar
½ c. butter or regular margarine
1 tsp. baking soda
1 tsp. ground nutmeg
1 egg
1 c. dairy sour cream
½ c. chopped pecans
Tangy Lemon Sauce (recipe follows)

Combine cake flour and brown sugar in bowl. Cut in butter until crumbly, using a pastry blender. Press half of the crumb mixture into greased 9″ square baking pan. Set aside.
Add baking soda and nutmeg to remaining crumb mixture; mix well. Stir in egg and sour cream; mix well. Spread batter over crumb mixture in pan. Sprinkle with pecans.
Bake in 350° oven 35 minutes, or until a cake tester or toothpick inserted in center comes out clean. Cool slightly in pan on rack.
Serve warm with Tangy Lemon Sauce.

Tangy Lemon Sauce

¾ c. sugar
4½ tsp. cornstarch
⅛ tsp. salt
1 c. water
2 tblsp. lemon juice
1 tsp. grated lemon rind
dash of ground mace
2 tblsp. butter or regular margarine
1 drop yellow food coloring

Combine sugar, cornstarch and salt in 2-qt. saucepan. Stir in water and lemon juice.

Cook over medium heat, stirring constantly, until mixture comes to a boil. Boil 1 minute. Remove from heat.

Gently stir in remaining ingredients. Serve warm.

Pumpkin Spice Cake

(12 servings)

2 c. raisins
1 c. walnuts
2 c. sifted flour
2 tsp. baking soda
2 tsp. ground cinnamon
1 tsp. ground ginger
½ tsp. ground cloves
½ tsp. salt
4 eggs
2 c. sugar
1 c. cooking oil
1 (16-oz.) can mashed pumpkin (2 c.)
Cream Cheese Frosting II (see page 62)

Coarsely chop raisins and walnuts. Toss lightly to combine. Set aside.

Sift together flour, baking soda, cinnamon, ginger, cloves and salt. Set aside.

Beat eggs until thick and lemon-colored, using an electric mixer at high speed. Gradually add sugar, beating well after each addition. Continue beating until thick.

Beat in oil and pumpkin, using low speed. Beat in flour mixture, using low speed. Stir in raisins and walnuts. Pour batter into greased 10″ tube pan.

Bake in 350° oven 60 minutes, or until top springs back when touched. Cool in pan on rack 10 minutes. Remove from pan. Cool on rack.

Frost sides and top of cake with Cream Cheese Frosting II.

Pineapple Upside-down Cake

(12 servings)

½ c. butter or regular margarine
1 c. packed brown sugar
1 (8¼-oz.) can crushed pineapple
2 c. sifted flour
2 tsp. baking powder
½ tsp. salt
⅔ c. butter or regular margarine
1½ c. sugar
3 eggs
½ tsp. almond extract
1 c. dairy sour cream
Sweetened Whipped Cream I (see page 63)

Combine ½ c. butter and brown sugar in 2-qt. saucepan. Cook over medium heat, stirring constantly, until mixture is bubbly. Immediately pour into ungreased 12x8x2″ (2-qt.) glass baking dish. Spoon undrained pineapple over brown sugar mixture. Set aside.

Sift together flour, baking powder and salt. Set aside.

Cream together ⅔ c. butter and sugar in bowl until light and fluffy, using an electric mixer at medium speed. Add eggs, one at a time, beating well after each addition. Blend in almond extract.

Gradually add dry ingredients alternately with sour cream to creamed mixture, beating well after each addition, using low speed. Pour batter in prepared baking dish.

Bake in 325° oven 55 minutes, or until a cake tester or toothpick inserted in center comes out clean. Loosen edges with metal spatula. Invert baking dish on rack. Remove baking dish. Cool cake slightly.

Serve warm with puffs of Sweetened Whipped Cream I.

Peach Upside-down Cake

(10 servings)

¼ c. butter or regular margarine
½ c. packed brown sugar
1 (16-oz.) can sliced peaches, drained
½ c. chopped walnuts
1¼ c. sifted cake flour
¾ c. sugar
2 tsp. baking powder
½ tsp. salt
⅓ c. shortening
½ c. milk
1 tsp. vanilla
1 egg
Sweetened Whipped Cream I (see page 63)

Melt butter in 8″ square baking pan over medium heat. Remove from heat. Stir in brown sugar. Arrange peach slices in brown sugar mixture in pan. Sprinkle with walnuts. Set aside.

Sift together cake flour, sugar, baking powder and salt into bowl. Add shortening, milk, vanilla and egg. Beat 2 minutes, using an electric mixer at medium speed. Pour batter into prepared pan.

Bake in 375° oven 35 minutes, or until a cake tester or toothpick inserted in center comes out clean. Cool in pan on rack 5 minutes. Loosen edges with metal spatula. Invert pan on rack. Remove pan.

Serve warm with puffs of Sweetened Whipped Cream I.

Skillet Pineapple Upside-down Cake

(10 servings)

2 (8¼-oz.) cans sliced pineapple in heavy syrup
¼ c. butter or regular margarine
⅓ c. sugar
⅓ c. packed brown sugar
7 red maraschino cherries, halved
8 pecan halves
1 c. sifted flour
¾ c. sugar
1½ tsp. baking powder
½ tsp. salt
¼ c. shortening
1 egg

Drain pineapple, reserving ½ c. of the syrup. Set aside.

Melt butter in 10″ oven-proof skillet over medium heat. Stir in ⅓ c. sugar and brown sugar. Remove from heat. Arrange pineapple, cherries and pecans in sugar mixture in skillet. Set aside.

Sift together flour, ¾ c. sugar, baking powder and salt into bowl. Add reserved pineapple syrup and shortening. Beat 2 minutes, using an electric mixer at medium speed. Add egg. Beat 2 minutes more. Pour batter evenly into prepared skillet.

Bake in 350° oven 40 minutes, or until a cake tester or toothpick inserted in center comes out clean. Cool in skillet on rack 5 minutes. Loosen edges with a metal spatula. Invert skillet on rack. Remove skillet. Cool cake slightly. Serve warm.

Pineapple-Carrot Cake

(16 servings)

2½ c. sifted flour
2 tsp. baking soda
1 tsp. salt
2 tsp. ground cinnamon
1½ c. cooking oil
3 eggs
2 c. sugar
2 tsp. vanilla
1 c. grated, pared carrots
1 (8¼-oz.) can crushed pineapple, drained
1 c. flaked coconut
1 c. chopped walnuts
Vanilla Glaze (recipe follows)

Sift together flour, baking soda, salt and cinnamon. Set aside.

Combine oil, eggs and sugar in bowl. Beat 2 minutes, using an electric mixer at medium speed. Blend in vanilla.

Gradually add dry ingredients, carrots, pineapple, coconut and walnuts to egg mixture, stirring to blend well. Pour batter into ungreased 13x9x2″ baking pan.

Bake in 350° oven 55 minutes, or until a cake tester or toothpick inserted in center comes out clean.

Immediately pour Vanilla Glaze over hot cake in pan. Cool in pan on rack.

Vanilla Glaze

1 c. sugar
1 tsp. baking soda
¼ c. butter or regular margarine
1 tblsp. light corn syrup
½ c. sour milk*
1 tsp. vanilla

Combine all ingredients in 2-qt. saucepan.

Cook over medium heat, stirring constantly, until mixture comes to a boil. Reduce heat to low and simmer 5 minutes. Remove from heat. Use immediately.

**Note:* To sour milk, place 1½ tsp. vinegar in measuring cup. Add enough milk to make ½ c.

Carrot Cake

(16 servings)

2 c. sifted flour
2 tsp. baking soda
1 tsp. salt
½ tsp. baking powder
3½ tsp. ground cinnamon
½ tsp. ground cloves
2 c. sugar
1½ c. cooking oil
4 eggs
3 c. grated, pared carrots
1 c. chopped pecans
Cream Cheese Frosting I (see page 61)

Sift together flour, baking soda, salt, baking powder, cinnamon and cloves. Set aside.

Combine sugar, oil and eggs in bowl. Beat until well blended, using an electric mixer at medium speed.

Gradually add dry ingredients alternately with carrots to egg mixture, beating well after each addition, using low speed. Stir in pecans. Pour batter into greased 13x9x2" baking pan.

Bake in 325° oven 65 minutes, or until a cake tester or toothpick inserted in center comes out clean. Cool in pan on rack.

Frost cake with Cream Cheese Frosting I.

Carrot Cake with Peanut Butter Pieces

(16 servings)

1½ c. sifted flour
2 tsp. ground cinnamon
1¼ tsp. baking soda
½ tsp. salt
¾ c. cooking oil
3 eggs
¾ c. sugar
½ c. packed brown sugar
1½ tsp. vanilla
2 c. grated, pared carrots
1 (12-oz.) pkg. peanut butter-flavored pieces
½ c. chopped walnuts
Cream Cheese Frosting IV (see page 62)

Sift together flour, cinnamon, baking soda and salt. Set aside.

Combine oil, eggs, sugar and brown sugar in bowl. Beat 2 minutes, using an electric mixer at medium speed. Blend in vanilla.

Gradually add dry ingredients alternately with carrots to egg mixture, beating well after each addition, using low speed. Stir in peanut butter pieces and walnuts. Pour batter into greased 13x9x2" baking pan.

Bake in 350° oven 35 minutes, or until a cake tester or toothpick inserted in center comes out clean. Cool in pan on rack.

Frost in pan with Cream Cheese Frosting IV.

Luscious Banana Layer Cake

(12 servings)

2 c. sifted cake flour
1 tsp. baking powder
1 tsp. baking soda
½ tsp. salt
½ c. butter or regular margarine
1½ c. sugar
1 egg
1 egg yolk
1 c. mashed bananas (3 small)
¾ c. buttermilk or sour milk*
1 tsp. vanilla
Snowy Frosting (see page 60)

Sift together cake flour, baking powder, baking soda and salt. Set aside.

Cream together butter and sugar in bowl until light and fluffy, using an electric mixer at medium speed. Add egg and egg yolk; beat well. Blend in bananas.

Gradually add dry ingredients alternately with buttermilk to creamed mixture, beating well after each addition, using low speed. Blend in vanilla. Spread batter evenly in 2 greased and floured 8″ square baking pans.

Bake in 375° oven 35 minutes, or until a cake tester or toothpick inserted in center comes out clean. Cool in pans on racks 10 minutes. Remove from pans. Cool on racks.

Fill and frost sides and top of cake with Snowy Frosting.

**Note:* To sour milk, place 2¼ tsp. vinegar in measuring cup. Add enough milk to make ¾ c.

Fantastic Date Cake

(9 servings)

1½ c. boiling water
1½ c. cut-up pitted dates
¼ c. butter or regular margarine
1 tsp. baking soda
1½ c. sifted flour
1 tsp. baking powder
½ tsp. salt
1 egg
1 c. sugar
1 tsp. vanilla
Date Topping (recipe follows)
Sweetened Whipped Cream I (see page 63)

Pour boiling water over dates, butter and baking soda in bowl. Let stand 10 minutes.

Meanwhile, sift together flour, baking powder and salt. Set aside.

Beat egg in bowl until thick and lemon-colored, using an electric mixer at high speed. Gradually add sugar, beating well after each addition. Continue beating until thick. Stir in date mixture.

Gradually add dry ingredients, beating at medium speed 2 minutes. Blend in vanilla. Pour batter into greased 9″ square baking pan.

Bake in 350° oven 30 minutes, or until a cake tester or toothpick inserted in center comes out clean.

Prepare Date Topping and spread over warm cake in pan. Serve slightly warm with puffs of Sweetened Whipped Cream I.

Date Topping

1 c. chopped pitted dates
¾ c. water
1 c. sugar
1 tblsp. butter or regular margarine
⅛ tsp. salt
½ c. chopped walnuts

Combine all ingredients in 2-qt. saucepan. Cook over medium heat, stirring constantly, until mixture comes to a boil. Cook, stirring constantly, 7 minutes or until thick. Remove from heat.

Hummingbird Cake

(16 servings)

3 c. sifted flour
1 tsp. baking soda
1 tsp. salt
1½ c. cooking oil
3 eggs
2 c. sugar
1½ tsp. vanilla
2 c. chopped bananas (2 to 3 medium)
1 (8¼-oz.) can crushed pineapple, drained
1½ c. chopped walnuts
½ c. chopped pitted dates
Tangy Orange Frosting (recipe follows)

Sift together flour, baking soda and salt. Set aside.

Combine cooking oil, eggs and sugar in bowl. Beat 2 minutes, using an electric mixer at medium speed. Blend in vanilla.

Add dry ingredients, bananas, pineapple, walnuts and dates to oil mixture; stir to blend. Pour into ungreased 13x9x2″ baking pan.

Bake in 350° oven 55 minutes, or until a cake tester or toothpick inserted in center comes out clean. Cool in pan on rack.

Frost in pan with Tangy Orange Frosting.

Tangy Orange Frosting

4 c. sifted confectioners' sugar
2 tblsp. butter or regular margarine, melted
¼ c. orange juice
2 tsp. grated orange peel

Combine all ingredients in bowl. Stir until smooth, using a wooden spoon. Makes 1½ c.

Cherry-Pecan Cake

(2 loaves)

1 lb. red candied cherries
4 c. chopped pecans
3¼ c. sifted flour
1 c. butter or regular margarine
3 c. sugar
½ tsp. ground mace
8 eggs, separated
⅓ c. bourbon or orange juice
additional bourbon or orange juice

Combine cherries, pecans and ¼ c. of the flour in bowl; toss to mix. Set aside.

Cream together butter, 2 c. of the sugar and mace in bowl until light and fluffy, using an electric mixer at medium speed. Add egg yolks, two at a time, beating well after each addition.

Gradually add remaining flour alternately with ⅓ c. bourbon to creamed mixture, beating well after each addition, using low speed. Stir in cherry mixture.

Beat egg whites in another bowl until foamy, using an electric mixer at high speed. Gradually add remaining sugar, beating until stiff glossy peaks form. Fold egg white mixture into batter. Pour batter into 2 greased and floured 9x5x3" loaf pans.

Bake in 350° oven 40 minutes. Cover with aluminum foil and bake 40 minutes more, or until a cake tester or toothpick inserted in center comes out clean. Cool in pans on racks 1 hour. Remove from pans. Cool on racks.

Soak 2 pieces of cheesecloth with additional bourbon or orange juice and wrap around each loaf. Then wrap each loaf in aluminum foil. Refrigerate several weeks. (Flavor improves on standing.)

Fruitcakes

These are the cakes to make well in advance of the time you plan to enjoy them. Let them mellow in a cool place for several weeks, stored in an airtight container or wrapped in cloths soaked with fruit juice or brandy. These cakes are baked longer and at lower temperatures than other butter cakes, but be sure not to overbake them in order to guarantee a firm, moist cake.

Elegant Fruitcake

(1 fruitcake)

8 oz. pitted dates, chopped
8 oz. red candied cherries, halved
4 oz. green candied cherries, halved
4 oz. chopped candied lemon peel
4 oz. chopped candied pineapple
1½ c. coarsely chopped pecans
1¼ c. golden raisins
1 c. plus 2 tblsp. dried currants
½ c. orange marmalade
½ c. bourbon
⅓ c. orange juice
3 tblsp. finely chopped candied ginger
1½ tsp. grated orange rind
½ tsp. lemon extract
½ tsp. vanilla
2 c. sifted flour
1 tsp. ground cinnamon
½ tsp. ground nutmeg
½ tsp. baking powder
½ tsp. salt
¼ tsp. ground cloves
¼ tsp. ground allspice
1 c. butter or regular margarine
1 c. sugar
6 eggs
Lemon Glaze I (recipe follows)
pecan halves
red and green candied cherry halves

Combine first 15 ingredients in large bowl. Let stand 1 hour.

Sift together flour, cinnamon, nutmeg, baking powder, salt, cloves and allspice. Set aside.

Cream together butter and sugar in another bowl until light and fluffy, using an electric mixer at medium speed. Add eggs, one at a time, beating well after each addition.

Gradually beat in dry ingredients, using low speed. Pour batter over fruit mixture; mix well with a wooden spoon. Spread batter in greased and floured 10″ tube pan.

Bake in 325° oven 2 hours, or until a cake tester or toothpick inserted in center comes out clean. Cool in pan on rack 10 minutes. Remove from pan. Cool on rack.

Frost top of cake with Lemon Glaze I. Decorate with pecans and cherry halves.

Lemon Glaze I

1½ c. sifted confectioners' sugar
2 tblsp. milk
2½ tsp. lemon juice

Combine all ingredients in bowl. Beat until smooth, using a wooden spoon. Makes ⅔ c.

Best-Ever Fruitcake

(2 fruitcakes)

3 c. raisins
2½ c. dried currants
8 oz. pitted dates, chopped
1 c. halved red maraschino cherries
1 c. chopped candied citron
2 c. chopped walnuts
2 c. chopped pecans
5 c. sifted flour
1 tsp. baking soda
1 tsp. baking powder
1 tsp. salt
1 tsp. ground cinnamon
½ tsp. ground nutmeg
¼ tsp. ground cloves
1¼ c. shortening
2 c. sugar
2 tblsp. light corn syrup
1 c. currant jelly
6 eggs
1 c. orange juice
Lemon Glaze II (recipe follows)

Combine raisins, currants, dates, cherries, citron, walnuts and pecans in large bowl. Set aside.

Sift together flour, baking soda, baking powder, salt, cinnamon, nutmeg and cloves. Set aside.

Cream together shortening and sugar in another bowl until light and fluffy, using an electric mixer at medium speed. Beat in corn syrup and currant jelly. Add eggs, one at a time, beating well after each addition.

Gradually add dry ingredients alternately with orange juice to creamed mixture, beating well after each addition, using low speed. Pour batter over fruit mixture; mix well with a wooden spoon. Spread batter into 2 greased and floured 10″ tube pans.

Bake in 275° oven 2 hours, or until a cake tester or toothpick inserted in center comes out clean. Cool in pans on racks 10 minutes. Remove from pans.

Brush Lemon Glaze II over warm fruitcakes. Cool fruitcakes on racks.

Wrap fruitcakes in aluminum foil and store in cool, dry place up to 2 months.

Lemon Glaze II

2 tblsp. light corn syrup
¼ c. sugar
¼ c. water
4 tsp. lemon juice

Combine all ingredients in small saucepan. Cook over medium heat, stirring constantly until mixture comes to a boil. Remove from heat. Cool 5 minutes.

Rich Fruitcake

(2 fruitcakes)

½ tsp. instant coffee powder
½ c. boiling water
2½ c. sifted flour
1 tsp. baking soda
½ tsp. salt
1 tsp. ground cinnamon
½ tsp. ground nutmeg
½ tsp. ground allspice
¼ tsp. ground cloves
½ c. butter or regular margarine
1 c. packed brown sugar
3 eggs
½ c. molasses
2½ c. raisins
1 c. mixed candied fruit
1 c. chopped, pitted dates
½ c. chopped pecans

Dissolve coffee powder in boiling water in bowl. Set aside.

Sift together flour, baking soda, salt, cinnamon, nutmeg, allspice and cloves. Set aside.

Cream together butter and brown sugar in another bowl until light and fluffy, using an electric mixer at medium speed. Add eggs, one at a time, beating well after each addition.

Stir molasses into coffee.

Gradually add dry ingredients alternately with molasses mixture to creamed mixture, beating well after each addition, using low speed. Stir in raisins, candied fruit, dates and pecans. Spread batter into 2 greased and waxed paper-lined 8¼x4½x2½" loaf pans.

Add enough hot water to a 13x9x2" baking pan or roasting pan to fill 1" deep. (This helps to moisten cake.) Place on lower rack in oven.

Bake cakes on top rack of 275° oven 2 hours, or until a cake tester or toothpick inserted in center comes out clean. Remove from pans. Cool on racks.

Wrap fruitcakes in aluminum foil. Store in a cool, dry place up to 2 months.

Glorious Golden Fruitcake

(1 fruitcake)

4 c. sifted flour
1½ tsp. baking powder
½ tsp. salt
4 c. chopped walnuts
1 c. golden raisins
½ c. chopped candied pineapple
½ c. chopped red candied cherries
½ c. chopped green candied cherries
1 tblsp. grated lemon rind
2 c. butter or regular margarine
2½ c. sugar
6 eggs
¼ c. milk
Pineapple Glaze (recipe follows)
pecan halves

Sift together flour, baking powder and salt. Set aside.

Combine walnuts, raisins, pineapple, red and green cherries, lemon rind and ¼ c. of the dry ingredients in bowl; toss to mix. Set aside.

Cream together butter and sugar in bowl until light and fluffy, using an electric mixer at medium speed. Add eggs, one at a time, beating well after each addition.

Gradually add dry ingredients alternately with milk to creamed mixture, beating well after each addition. Stir in walnut mixture. Pour batter into greased and waxed paper-lined 10" tube pan.

Bake in 275° oven 2 hours 45 minutes, or until a cake tester or toothpick inserted in center comes out clean. Cool in pan on rack 30 minutes. Remove from pan. Cool on rack.

Wrap fruitcake tightly in foil. Store in refrigerator up to 4 weeks.

To serve, drizzle fruitcake with Pineapple Glaze. Decorate with pecan halves.

Pineapple Glaze

1 c. sifted confectioners' sugar
2 tblsp. pineapple juice

Combine confectioners' sugar and pineapple juice in bowl. Stir until smooth, using a wooden spoon.

Miniature Fruitcakes

(10 small fruitcakes)

8 oz. pitted chopped dates
8 oz. red candied cherries, halved
8 oz. green candied cherries, halved
8 oz. mixed candied fruit
2 c. chopped pecans
1 (12-oz.) pkg. semisweet chocolate pieces
½ c. apple juice
3 c. sifted flour
2 tsp. salt
6 eggs
1 c. sugar
2 tsp. vanilla
Apple-Lemon Glaze (recipe follows)

Combine dates, red and green cherries, candied fruit, pecans and chocolate pieces in large bowl. Add apple juice; mix well. Set aside.

Sift together flour and salt. Set aside.

Beat eggs until thick and lemon-colored, using an electric mixer at high speed. Gradually add sugar, beating well after each addition. Continue beating until thick. Blend in vanilla.

Beat in dry ingredients, using low speed. Pour batter over fruit mixture. Mix well. Spread batter in 10 greased and floured 4⅜x2⅜x1½″ loaf pans.

Bake in 325° oven 35 minutes, or until a cake tester or toothpick inserted in center comes out clean. Cool in pans on racks 10 minutes. Remove from pans. Cool on racks.

Spread tops with Apple-Lemon Glaze.

Apple-Lemon Glaze

3 c. sifted confectioners' sugar
6 tblsp. apple juice
1 tsp. grated lemon rind

Combine all ingredients in bowl. Mix well, using a wooden spoon. Makes 1 c.

Sugarplum Cake

(12 servings)

12 oz. miniature candy orange slices, chopped
8 oz. pitted dates, chopped
1½ c. chopped pecans
1½ c. flaked coconut
2 tsp. grated orange rind
4 c. sifted flour
1 tsp. baking soda
¾ c. butter or regular margarine
1¾ c. sugar
4 eggs
1 tblsp. lemon juice
1 c. buttermilk
Orange Glaze (recipe follows)

Combine chopped candy orange slices, dates, pecans, coconut, orange rind and ½ c. of the flour in large bowl; toss to mix. Set aside.

Sift together remaining flour and baking soda. Set aside.

Cream together butter and sugar in another bowl until light and fluffy, using an electric mixer at medium speed. Add eggs, one at a time, beating well after each addition. Blend in lemon juice.

Gradually add dry ingredients alternately with buttermilk to creamed mixture, beating well after each addition, using low speed. Stir in candy-nut mixture. Spread batter in greased and floured 10″ tube pan.

Bake in 300° oven 1 hour 40 minutes, or until a cake tester or toothpick inserted in center comes out clean. Cool in pan on rack 10 minutes. Remove from pan. Cool on rack.

Generously pierce surface of cake with the tines of a fork. Slowly pour Orange Glaze over cake.

Orange Glaze

1 c. sifted confectioners' sugar
3 tblsp. orange juice
1 tsp. grated orange rind

Combine all ingredients in small saucepan. Cook over low heat, stirring constantly, until mixture comes to a boil.

Remove from heat. Cool about 15 minutes.

Pound cakes

These recipes are good choices for cakes that will be cut up and reassembled in novelty shapes because the firm texture of a pound cake allows it to withstand more handling than most. The pound cakes our great-grandmothers baked were even more dense; those recipes called for a pound of flour, a pound of butter and a pound of eggs, and the only leavening used was the air that could be beaten into the batter by hand.

Old-fashioned Pound Cake

(12 servings)

1 c. butter or regular margarine
1⅔ c. sugar
5 eggs
1 tsp. vanilla
2 c. sifted flour
½ c. milk

Cream together butter and sugar in bowl until light and fluffy, using an electric mixer at medium speed. Add eggs, one at a time, beating well after each addition. Blend in vanilla (total beating time: 10 minutes).

Gradually add flour alternately with milk to creamed mixture, beating well after each addition, using low speed. Pour batter into greased 10″ fluted tube pan.

Bake in 350° oven 1 hour, or until a cake tester or toothpick inserted in center comes out clean. Cool in pan on rack 10 minutes. Remove from pan. Cool on rack.

Heirloom Pound Cake

(12 servings)

2 c. sifted flour
1 tsp. mace
¼ tsp. salt
1 c. butter or regular margarine
2 c. sugar
5 eggs

Sift together flour, mace and salt. Set aside.

Cream together butter and sugar in bowl until light and fluffy, using an electric mixer at medium speed. Add eggs, one at a time, beating well after each addition (total beating time: 10 minutes).

Gradually add dry ingredients to creamed mixture, beating well after each addition, using low speed. Pour batter into well greased 10″ fluted tube pan.

Bake in 350° oven 50 minutes, or until a cake tester or toothpick inserted in center comes out clean. Cool in pan on rack 10 minutes. Remove from pan. Cool on rack.

Rich Pound Cake

(18 servings)

2 c. butter or regular margarine
1 (1-lb.) box confectioners' sugar, sifted
6 eggs
1 tblsp. vanilla
3 c. sifted cake flour
confectioners' sugar

Cream together butter and 1 lb. confectioners' sugar in bowl until light and fluffy, using an electric mixer at medium speed. Add eggs, one at a time, beating well after each addition. Blend in vanilla (total beating time: 10 minutes).

Gradually add cake flour to creamed mixture, beating well after each addition, using low speed. Pour batter into 2 greased 9x5x3″ loaf pans.

Bake in 350° oven 45 minutes, or until a cake tester or toothpick inserted in center comes out clean.

Cool in pans on racks 10 minutes. Remove from pans. Cool on racks.

Sprinkle with confectioners' sugar.

Million-Dollar Pound Cake

(12 servings)

3 c. sifted flour
½ tsp. salt
¼ tsp. baking soda
½ c. butter or regular margarine
½ c. shortening
3 c. sugar
6 eggs
2 tsp. lemon extract
1 tsp. vanilla
1 c. buttermilk
Creamy Frosting (see page 60)

Sift together flour, salt and baking soda. Set aside.

Cream together butter, shortening and sugar in bowl until light and fluffy, using an electric mixer at medium speed. Add eggs, one at a time, beating well after each addition. Blend in lemon extract and vanilla (total beating time: 10 minutes).

Gradually add dry ingredients alternately with buttermilk to creamed mixture, beating well after each addition, using low speed. Pour batter into greased and floured 10″ tube pan.

Bake in 325° oven 1 hour 20 minutes, or until a cake tester or toothpick inserted in center comes out clean. Cool in pan on rack 10 minutes. Remove from pan. Cool on rack.

Frost sides and top of cake with Creamy Frosting.

Dolores' Pound Cake

(24 servings)

5 c. sifted flour
2 tsp. baking powder
2 c. butter or regular margarine
3 c. sugar
8 eggs
1 tsp. vanilla
1 c. milk

Sift together flour and baking powder. Set aside.

Cream together butter and sugar in bowl until light and fluffy, using an electric mixer at medium speed. Add eggs, one at a time, beating well after each addition. Blend in vanilla (total beating time: 10 minutes).

Gradually add dry ingredients alternately with milk to creamed mixture, beating well after each addition, using low speed. Pour batter into greased and floured 17x13x1" baking pan or disposable aluminum pan.

Bake in 325° oven 1 hour 15 minutes, or until a cake tester or toothpick inserted in center comes out clean. Cool in pan on rack.

Frost in pan as you wish.

Chocolate Pound Cake

(12 servings)

2½ c. sifted flour
1 c. baking cocoa
2 tsp. baking powder
1 tsp. salt
1½ c. butter or regular margarine
3 c. sugar
5 eggs
2½ tsp. vanilla
1½ c. buttermilk or sour milk*
Butter-Rum Glaze (recipe follows)
pecan or walnut halves

Sift together flour, cocoa, baking powder and salt. Set aside.

Cream together butter and sugar in bowl until light and fluffy, using an electric mixer at medium speed. Add eggs, one at a time, beating well after each addition. Blend in vanilla (total beating time: 10 minutes).

Gradually add dry ingredients alternately with buttermilk to creamed mixture, beating well after each addition. Pour batter into greased 10" fluted tube pan.

Bake in 325° oven 1 hour 20 minutes, or until a cake tester or toothpick inserted in center comes out clean. Cool in pan on rack 10 minutes. Remove from pan. Cool on rack.

Pour Butter-Rum Glaze over cake and decorate with pecan halves.

**Note:* To sour milk, place 4½ tsp. vinegar in measuring cup. Add enough milk to make 1½ c.

Butter-Rum Glaze

2 c. sifted confectioners' sugar
⅓ c. butter or regular margarine, melted
½ tsp. rum flavoring*
1 to 2 tblsp. water*

Combine confectioners' sugar, melted butter and rum flavoring in bowl. Blend well, using a wooden spoon. Blend in enough water, 1 tsp. at a time, to make glaze thin enough to pour.

**Note:* 2 tblsp. light rum may be substituted for rum flavoring and water.

Grandma's Chocolate Pound Cake

(12 servings)

3 c. sifted flour
4 tblsp. baking cocoa
½ tsp. baking powder
½ tsp. salt
1 c. butter or regular margarine
½ c. shortening
2 c. sugar
5 eggs
1½ tsp. vanilla
1 c. milk

Sift together flour, cocoa, baking powder and salt. Set aside.

Cream together butter, shortening and sugar in bowl until light and fluffy, using an electric mixer at medium speed. Add eggs, one at a time, beating well after each addition. Blend in vanilla (total beating time: 10 minutes).

Gradually add dry ingredients alternately with

milk to creamed mixture, beating well after each addition, using low speed. Pour batter into greased 10" tube pan.

Bake in 325° oven 1 hour 20 minutes, or until a cake tester or toothpick inserted in center comes out clean. Cool in pan on rack 10 minutes. Remove from pan. Cool on rack.

Coconut Pound Cake

(12 servings)

3 c. sifted flour
2 tsp. baking powder
¼ tsp. salt
1 c. butter or regular margarine
1 (1-lb.) box confectioners' sugar, sifted
4 eggs
1 tsp. vanilla
½ c. milk
1⅔ c. flaked coconut
1 tsp. grated lemon rind

Sift together flour, baking powder and salt. Set aside.

Cream together butter and confectioners' sugar in bowl until light and fluffy, using an electric mixer at medium speed. Add eggs, one at a time, beating well after each addition. Blend in vanilla (total beating time: 10 minutes).

Gradually add dry ingredients alternately with milk to creamed mixture, beating well after each addition, using low speed. Blend in coconut and lemon rind. Pour batter into greased and floured 10" fluted tube pan.

Bake in 350° oven 35 minutes. Reduce temperature to 325° and bake 35 minutes more, or until a cake tester or toothpick inserted in center comes out clean. Cool in pan on rack 10 minutes. Remove from pan. Cool on rack.

Pumpkin Pound Cake

(12 servings)

3 c. sifted flour
4 tsp. baking powder
¼ tsp. baking soda
½ tsp. salt
1 c. butter or regular margarine
1 c. sugar
1 c. packed brown sugar
2 eggs
1 c. canned or mashed, cooked pumpkin
1 tsp. lemon extract
½ c. milk
1 c. chopped walnuts
confectioners' sugar

Sift together flour, baking powder, baking soda and salt. Set aside.

Cream together butter, sugar and brown sugar in bowl until light and fluffy, using an electric mixer at medium speed. Add eggs, one at a time, beating well after each addition. Blend in pumpkin and lemon extract (total beating time: 10 minutes).

Gradually add dry ingredients alternately with milk to creamed mixture, beating well after each addition, using low speed. Stir in walnuts. Pour batter into greased 10" tube pan.

Bake in 325° oven 1 hour 20 minutes, or until a cake tester or toothpick inserted in center comes out clean. Cool in pan on rack 10 minutes. Remove from pan. Cool on rack.

Sprinkle with confectioners' sugar.

Pound Cake with Peanut Butter Pieces

(12 servings)

3 c. sifted flour
1½ tsp. baking powder
1½ tsp. baking soda
¼ tsp. salt
¾ c. butter or regular margarine
1½ c. sugar
3 eggs
1 tsp. vanilla
1½ c. sour cream
1 (12-oz.) pkg. peanut butter-flavored pieces
Streusel Swirl (recipe follows)
Peanut Butter Glaze (recipe follows)

Sift together flour, baking powder, baking soda and salt. Set aside.

Cream together butter and sugar in bowl until light and fluffy, using an electric mixer at medium speed. Add eggs, one at a time, beating well after each addition. Blend in vanilla (total beating time: 10 minutes).

Gradually add dry ingredients alternately with sour cream to creamed mixture, beating well after each addition, using low speed. Stir in peanut butter pieces. Pour half of the batter into greased 10″ fluted tube pan. Sprinkle Streusel Swirl evenly over batter. Spread remaining batter evenly on top.

Bake in 350° oven 65 minutes, or until a cake tester or toothpick inserted in center comes out clean. Cool in pan on rack 10 minutes. Remove from pan. Cool on rack.

Pour Peanut Butter Glaze over the top of cake.

Streusel Swirl

¼ c. packed brown sugar
¼ c. finely chopped walnuts
½ tsp. ground cinnamon

Combine all ingredients in bowl. Mix well.

Peanut Butter Glaze

⅓ c. sugar
¼ c. water
1 c. peanut butter-flavored pieces
2 tblsp. marshmallow creme
hot water

Combine sugar and ¼ c. water in small saucepan. Bring to boil over medium heat. Remove from heat; add peanut butter pieces. Stir until smooth.

Stir in marshmallow creme. Blend in enough hot water, ½ tsp. at a time, to make glaze thin enough to pour. Makes 1 c.

Angel food cakes

Light and airy, these are true foam cakes, leavened entirely with air and made without shortening. An angel food cake is always baked in an ungreased pan so that as it bakes it can rise up the sides of the pan to its full height.

Special care is needed in using eggs in these recipes. The eggs should be separated while still cold, and there mustn't be even a smidgen of yolk in the egg white mixture. Let the egg whites come to room temperature before beating them together with the cream of tartar and salt; then, once they're foamy, be sure to add the sugar gradually until the mixture is stiff and glossy but not dry. To test whether you've beaten the egg whites long enough, draw a spatula through them; if they retain their shape, they're ready. Further beating will reduce the volume and coarsen the texture of the finished cake.

Cake flour helps give these cakes their light texture, and sifting it together with the sugar three or four times produces the highest, lightest cakes possible. As you add the flour mixture to the egg whites, fold it in gently by hand with an under-and-over motion, using a spatula to bring the egg whites up over the flour and fold the flour into the egg whites. About 15 gentle strokes after each addition of flour are enough; a heavy hand will release the precious air that gives the cakes its volume.

Angel food cakes should be baked on the lower rack of the oven. Five minutes before the end of the baking time, check for doneness; if the cake has a golden brown crust and the top springs back when you touch it lightly with your finger, the cake is done.

Let these cakes cool in their pans, inverted over a funnel or a bottle, for at least two hours before you remove them; if you try to remove them before they're completely cool, they may collapse.

Super Angel Food Cake

(12 servings)

1 c. sifted cake flour
1½ c. sifted confectioners' sugar
1½ c. egg whites (about 12)
1½ tsp. cream of tartar
¼ tsp. salt
1 c. sugar
1 tsp. vanilla

Sift together cake flour and confectioners' sugar 3 times. Set aside.

Beat egg whites, cream of tartar and salt in large bowl until foamy, using an electric mixer at high speed. Gradually add sugar, 2 tblsp. at a time, beating until stiff glossy peaks form. Blend in vanilla.

Add flour mixture one-fourth at a time, folding about 15 strokes after each addition. Turn batter into ungreased 10″ tube pan. Pull a metal spatula through batter once to break large air bubbles.

Bake in 325° oven 65 minutes, or until top springs back when touched. Invert tube pan on funnel or bottle to cool. When completely cool, remove cake from pan.

Party Angel Food Cake

(12 servings)

1 c. plus 2 tblsp. sifted cake flour
¾ c. sugar
1⅔ c. egg whites (about 13)
1½ tsp. cream of tartar
½ tsp. salt
1 c. sugar
1 tsp. vanilla
½ tsp. almond extract
10 red maraschino cherries, chopped
½ c. chopped pecans
7-Minute Frosting (see page 62)
red maraschino cherries with stems

Sift together cake flour and ¾ c. sugar 4 times. Set aside.

Beat egg whites, cream of tartar and salt in large bowl until foamy, using an electric mixer at high speed. Gradually add 1 c. sugar, 2 tblsp. at a time, beating until stiff glossy peaks form. Blend in vanilla and almond extract.

Add flour mixture one-fourth at a time, folding about 15 strokes after each addition. Fold in chopped cherries and pecans. Turn batter into ungreased 10″ tube pan. Pull a metal spatula through batter once to break large air bubbles.

Bake in 350° oven 45 minutes, or until top springs back when touched. Invert tube pan on funnel or bottle to cool. When completely cool, remove cake from pan.

Frost with 7-Minute Frosting and decorate with whole maraschino cherries.

Peppermint Angel Food Cake

(12 servings)

1 c. sifted cake flour
1 c. sifted confectioners' sugar
1⅔ c. egg whites (about 13)
1½ tsp. cream of tartar
¼ tsp. salt
1 c. sugar
1 tsp. vanilla
½ tsp. peppermint extract
12 drops red food coloring
2 drops peppermint extract
7-Minute Frosting (see page 62)
red food coloring

Sift together cake flour and confectioners' sugar 4 times. Set aside.

Beat egg whites, cream of tartar and salt in large bowl until foamy, using an electric mixer at high speed. Gradually add sugar, 2 tblsp. at a time, beating until stiff glossy peaks form.

Add flour mixture one-fourth at a time, folding about 15 strokes after each addition. Divide batter in half. Fold vanilla into half of the batter. Fold ½ tsp. peppermint extract and 12 drops food coloring into remaining half.

Alternate spoonfuls of pink and white batter in ungreased 10″ tube pan. Swirl batter with a metal spatula.

Bake in 325° oven 50 minutes, or until top springs back when touched. Invert tube pan on funnel or bottle to cool. When completely cool, remove cake from pan.

Add 2 drops peppermint extract to 7-Minute Frosting. Tint frosting pale pink with red food coloring. Remove ½ c. frosting and tint dark pink by adding more red food coloring. Frost cake with pale pink frosting. Using a spoon, swirl dark pink frosting over cake.

Strawberry Angel Surprise

(12 servings)

1 (3-oz.) pkg. strawberry-flavored gelatin
1 c. boiling water
20 drops red food coloring
1 (10″) angel food cake
1½ c. heavy cream, whipped
1½ c. sliced fresh strawberries
½ tsp. vanilla
Strawberry Cream (recipe follows)

Dissolve gelatin in boiling water in bowl. Stir in food coloring. Refrigerate until thick and syrupy.

Place cake on serving plate. Cut a 1″ slice

from top of cake and set aside. Cut down into cake 1″ from outer edge and 1″ from hole. Remove cake between cuts, forming a cavity all around with a 1″ base at bottom.

Fold thickened gelatin mixture into whipped cream. Then fold in strawberries and vanilla. Spoon into cake shell. Replace top of cake and frost with Strawberry Cream. Refrigerate 4 hours before serving.

Strawberry Cream

1½ c. sliced fresh strawberries
¼ c. confectioners' sugar
1½ c. heavy cream, whipped

Combine strawberries and sugar in bowl; let stand 30 minutes. Fold strawberry mixture into whipped cream. Makes 4½ c.

Daffodil Cake

(12 servings)

1 c. sifted cake flour
¾ c. sugar
1½ c. egg whites (about 12)
1½ tsp. cream of tartar
¼ tsp. salt
¾ c. sugar
2 tsp. vanilla
½ tsp. almond extract
6 egg yolks

Sift together cake flour and ¾ c. sugar. Set aside.

Beat egg whites, cream of tartar and salt in large bowl until foamy, using an electric mixer at high speed. Gradually add ¾ c. sugar, 2 tblsp. at a time, beating until stiff glossy peaks form. Blend in vanilla and almond extract.

Add flour mixture one-fourth at a time, folding about 15 strokes after each addition. Set aside.

Beat egg yolks in small bowl until thick and lemon-colored, using an electric mixer at high speed. Fold egg yolk mixture into half of batter.

Spoon yellow and white batters alternately into ungreased 10″ tube pan. Swirl batter with a metal spatula.

Bake at 375° on lowest shelf of oven 35 to 40 minutes, or until top is dry and springs back when touched. Invert tube pan on funnel or bottle to cool. When completely cool, remove cake from pan.

Sponge cakes

Many combinations of ingredients, several methods of mixing and several shapes of pans can produce an excellent sponge cake.

The most important constant in sponge cakes is the way the eggs are beaten. If you don't beat the eggs until they thicken and become creamy and pale yellow, even the presence of baking powder won't produce an airy cake. But if you follow the directions in these recipes, you'll have a light and lovely cake that can highlight a multitude of occasions.

Golden Sponge Cake

(12 servings)

6 eggs, separated
1½ c. sugar
½ c. cold water
1 tsp. vanilla
1½ c. sifted cake flour
¾ tsp. cream of tartar
¼ tsp. salt

Beat together egg yolks, ¾ c. of the sugar, water and vanilla in bowl until thick and lemon-colored, using an electric mixer at high speed. Blend in flour at low speed.

Beat egg whites, cream of tartar and salt in another bowl until foamy, using an electric mixer at high speed. Gradually add remaining sugar, beating until stiff glossy peaks form.

Fold egg yolk mixture into egg white mixture. Pour into ungreased 10″ tube pan. Pull a metal spatula through batter once to break large air bubbles.

Bake in 325° oven 1 hour, or until top is dry and springs back when touched. Invert tube pan on funnel or bottle to cool. When completely cool, remove cake from pan.

Lemon Sponge Cake

(12 servings)

8 eggs, separated
1½ c. sugar
2 tblsp. cold water
½ tsp. vanilla
½ tsp. almond extract
½ tsp. lemon extract
1¼ c. sifted flour
½ tsp. cream of tartar
½ tsp. salt
confectioners' sugar

Combine egg yolks, ½ c. of the sugar, water, vanilla, almond extract and lemon extract in bowl. Beat with an electric mixer at high speed, about 5 minutes, or until thick and lemon-colored. Stir in flour all at once.

Beat egg whites, cream of tartar and salt in another bowl until foamy, using an electric mixer at high speed. Gradually add remaining sugar, beating until stiff glossy peaks form.

Gradually fold egg yolk mixture into egg white mixture. Pour batter into ungreased 10″ tube pan. Pull a metal spatula through batter once to break large air bubbles.

Bake in 325° oven 60 to 65 minutes, or until top springs back when touched. Invert tube pan on funnel or bottle to cool. When completely cool, remove cake from pan.

Sprinkle with confectioners' sugar.

Lazy Daisy Cake

(9 servings)

1 c. sifted flour
1 tsp. baking powder
¼ tsp. salt
2 tblsp. butter or regular margarine
½ c. milk
2 eggs
1 c. sugar
1 tsp. vanilla
Coconut-Pecan Topping (recipe follows)

Sift together flour, baking powder and salt. Set aside.

Heat butter and milk over low heat until butter melts. Keep warm.

Beat eggs and sugar in bowl 2 minutes, using an electric mixer at medium speed. Gradually add dry ingredients and vanilla, beating well after each addition, using low speed. Add warm milk mixture, beating until blended. Pour batter into greased 9″ square baking pan.

Bake in 375° oven 20 minutes, or until top springs back when touched. Cool in pan on rack 10 minutes.

Frost warm cake with Coconut-Pecan Topping and broil as directed. Cool in pan on rack.

Coconut-Pecan Topping

½ c. butter or regular margarine
¾ c. packed brown sugar
1 c. flaked coconut
½ c. chopped pecans
4 tblsp. light cream

Combine all ingredients in small saucepan. Cook over medium heat until mixture comes to a boil. Remove from heat. Makes 2 c.

Spread frosting over top of cake in pan. Broil 3″ from source of heat 1 minute or until golden brown and bubbly.

Strawberry Sponge Shortcake

(8 servings)

⅓ c. sifted flour
¼ c. cornstarch
⅛ tsp. salt
2 eggs
⅓ c. sugar
1 c. heavy cream, whipped
Strawberry Filling (recipe follows)
whole strawberries

Sift together flour, cornstarch and salt. Set aside.

Beat eggs in bowl until thick and lemon-colored, using an electric mixer at high speed. Gradually add sugar, beating until light.

Beat in dry ingredients at low speed. Pour batter into greased and waxed paper-lined 8″ round baking pan.

Bake in 350° oven 20 minutes, or until top springs back when touched. Cool in pan on rack 10 minutes. Remove from pan. Cool on rack.

Cut layer horizontally into 2 equal layers. Fill layers with half of the whipped cream and half of the Strawberry Filling.

Spread top with remaining Strawberry Filling. Decorate with remaining whipped cream and strawberries.

Strawberry Filling

1 pt. strawberries, hulled
¼ c. sugar
1 tblsp. cornstarch
½ c. water

Crush ½ c. of the strawberries. Slice remaining strawberries.

Combine crushed strawberries, sugar, cornstarch and water in small saucepan.

Cook over medium heat, stirring constantly, until mixture comes to a boil. Reduce heat to low and simmer 5 minutes. Stir in sliced strawberries.

Remove from heat. Cool completely. Makes 2 c.

Fresh Fruit Sponge Cake

(8 servings)

⅓ c. sifted flour
¼ c. cornstarch
⅛ tsp. salt
2 eggs
⅓ c. sugar
2 c. assorted fresh fruits (such as sliced peaches, sliced strawberries, grapes)
Fruit Glaze (recipe follows)
Sweetened Whipped Cream I (see page 63)

Sift together flour, cornstarch and salt. Set aside.

Beat eggs in bowl until thick and lemon-colored, using an electric mixer at high speed. Gradually add sugar, beating until light.

Beat in dry ingredients at low speed. Pour batter into greased and waxed paper-lined 9″ round baking pan.

Bake in 350° oven 20 minutes, or until top springs back when touched. Cool in pan on rack 10 minutes. Remove from pan; cool on rack.

Arrange fruit as desired on top of cake. Pour Fruit Glaze evenly over fruit and let stand at room temperature 30 minutes or until set.

Serve with Sweetened Whipped Cream I.

Fruit Glaze

1 c. apple juice
1 tblsp. lemon juice
1 tblsp. cornstarch

Combine all ingredients in small saucepan.

Cook over medium heat, stirring constantly, until mixture comes to a boil. Simmer over low heat 5 minutes.

Remove from heat and cool 5 minutes. Makes 1 c.

Peanut Butter-and-Jelly Roll

(8 servings)

1 c. sifted cake flour
1 tsp. baking powder
¼ tsp. salt
3 eggs
1 c. sugar
⅓ c. water
1 tsp. vanilla
confectioners' sugar
1 c. currant or strawberry jelly
Creamy Peanut Butter Frosting (recipe follows)
3 tblsp. chopped peanuts

Sift together cake flour, baking powder and salt. Set aside.

Beat eggs and sugar in bowl until thick and lemon-colored, using an electric mixer at high speed. Blend in water and vanilla.

Blend in dry ingredients at low speed. Pour batter into greased and waxed paper-lined 15½x10½x1″ jelly roll pan.

Bake in 350° oven 15 minutes, or until top springs back when touched.

Loosen cake around edges with a metal spatula. Turn cake out on a linen dish towel dusted with confectioners' sugar. Carefully peel off waxed paper. Trim brown crust from edges. Roll up cake, starting at narrow end, rolling up towel with cake. Cool on rack.

Unroll cake and spread with jelly to within ½″ of edges. Reroll cake, using towel to help make a tight roll. Place cake roll seam side down.

Frost cake with Creamy Peanut Butter Frosting and sprinkle with peanuts.

Creamy Peanut Butter Frosting

½ (3-oz.) pkg. cream cheese, softened (1½ oz.)
2 tblsp. smooth peanut butter
1 c. sifted confectioners' sugar
1 tblsp. milk
¼ tsp. vanilla

Cream together cream cheese and peanut butter in bowl until light and fluffy, using an electric mixer at medium speed. Stir in remaining ingredients. Makes 1 c.

My Favorite Jelly Roll

(8 servings)

¾ c. sifted cake flour
¾ tsp. baking powder
¼ tsp. salt
5 eggs
¾ c. sugar
½ tsp. almond extract
confectioners' sugar
1 c. apricot preserves (or any other jam or jelly)

Sift together cake flour, baking powder and salt. Set aside.

Combine eggs, ¾ c. sugar and almond extract in bowl. Beat with an electric mixer at high speed, about 5 minutes, until thick and lemon-colored.

Fold dry ingredients into egg mixture. Spread batter in greased and waxed paper-lined 15½x10½x1" jelly roll pan.

Bake in 350° oven 20 minutes, or until top springs back when touched.

Loosen cake around edges with a metal spatula. Turn cake out on a linen dish towel dusted with confectioners' sugar. Carefully peel off waxed paper. Trim brown crust from edges. Roll up cake, starting at narrow end, rolling up towel with cake. Cool on rack.

Unroll cake and spread with apricot preserves to within ½" of edges. Reroll cake, using towel to help make a tight roll. Place cake roll seam side down.

Applesauce Roll

(8 servings)

½ c. raisins
boiling water
1 c. sifted flour
½ tsp. baking powder
½ tsp. baking soda
½ tsp. cinnamon
¼ tsp. ground cloves
¼ tsp. salt
3 eggs
¾ c. sugar
½ c. applesauce
confectioners' sugar
Cinnamon Whipped Cream (recipe follows)

Place raisins in bowl with enough boiling water to cover. Let stand 5 minutes. Drain; set aside.

Sift together flour, baking powder, baking soda, cinnamon, cloves and salt; set aside.

Combine eggs and sugar in bowl. Beat with an electric mixer at high speed, about 5 minutes, until thick and lemon-colored.

Fold dry ingredients into egg mixture. Fold in applesauce and raisins. Spread batter in greased and waxed paper-lined 15½x10½x1" jelly roll pan.

Bake in 350° oven 20 minutes, or until top springs back when touched.

Loosen cake around edges with a metal spatula. Turn cake out on linen dish towel dusted with confectioners' sugar. Carefully peel off waxed paper. Trim brown crust from edges. Roll up cake, starting at narrow end, rolling up towel with cake. Cool on rack.

Unroll cake and spread with Cinnamon Whipped Cream to within ½" of edges. Reroll cake, using towel to help make a tight roll. Place cake roll seam side down.

Cinnamon Whipped Cream

1 c. heavy cream
2 tblsp. sugar
½ tsp. vanilla
¼ tsp. cinnamon

Beat all ingredients in chilled bowl until soft peaks form, using an electric mixer at high speed. Makes 2 c.

Orange Sponge Roll

(8 servings)

1 c. sifted flour
1 tsp. baking powder
½ tsp. salt
3 eggs
1 c. sugar
1 tsp. vanilla
⅓ c. hot orange juice
2 tblsp. confectioners' sugar
Orange Filling (recipe follows)

Sift together flour, baking powder and salt. Set aside.

Beat eggs in bowl until thick and lemon-colored, using an electric mixer at high speed. Gradually add sugar, beating well after each addition. Beat in vanilla.

Fold dry ingredients into egg mixture. Add hot orange juice. Beat until smooth. Spread batter in greased and waxed paper-lined 15½x10½x1" jelly roll pan.

Bake in 375° oven 12 minutes, or until top springs back when touched.

Loosen cake around edges with a metal spatula. Turn cake out on linen dish towel dusted with confectioners' sugar. Carefully peel off waxed paper. Trim brown crust from edges. Roll up cake, starting at narrow end, rolling up towel with cake. Cool on rack.

Unroll cake and spread with Orange Filling to within ½" of edges. Reroll cake, using towel to help make a tight roll. Place cake roll seam side down.

Orange Filling

½ c. sugar
3 tblsp. cornstarch
¼ tsp. salt
¾ c. water
1 tblsp. butter
1 tblsp. grated orange rind
¼ c. orange juice

Combine sugar, cornstarch and salt in small saucepan. Stir in water.

Cook over medium heat, stirring constantly, 5 minutes, or until mixture boils and thickens. Cook 1 minute more. Remove from heat.

Stir in butter, orange rind and orange juice. Cool to room temperature. Makes 1¼ c.

Chocolate Cake Roll

(8 servings)

¼ c. sifted flour
¼ c. baking cocoa
2 tblsp. cornstarch
⅛ tsp. salt
3 eggs, separated
⅓ c. sugar
1 tblsp. cooking oil
1 tblsp. water
baking cocoa
Custard Filling (recipe follows)
Mocha Creme Frosting (recipe follows)
chopped pistachio nuts or almonds

Sift together flour, baking cocoa, cornstarch and salt. Set aside.

Beat egg whites in bowl until foamy, using an electric mixer at high speed. Gradually add sugar, 2 tblsp. at a time, beating until stiff glossy peaks form. Set aside.

Beat egg yolks in another bowl until thick and lemon-colored, using an electric mixer at high speed.

Gradually fold egg yolks into egg white mixture.

Gradually fold dry ingredients, oil and water into egg mixture. Spread batter in greased and waxed paper-lined 15½x10½x1" jelly roll pan.

Bake in 400° oven 15 minutes, or until top springs back when touched.

Loosen cake around edges with a metal spatula. Turn cake out on linen dish towel dusted with baking cocoa. Carefully peel off waxed paper. Trim brown crust from edges. Roll up cake, starting at narrow end, rolling up towel with cake. Cool slightly.

Meanwhile, prepare Custard Filling.

Unroll cake and spread with Custard Filling to within ½" of edges. Reroll cake, using towel to help make a tight roll. Place cake roll seam side down.

Frost with Mocha Creme Frosting. Using a dinner fork, run tines of fork lengthwise along frosted cake. Sprinkle top with pistachios or almonds. Refrigerate. About 30 minutes before serving, remove from refrigerator.

Custard Filling

½ c. sugar
¼ c. cornstarch

1/8 tsp. salt
2 c. milk
3 egg yolks, beaten
1 1/2 tsp. vanilla

Combine sugar, cornstarch and salt in 2-qt. saucepan. Gradually stir in milk.

Cook over medium heat, stirring constantly, until mixture boils and thickens. Add some of the hot pudding mixture to egg yolks. Then stir egg yolk mixture into remaining hot pudding mixture. Cook 1 minute more.

Remove from heat. Stir in vanilla. Cool completely. Makes 2 3/4 c.

Mocha Creme Frosting

1 (6-oz.) pkg. semisweet chocolate pieces
1 tsp. instant coffee powder
1/2 c. butter or regular margarine
2 tblsp. brandy or water
1/2 c. sifted confectioners' sugar

Melt chocolate pieces over hot (not boiling) water in top of double boiler. When chocolate is melted, add coffee powder and stir until dissolved. Remove from heat. Cool completely.

Combine chocolate mixture, butter and brandy in bowl. Beat until smooth and creamy, using an electric mixer at medium speed.

Gradually add sugar to creamed mixture, beating well after each addition, using low speed.

Cool until mixture is thick enough to spread. Makes 1 1/3 c.

Bûche de Noel

(8 servings)

1/2 c. sifted cake flour
1/3 c. baking cocoa
3/4 c. sugar
1/2 tsp. baking powder
1/4 tsp. salt
4 eggs
1 tsp. vanilla
baking cocoa
Coffee Cream Filling (recipe follows)
Dark Chocolate Frosting (recipe follows)

Sift together cake flour, 1/3 c. cocoa, 1/4 c. of the sugar, baking powder and salt 4 times. Set aside.

Beat eggs and remaining sugar in bowl until thick and lemon-colored, using an electric mixer at high speed. Blend in vanilla.

Gently fold dry ingredients into egg mixture. Pour batter into waxed paper-lined 15 1/2x10 1/2x1" jelly roll pan.

Bake in 400° oven 13 minutes, or until top springs back when touched. Loosen cake around edges with a metal spatula. Turn out on dish towel sprinkled with sifted cocoa. Carefully peel off waxed paper. Trim crisp edges. Roll up, starting at narrow side, rolling towel up with cake. Cool on rack.

Unroll cake and spread with Coffee Cream Filling. Reroll cake, using towel to help make a tight roll. Place seam side down. Frost cake roll with Dark Chocolate Frosting.

Coffee Cream Filling

1 1/2 c. heavy cream
2 tblsp. sugar
2 1/2 tsp. instant coffee powder
1/2 tsp. vanilla

Combine all ingredients in bowl. Refrigerate 1 hour, or until coffee is dissolved.

Beat coffee mixture until soft peaks form, using an electric mixer at high speed.

Dark Chocolate Frosting

2 (1-oz.) squares unsweetened chocolate
1/4 c. butter or regular margarine
2 c. sifted confectioners' sugar
1/2 tsp. vanilla
3-4 tblsp. milk

Melt chocolate and butter in 2-qt. saucepan over low heat. Remove from heat. Stir in confectioners' sugar and vanilla, using a wooden spoon. Beat in milk, 1 tblsp. at a time, until smooth and creamy.

Chiffon cakes

Unlike both sponge cakes and angel food cakes, chiffon cakes are made with cooking oil, and other ingredients are combined differently, too. The dry ingredients are sifted together into a bowl; then a well is made in the center of the dry ingredients. The cooking oil, egg yolks, water and flavorings are added and beaten together until smooth before being folded into the stiffly beaten egg whites.

Like angel food cakes, chiffon cakes are always baked in ungreased pans so that they can rise high and handsome.

Lemon Chiffon Cake

(12 servings)

1 c. egg whites (about 8)
½ tsp. cream of tartar
1¾ c. plus 2 tblsp. sifted flour
1½ c. sugar
3 tsp. baking powder
1 tsp. salt
½ c. cooking oil
5 egg yolks
½ c. water
¼ c. lemon juice
2 tsp. grated lemon rind
Boiled Frosting (see page 62)

Beat egg whites and cream of tartar in bowl until very stiff peaks form, using an electric mixer at high speed. Set aside.

Sift together flour, sugar, baking powder and salt into another bowl. Make a well in the center. Add oil, egg yolks, water, lemon juice and lemon rind. Beat 1 minute, using an electric mixer at low speed.

Gradually pour lemon mixture over egg whites, folding just until blended. Pour batter into ungreased 10″ tube pan. Pull a metal spatula through batter once to break large air bubbles.

Bake in 325° oven 55 minutes. Increase temperature to 350° and bake 10 minutes more, or until top springs back when touched. Invert pan on funnel or bottle to cool. When completely cool, remove cake from pan.

Frost sides and top of cake with Boiled Frosting.

Chocolate Chip Chiffon Cake

(12 servings)

7 egg whites
½ tsp. cream of tartar
2¼ c. sifted cake flour
1¾ c. sugar
3 tsp. baking powder
1 tsp. salt
½ c. cooking oil
5 egg yolks
¾ c. cold water
2 tsp. vanilla
3 (1-oz.) squares unsweetened chocolate, finely grated
Creamy Vanilla Frosting (recipe follows)

Beat egg whites and cream of tartar in bowl until very stiff peaks form, using an electric mixer at high speed. Set aside.

Sift together cake flour, sugar, baking powder and salt into another bowl. Make a well in the center. Add oil, egg yolks, water and vanilla. Beat 1 minute, using an electric mixer at low speed.

Gradually pour egg yolk mixture over egg whites, folding just until blended. Sprinkle with grated chocolate, and fold chocolate into batter. Pour batter into ungreased 10″ tube pan. Pull a metal spatula through batter once to break large air bubbles.

Bake in 325° oven 55 minutes. Increase temperature to 350° and bake 10 to 15 minutes more, or until top springs back when touched. Invert tube pan on funnel or bottle to cool.

When completely cool, remove cake from pan.

Frost sides and top of cake with Creamy Vanilla Frosting.

Creamy Vanilla Frosting

2 eggs
3 tblsp. cornstarch
2 c. milk
1 tsp. vanilla
1 c. butter
1½ c. sifted confectioners' sugar

Beat eggs in 2-qt. saucepan until well blended. Add cornstarch and milk. Mix well.

Cook over medium heat, stirring constantly, until mixture boils and thickens. Cook 1 minute more. Remove from heat. Stir in vanilla. Cool completely.

Add butter and sugar. Beat until light and fluffy, using an electric mixer at medium speed. Makes 3 c.

Cocoa Chiffon Cake

(12 servings)

½ c. baking cocoa
¾ c. boiling water
8 eggs, separated
½ tsp. cream of tartar
1¾ c. sifted cake flour
1¾ c. sugar
1½ tsp. baking soda
1 tsp. salt
½ c. cooking oil
2 tsp. vanilla
Fluffy Chocolate Frosting (recipe follows)

Combine cocoa and boiling water in bowl; stir to blend. Set aside to cool.

Beat egg whites and cream of tartar in bowl until very stiff peaks form, using an electric mixer at high speed. Set aside.

Sift together cake flour, sugar, baking soda and salt into another bowl. Make a well in the center. Add oil, vanilla, egg yolks and cocoa mixture. Beat 1 minute, using an electric mixer at low speed.

Gradually pour chocolate mixture over egg white mixture, folding just until blended. Pour batter into ungreased 10″ tube pan. Pull a metal spatula through batter once to break large air bubbles.

Bake in 325° oven 55 minutes. Increase temperature to 350° and bake 10 minutes longer, or until top springs back when touched. Invert tube pan on funnel or bottle to cool. When completely cool, remove cake from pan.

Frost sides and top of cake with Fluffy Chocolate Frosting.

Fluffy Chocolate Frosting

2 egg whites
1½ c. sugar
⅓ c. water
¼ tsp. cream of tartar
1 tsp. vanilla
2 (1-oz.) squares unsweetened chocolate, melted and cooled

Combine egg whites, sugar, water and cream of tartar in top of double boiler. Beat, using an electric mixer at medium speed, 1 minute.

Place over simmering water. Cook 7 minutes, beating constantly at high speed, until soft glossy peaks form. Remove from hot water. Beat in vanilla. Fold in melted chocolate. Makes 4 c.

Mahogany Chiffon Cake

(12 servings)

⅓ c. freeze-dried coffee
¾ c. boiling water
7 eggs, separated
½ tsp. cream of tartar
1¾ c. sifted cake flour
1⅔ c. sugar
⅓ c. baking cocoa
1½ tsp. baking soda
1 tsp. salt
½ c. cooking oil
2 tsp. vanilla
Mocha Seafoam Frosting (recipe follows)

Combine coffee and boiling water in small bowl; stir to blend. Cool completely.

Beat egg whites and cream of tartar in bowl until very stiff peaks form, using an electric mixer at high speed. Set aside.

Sift together cake flour, sugar, baking cocoa, baking soda and salt into another bowl. Make a well in the center. Add oil, vanilla, egg yolks and coffee mixture. Beat 1 minute, using an electric mixer at low speed.

Gradually pour coffee mixture over egg white mixture, folding just until blended. Pour batter into ungreased 10″ tube pan. Pull a metal spatula through batter once to break large air bubbles.

Bake in 325° oven 55 minutes. Increase temperature to 350° and bake 10 minutes more, or until top springs back when touched. Invert tube pan on funnel or bottle to cool. When completely cool, remove cake from pan.

Frost sides and top of cake with Mocha Seafoam Frosting.

Mocha Seafoam Frosting

1 tsp. freeze-dried coffee
⅓ c. boiling water
2 egg whites
1½ c. packed brown sugar
⅛ tsp. cream of tartar
⅛ tsp. salt

Combine coffee and boiling water in small bowl; stir to blend. Cool completely.

Combine coffee mixture and remaining ingredients in top of double boiler. Beat 1 minute, using an electric mixer at high speed. Place over simmering water.

Cook 7 minutes, beating constantly with an electric mixer at high speed, until soft glossy peaks form. Remove from heat. Makes 5 c.

Coffee Chiffon Layer Cake

(12 servings)

2 eggs, separated
1½ c. sugar
4 tsp. instant coffee powder
½ c. hot water
½ c. milk
⅛ tsp. baking soda
2¼ c. sifted cake flour
3 tsp. baking powder
1 tsp. salt
⅓ c. oil
2 tsp. vanilla
Coffee Fluff Frosting (recipe follows)

Beat egg whites in bowl until foamy, using an electric mixer at high speed. Gradually add ½ c. of the sugar, beating until stiff glossy peaks form. Set aside.

Dissolve instant coffee in hot water and cool to room temperature. Combine with milk and baking soda. Set aside.

Sift together cake flour, remaining sugar, baking powder and salt into bowl. Add oil, vanilla and half of the coffee mixture. Beat 1 minute, using an electric mixer at low speed. Add 2 egg yolks and remaining coffee mixture; beat 1 minute.

Gradually fold flour mixture into egg white mixture. Pour batter into 2 greased and waxed paper-lined 9" round baking pans.

Bake in 350° oven 30 minutes, or until top springs back when touched. Cool 10 minutes. Remove from pans. Cool on racks.

Fill and frost sides and top of cake with Coffee Fluff Frosting. Refrigerate until ready to serve.

Coffee Fluff Frosting

1½ c. heavy cream
3 tblsp. sugar
2 tsp. instant coffee powder
½ tsp. vanilla

Combine all ingredients in bowl. Refrigerate 20 minutes. Whip until soft peaks form, using an electric mixer at high speed. Makes 3 c.

Cakes to microwave

Old-fashioned flavor doesn't have to be created conventionally, and here are ten new recipes for cakes and frostings that can be microwaved, including a traditionally rich fruitcake. All these cakes can be baked in 17 minutes or less in standard-size glass baking dishes or casseroles. Once you've experienced the fun of seeing Pumpkin-Raisin Cupcakes rise in the microwave in just two minutes or used our one-bowl recipe for a big-batch Chocolate Sour Cream Cake, you'll become converted to microwave cake cookery.

Sour Cream Chocolate Cake

(16 servings)

cooking oil
sugar
2¼ c. sifted flour
1 c. sugar
⅓ c. baking cocoa
1 tsp. baking soda
½ tsp. salt
2 eggs
1 c. dairy sour cream
½ c. cooking oil
½ c. milk
1 tsp. vanilla
Microwaved Chocolate Icing (recipe follows)

Oil a microwave-safe 12-c. fluted tube pan or 3-qt. casserole, using about ½ tsp. cooking oil. Sprinkle with a little sugar, turning to coat all sides of dish. (If using casserole, oil and sugar a 2½"-diameter drinking glass and place in center of casserole.) Set aside.

Sift together flour, 1 c. sugar, cocoa, baking soda and salt into bowl. Make a well in center and add eggs, sour cream, ½ c. oil, milk and vanilla. Beat ½ minute, using an electric mixer at low speed. Mix 1 minute more, using medium speed. Pour batter into prepared pan.

Microwave (medium setting) 11 minutes, rotating dish one-quarter turn every 3 minutes. Continue microwaving (high setting) 3 to 6 minutes, or until cake pulls away from sides and center of pan. Cool in pan on wooden board or heat-proof surface 15 minutes. Remove from pan and place on serving plate. Cool.

Spread Microwaved Chocolate Icing over cooled cake, allowing icing to drip down sides.

Microwaved Chocolate Icing

2 tblsp. butter or regular margarine
3 tblsp. milk
2 tblsp. baking cocoa
1¼ c. sifted confectioners' sugar
¼ tsp. vanilla

Place butter and milk in microwave-safe bowl.

Microwave (high setting) 45 seconds or until it comes to a boil. Gradually stir in remaining ingredients. Mix until smooth, using a wooden spoon.

Old-fashioned Spice Cake

(10 servings)

2 c. sifted flour
1¼ tsp. baking powder
1 tsp. baking soda
1½ tsp. ground cinnamon
1¼ tsp. ground nutmeg
¾ tsp. ground allspice
½ tsp. salt
1¼ c. packed brown sugar
¾ c. shortening
⅔ c. buttermilk
4 eggs
Whipped Frosting (recipe follows)

Sift together flour, baking powder, baking soda, cinnamon, nutmeg, allspice and salt in bowl. Add brown sugar, shortening, buttermilk and eggs. Beat ½ minute, using an electric mixer at low speed. Beat 2 minutes more, using medium speed. Pour batter into 2 waxed paper-lined 8" or 9" round glass baking dishes.

Microwave (medium setting), one dish at a time, 8 minutes, rotating dish one-quarter turn every 2 minutes. Microwave (high setting) 1 to 3 minutes, or until cake pulls away from sides of dish. Cool in dish on wooden board or heat-proof surface 5 to 10 minutes. Remove from dish. Cool on rack.

Fill and frost sides and top of cake with Whipped Frosting.

Whipped Frosting

⅓ c. milk
½ c. packed brown sugar
½ c. butter or regular margarine
⅓ c. shortening
3 tblsp. flour
¾ c. sifted confectioners' sugar

Measure milk in 1-c. glass measuring cup. Add brown sugar.

Microwave (high setting) 45 seconds, or until milk is warm. Stir to dissolve brown sugar. Set aside.

Cream together butter and shortening in bowl, using an electric mixer at medium speed. Add flour; beat well.

Beat in milk-sugar mixture, using high speed. (Mixture will look curdled.) Gradually add confectioners' sugar, beating well. Beat 5 minutes, or until frosting holds stiff peaks, using high speed.

Pumpkin-Raisin Cupcakes

(18 servings)

1 c. sifted flour
1 tsp. ground cinnamon
½ tsp. baking powder
½ tsp. baking soda
¼ tsp. salt
2 eggs, slightly beaten
1 c. cooked, mashed pumpkin
⅔ c. packed brown sugar
½ c. cooking oil
½ tsp. vanilla
½ c. raisins
Microwaved Cream Cheese Frosting
(recipe follows)

Sift together flour, cinnamon, baking powder, baking soda and salt. Set aside.

Combine eggs, pumpkin, brown sugar, oil and vanilla in bowl. Mix until smooth. Stir in dry ingredients and raisins, blending well. Spoon batter into 16 double paper-lined microwave-safe (6-oz.) custard cups, filling half full.

Microwave (high setting), 6 at a time, 1¾ to 2¼ minutes, or until cupcakes are almost dry on top, rotating cups one-quarter turn after 1 minute. Remove from custard cups; cool on rack.

Frost cupcakes with Microwaved Cream Cheese Frosting.

Microwaved Cream Cheese Frosting

1½ oz. cream cheese
1½ tblsp. butter or regular margarine
¾ c. to 1 c. sifted confectioners' sugar
½ tsp. vanilla

Place cream cheese and butter in microwave-safe bowl. Microwave (high setting) 15 seconds to soften. Stir with a fork until blended. Gradually add confectioners' sugar and vanilla, beating with a fork until smooth.

Good-for-You Banana Cake

(6 servings)

¼ c. packed brown sugar
1 tsp. ground cinnamon
⅓ c. finely chopped walnuts
1 c. stirred whole-wheat flour
¾ c. sifted all-purpose flour
1 tsp. baking soda
½ tsp. salt
⅔ c. shortening
½ c. packed brown sugar
2 eggs
1 tsp. vanilla
1 c. very ripe mashed banana
¼ c. milk

Combine ¼ c. brown sugar, cinnamon and walnuts in bowl. Mix well. Set aside.

Stir together whole-wheat flour, all-purpose flour, baking soda and salt. Set aside.

Cream together shortening and ½ c. brown sugar in bowl, using an electric mixer at medium speed. Beat in eggs, vanilla and banana.

Gradually add flour mixture alternately with milk, beating well after each addition. Pour batter into greased 8" square glass baking dish, spreading batter slightly higher in corners. Sprinkle evenly with walnut mixture.

Microwave (medium setting) 9 minutes, rotating dish one-quarter turn every 2 minutes. Place small pieces of aluminum foil over cooked areas of cake. (Check the use-and-care manual for your microwave oven before using foil, because the magnetron tubes on some ovens can be damaged by foil.)

Microwave (high setting) 4 to 5 minutes, or until cake pulls away from sides of dish and top is done. Cool in dish on wooden board or heat-proof surface. Serve warm or cool.

Zucchini-Pecan Cake

(8 to 12 servings)

cooking oil
3 tblsp. fine graham cracker crumbs
1¼ c. sifted flour
¾ tsp. baking powder
½ tsp. salt
½ c. butter or regular margarine
½ c. packed brown sugar
¼ c. sugar
2 eggs
1 tsp. vanilla
1 tblsp. milk
1½ c. shredded zucchini
½ c. finely chopped pecans
Brown Sugar Glaze (recipe follows)

Oil a microwave-safe 6-c. ring mold or 2-qt. glass casserole, using about ½ tsp. cooking oil. Sprinkle generously with graham cracker crumbs, turning to coat all sides of dish. Leave excess crumbs in dish. (If using casserole, oil and coat with crumbs a 2½"-diameter drinking glass and place in center of casserole.) Set aside.

Sift together flour, baking powder and salt. Set aside.

Cream together butter, brown sugar and sugar in bowl, using an electric mixer at medium speed. Beat in eggs, vanilla and milk. Add dry ingredients, mixing well, using low speed. Stir in zucchini and pecans. Pour batter into prepared dish.

Microwave (medium setting) 10 minutes, rotating dish one-quarter turn every 2 minutes.

Microwave (high setting) 2 to 4 minutes, or until cake pulls away from sides and center of dish. Cool in dish on wooden board or heat-proof surface 10 minutes. Remove from dish and cool on serving plate.

Drizzle Brown Sugar Glaze over cooled cake.

Brown Sugar Glaze

2 tblsp. butter or regular margarine
2 tblsp. packed brown sugar
2 tblsp. milk
1 ¼ c. sifted confectioners' sugar
½ tsp. vanilla

Place butter, brown sugar and milk in microwave-safe bowl.

Microwave (high setting) 1½ minutes, or until mixture boils for ½ minute. Gradually stir in confectioners' sugar and vanilla. Mix until smooth, using a wooden spoon.

Let stand 5 minutes to cool before using. (Glaze thickens as it cools.)

Dark Fruitcake

(2 loaves)

cooking oil
2 tblsp. sugar
2 tsp. ground cinnamon
1 lb. mixed candied fruit
1½ c. sifted flour
1 tsp. ground cinnamon
½ tsp. ground allspice
½ tsp. ground nutmeg
¼ tsp. ground cloves
½ tsp. baking powder
½ tsp. baking soda
½ tsp. salt
3 eggs
¾ c. packed brown sugar
½ c. cooking oil
2 tblsp. dark molasses
½ c. apple juice
1 c. finely chopped apple
1 c. raisins
1 ¼ c. coarsely chopped pecans or walnuts

Lightly oil 2 microwave-safe 8¼x4½x2¾" (1½-qt.) loaf dishes. Combine sugar and 2 tsp. cinnamon in bowl. Mix well. Sprinkle some of the mixture in dishes, turning dishes to coat all sides. Set aside. Reserve remaining sugar mixture.

Combine candied fruit and ¼ c. of the flour in bowl; toss to mix. Set aside.

Sift together remaining flour, 1 tsp. cinnamon, allspice, nutmeg, cloves, baking powder, baking soda and salt. Set aside.

Beat eggs, brown sugar, ½ c. oil and molasses in bowl until well blended, using an electric mixer at medium speed. Add apple juice and half of the dry ingredients, stirring well. Add remaining dry ingredients and chopped apple. Mix well. Stir in candied fruit mixture, raisins and nuts. Pour batter into prepared dishes, pushing fruit and nuts into batter. Sprinkle with reserved sugar mixture.

Microwave (medium setting) 12 minutes, 1 dish at a time, rotating dish one-quarter turn every 3 minutes. Place small pieces of aluminum foil over cooked areas of cake. (Check the use-and-care manual for your microwave oven before using foil, because the magnetron tubes on some ovens can be damaged by foil.)

Microwave (high setting) 2 to 4 minutes, or until cake pulls away from sides of dish and top is done. Cool in dish on wooden board or heat-proof surface 10 minutes. Remove from dish and cool on rack. Wrap in aluminum foil and store in refrigerator or freezer.

2

Then the Frosting

Though some cakes are best served plain or with a simple dusting of confectioners' sugar, the crowning touch for most cakes is the frosting. Variations of frostings are endless, but they generally fit into three basic categories: butter creams, fluffy cooked frostings and cooked fudge frostings.

Butter cream frostings are the easiest to make because they don't require cooking. Butter, margarine, solid shortening or a combination of these ingredients is creamed together with confectioners' sugar and thinned with a liquid, usually milk, to make a smooth, creamy, spreadable frosting.

Frosting that is too soft will slide off your cake, but frosting that is too stiff can tear the cake or have a dry, unappetizing appearance. In hot humid weather, less liquid may be needed to make a butter cream frosting, and if your frosting is too soft, a little confectioners' sugar can be added. Too stiff a butter cream frosting can be thinned by blending in a little more liquid.

If you're using a butter cream in a decorating tube, it may be necessary to add more confectioners' sugar so that your piped decorations will hold their definition.

Butter cream frostings have good keeping qualities, so they're ideal for cakes you plan to pack in lunch boxes or transport to picnics. If you must freeze a frosted cake, use a butter cream frosting—it will hold up admirably.

Fluffy cooked frostings are made with beaten egg whites and will ice any cake to perfection with soft, beautiful swirls.

Our 7-Minute Frosting, Boiled Frosting, White Mountain Frosting and Divinity Frosting are all fluffy cooked frostings.

Cakes iced with fluffy cooked frostings are best eaten the same day because these frostings have a tendency to become sugary after a day or two. Don't try to make this type of frosting on a damp or humid day.

Cooked fudge frostings such as our Penuche or Caramel Frostings are exactly what their name implies, but softer than candy so they can be spread. These frostings are cooked, cooled and beaten like fudge. Like fudge, they set up quickly, so you must work rapidly when icing your cake. If a cooked fudge frosting becomes too thick, try setting the bowl of frosting in a pan of hot water and beating in a little liquid.

Also included in this chapter are recipes for whipped cream icings, which are used for simple but luxuriant frostings, and Royal Icing, used only to make flowers and other fancy trims with which to decorate your frosted cake.

In addition to using these recipes, you may sometimes wish to take a shortcut by using purchased products: canned butter cream-type frostings; packaged frosting mixes, including fluffy frosting mixes similar to our fluffy cooked frostings; and dessert topping mixes, which may be substituted for whipped cream.

RECIPES

Basic Vanilla Butter Cream Icing

½ c. butter or regular margarine
3⅓ c. sifted confectioners' sugar
½ tsp. vanilla
3 tblsp. milk

Cream together butter, confectioners' sugar and vanilla in bowl, using an electric mixer at low speed.

Gradually add milk, beating until smooth and creamy, using medium speed. Makes 2 c.

Best Butter Cream Decorating Icing

½ c. butter or regular margarine
1 (1-lb.) box confectioners' sugar, sifted
2 egg whites
1 tsp. vanilla
milk

Cream butter in bowl, using an electric mixer at medium speed.

Add confectioners' sugar, egg whites and vanilla; blend until smooth and creamy, using low speed. If necessary, add a little milk to make desired consistency. Makes 2¼ c.

Basic Cake Icing

2¼ c. sifted confectioners' sugar
1 c. shortening
¼ c. milk
½ tsp. vanilla

Combine all ingredients in bowl. Beat until moistened, using an electric mixer at low speed. Beat at high speed 5 minutes or until light and creamy.

Creamy Frosting

4 c. sifted confectioners' sugar
½ c. shortening
¼ c. milk
½ tsp. lemon extract
½ tsp. vanilla
dash of salt

Combine all ingredients in bowl. Beat until smooth and creamy, using a wooden spoon. Makes 2⅓ c.

Snowy Frosting

4 c. sifted confectioners' sugar
½ c. butter or regular margarine
½ c. shortening
2 egg whites
1 tsp. coconut extract

Combine all ingredients in bowl. Beat until smooth and creamy, using an electric mixer at low speed. Makes 2½ c.

Creamy Pineapple Frosting

1 (8½-oz.) can crushed pineapple
¼ c. butter or regular margarine
¼ c. shortening
3 c. sifted confectioners' sugar
½ tsp. grated lemon rind
¼ tsp. vanilla
⅛ tsp. salt

Drain pineapple and blot dry with paper towels.

Combine butter, shortening, 2 c. of the confectioners' sugar, drained pineapple, lemon rind, vanilla and salt in bowl. Beat until smooth, using a wooden spoon.

Stir in remaining confectioners' sugar. Makes 1⅓ c.

Lemon Decorating Icing

4½ c. sifted confectioners' sugar
¾ c. shortening
6 tblsp. milk
1 tsp. lemon extract

Combine all ingredients in bowl. Beat with an electric mixer at low speed 5 minutes or until smooth and creamy. Makes 2 c.

Coffee Frosting

1 tsp. instant coffee granules
3 tblsp. water
½ c. butter or regular margarine
4 c. sifted confectioners' sugar
1 tsp. vanilla

Dissolve coffee granules in water in bowl. Add remaining ingredients. Mix well, using an electric mixer at low speed.

Beat until smooth and creamy, using medium speed. Makes 2 c.

Chocolate Frosting

3 (1-oz.) squares unsweetened chocolate
2 tblsp. butter or regular margarine
2 c. sifted confectioners' sugar
3 tblsp. milk

Melt chocolate and butter in 2-qt. saucepan over low heat. Remove from heat.

Add confectioners' sugar and milk and beat with a wooden spoon until smooth and just thick enough to spread. Makes 1 c.

Chocolate Butter Cream Icing

6 tblsp. butter or regular margarine
1 (1-oz.) square unsweetened chocolate, melted and cooled
1 tsp. vanilla
⅛ tsp. salt
1 (1-lb.) box confectioners' sugar, sifted
3 to 4 tblsp. milk

Combine butter, melted chocolate, vanilla and salt in bowl. Beat until blended, using an electric mixer at medium speed.

Gradually add confectioners' sugar, using low speed. Add milk and beat until smooth and creamy, using medium speed. Makes 2¼ c.

Rich Chocolate Icing

4 c. sifted confectioners' sugar
1 c. butter or regular margarine
3 (1-oz.) squares unsweetened chocolate, melted and cooled
1 tsp. vanilla
3 tblsp. milk

Combine confectioners' sugar, butter, melted chocolate and vanilla in bowl. Beat until blended, using an electric mixer at low speed. Gradually add milk, beating until smooth and creamy, using medium speed. Makes 3⅓ c.

Chocolate Icing

2 (1-oz.) squares unsweetened chocolate
2 tsp. butter or regular margarine
2 c. sifted confectioners' sugar
3 tblsp. hot water

Melt chocolate and butter in top of double boiler over hot water. Remove from hot water.

Add confectioners' sugar and 3 tblsp. hot water. Beat until smooth, using a wooden spoon. (Icing will be stiff. If it's too stiff to pipe, stir in a little more hot water.) Makes about 1 c.

Chocolate Cream Cheese Frosting

1 (8-oz.) pkg. cream cheese, softened
2 (1-oz.) squares unsweetened chocolate, melted and cooled
1 tsp. vanilla
3 c. sifted confectioners' sugar

Beat cream cheese in bowl until light and fluffy, using an electric mixer at medium speed. Blend in chocolate and vanilla.

Gradually beat in confectioners' sugar, using low speed. Continue beating until smooth and creamy. Makes 2 c.

Cream Cheese Frosting I

½ (8-oz.) pkg. cream cheese, softened
2 tblsp. butter or regular margarine
1 tsp. vanilla
2 c. sifted confectioners' sugar

Cream together cream cheese and butter in bowl until light and fluffy, using an electric mixer at medium speed. Blend in vanilla.

Gradually add confectioners' sugar, beating well after each addition, using low speed. Continue beating until smooth and creamy. Makes 1½ c.

Cream Cheese Frosting II

1 (8-oz.) pkg. cream cheese, softened
1 tblsp. butter or regular margarine
1 tsp. almond extract
1 (1-lb.) box confectioners' sugar, sifted

Cream together cream cheese and butter in bowl until light and fluffy, using an electric mixer at medium speed. Blend in almond extract.

Gradually add confectioners' sugar, beating well after each addition, using low speed. Continue beating until smooth and creamy. Makes 3 c.

Cream Cheese Frosting III

1 (8-oz.) pkg. cream cheese, softened
½ c. butter or regular margarine
1 tsp. vanilla
1 (1-lb.) box confectioners' sugar, sifted

Cream together cream cheese and butter in bowl until light and fluffy, using an electric mixer at medium speed. Blend in vanilla.

Gradually add confectioners' sugar, beating well after each addition, using low speed. Continue beating until smooth and creamy. Makes 3 c.

Cream Cheese Frosting IV

½ (8-oz.) pkg. cream cheese, softened
⅓ c. butter or regular margarine
1½ tsp. vanilla
3 c. sifted confectioners' sugar

Cream together cream cheese and butter in bowl until light and fluffy, using an electric mixer at medium speed. Blend in vanilla.

Gradually add confectioners' sugar, beating well after each addition, using low speed. Continue beating until smooth and creamy. Makes 1½ c.

7-Minute Frosting

2 egg whites
1½ c. sugar
⅓ c. water
¼ tsp. cream of tartar
1 tsp. vanilla

Combine egg whites, sugar, water and cream of tartar in top of double boiler. Beat 1 minute, using an electric mixer at medium speed.

Place over simmering water. Cook 7 minutes, beating constantly at high speed, until soft glossy peaks form. Remove from hot water. Beat in vanilla. Makes 4 c.

Boiled Frosting

½ c. water
1½ c. sugar
3 egg whites
½ tsp. cream of tartar
1 tsp. vanilla

Combine water and sugar in 2-qt. saucepan. Cook over high heat until temperature reaches 238° (soft ball) on candy thermometer.

Meanwhile, beat egg whites, cream of tartar and vanilla in bowl until stiff peaks form, using an electric mixer at high speed.

Slowly pour hot syrup over egg white mixture, beating constantly at high speed until stiff glossy peaks form, 3 to 5 minutes. Makes 4 c.

White Mountain Frosting

½ c. sugar
¼ c. light corn syrup
2 tblsp. water
2 egg whites
1 tsp. vanilla

Combine sugar, corn syrup and water in small saucepan. Cook over medium heat until temperature reaches 242° on candy thermometer.

Meanwhile, beat egg whites in bowl until stiff peaks form, using an electric mixer at high speed.

Slowly pour hot syrup over egg whites, beating constantly at high speed until stiff glossy peaks form. Beat in vanilla. Makes 3½ c.

Divinity Frosting

⅔ c. water
½ c. sugar
4 tblsp. light corn syrup
½ tsp. salt
2 egg whites
½ tsp. cream of tartar
1 tsp. vanilla

Combine water, sugar, corn syrup and salt in 2-qt. saucepan. Cook over high heat until temperature reaches 232° (soft ball) on candy thermometer.

Meanwhile, beat egg whites, cream of tartar and vanilla in bowl until stiff peaks form, using an electric mixer at high speed.

Slowly pour hot syrup over egg white mixture, beating constantly at high speed until stiff glossy peaks form, 3 to 5 minutes. Makes 2½ c.

Penuche Frosting

½ c. butter or regular margarine
1 c. packed brown sugar
¼ c. milk
2 c. sifted confectioners' sugar

Melt butter in 2-qt. saucepan over medium heat. Add brown sugar. Cook, stirring constantly, until mixture comes to a boil. Boil 2 minutes, stirring constantly. Stir in milk; return to boiling.

Remove from heat and cool to lukewarm. Stir in confectioners' sugar and beat with a wooden spoon until frosting is thick enough to spread. Makes 1¾ c.

Fast-cook Frosting

3 tblsp. flour
¾ c. milk
6 tblsp. butter or regular margarine
6 tblsp. shortening
¾ c. sugar
1 ½ tsp. vanilla
dash of salt

Combine flour and milk in jar. Cover and shake until well blended. Pour into small saucepan. Cook over medium heat 5 to 8 minutes, stirring constantly, until mixture boils and thickens. Remove from heat and cool well.

Cream together remaining ingredients in bowl until light and fluffy, using an electric mixer at medium speed. Add flour mixture, beating until smooth and creamy. Makes 2½ c.

Thin Glaze

1 c. sifted confectioners' sugar
2 tblsp. milk
½ tsp. vanilla

Combine all ingredients in bowl. Beat until smooth, using a wooden spoon. Makes ⅓ c.

Sweetened Whipped Cream I

1 c. heavy cream
2 tblsp. sugar
½ tsp. vanilla

Combine all ingredients in chilled bowl. Beat until soft peaks form, using an electric mixer at high speed. Makes about 2 c.

Sweetened Whipped Cream II

2 c. heavy cream
¼ c. sugar
1 tsp. vanilla

Combine all ingredients in chilled bowl. Beat until soft peaks form, using an electric mixer at high speed. Makes about 4 c.

Whipped Cream Icing

1 tsp. unflavored gelatin
4 tsp. cold water
1 c. heavy cream, well chilled
¼ c. confectioners' sugar
½ tsp. vanilla

Combine gelatin and cold water in small saucepan. Let stand 5 minutes to soften.

Place over low heat, stirring constantly, until gelatin dissolves completely, about 3 minutes. Remove from heat; cool slightly.

Whip cream, confectioners' sugar and vanilla until thickened, using an electric mixer at low speed. Continuing to beat at low speed, gradually add gelatin to whipped cream mixture. Beat until stiff peaks form, using high speed. Makes about 2 c.

Royal Icing

1 (1-lb.) box confectioners' sugar, sifted
3 egg whites
1 tsp. cream of tartar
1 tsp. vanilla

Combine all ingredients in bowl. Beat until moistened, using an electric mixer at low speed. Continue beating until stiff glossy peaks form, using high speed.

Keep icing covered with wet paper towels or cloth at all times.

Store unused icing in covered plastic container in refrigerator up to 2 weeks.

To use, bring to room temperature and beat until stiff peaks form, using an electric mixer at high speed. Makes 2½ c.

Run Sugar

Prepare Royal Icing as above but beat just until stiff, using an electric mixer at low speed. Tint icing if needed and pipe outline as needed for specific design.

Thin remaining icing to be used for filling in the outlines by adding water, a few drops at a time, and stirring gently. Icing is the proper consistency when a spoonful dropped back into bowl will blend in and disappear completely by the count of 10.

TINTING ICING

Color brings cake decorations to life, and it's easy to tint icing. Paste food colors work best because they won't thin decorating icings as liquid food colors do. When tinting icing, keep in mind these tips:
*Colors intensify one or two hours after tinting.
*Add the paste food color a little at a time until you have the color you want. To add just a bit of color, use a toothpick. Stir the color into a small amount of icing first, and then mix the tinted icing with the rest.
*To avoid transferring icing to paste food colors, use a clean toothpick each time you remove color from the jar.
*Always tint the entire amount of icing you'll need for a cake all at once, because it's very difficult to match any color.
*You'll need more paste color to make deep, richly hued icings.
*Royal icing requires more paste color than butter cream icings to achieve the same intensity of color.
*To restore the consistency of paste colors that have dried during storage, add a few drops of glycerin. It's available at drugstores.

FROSTING A LAYER CAKE IN SOFT SWIRLS

In a hurry? You can turn a simple cake into a lovely centerpiece just by swirling the frosting in a graceful pattern.

This is the easiest way of all to create a stunning layer cake, because there's no need to be sure the top layer is perfectly flat—in fact, a layer cake with a slightly rounded top will look even more attractive.

1. CHOOSE THE BOTTOM LAYER. If one layer is higher than the other, place it on the bottom. Center it on the serving plate, top side down.
2. FILL THE CAKE. Spread the filling or frosting over the bottom layer, almost to the edge. Add the second layer, top side up, being sure the edges are even and the cake is of uniform height.

3. FROST THE SIDES. Brush crumbs from the sides of the cake layers and thinly frost the sides of the cake.
4. SWIRL THE SIDES. Add more frosting to the sides of the cake, making graceful swirls by pulling a metal spatula through the frosting in upward strokes.
5. FROST THE TOP. Pile frosting on top of the cake. Spread the frosting so that it touches the frosting on the sides.
6. FINISH THE TOP. Pull a spatula over the top of the cake, making irregular swirls.

Fill the cake

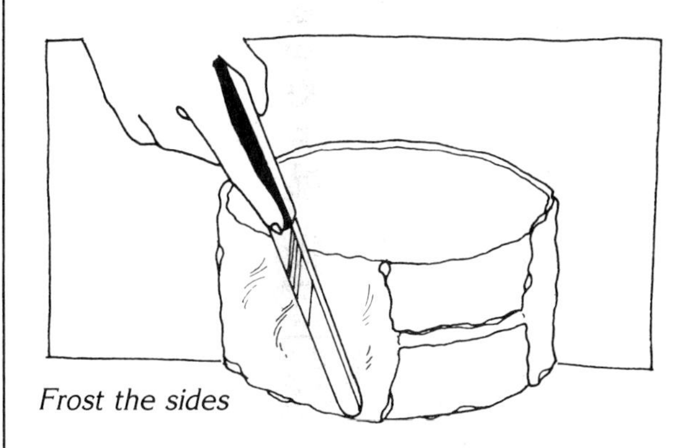

Frost the sides

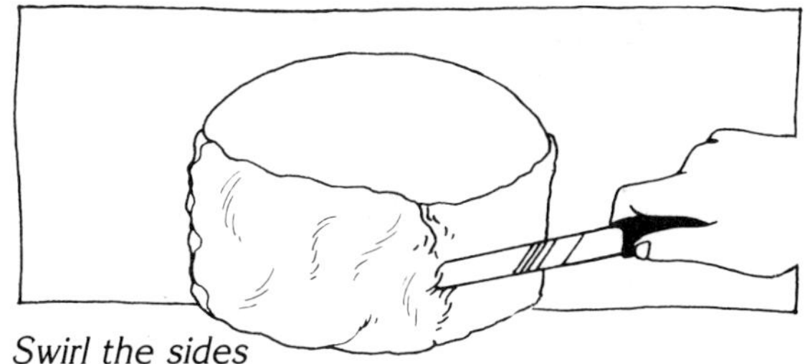

Swirl the sides

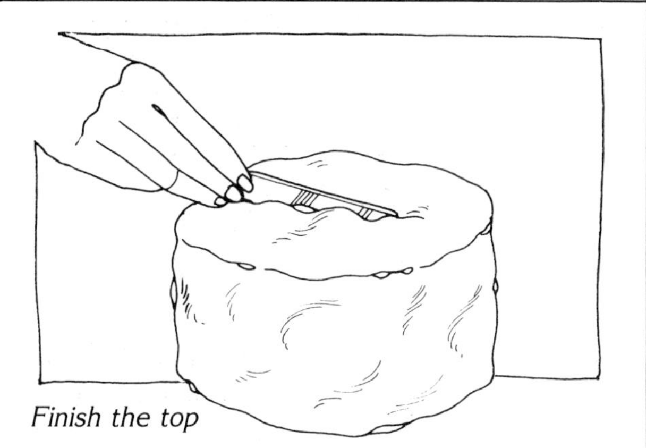

Finish the top

DECORATING WITH TUBES

In this section you'll find everything you need to know about using decorating bags and tubes to create perfectly glorious cakes!

Decorating utensils

Some of the decorated cakes we show in this book can be made without using any of the items on this list, but if you want to explore the full range of decorating possibilities, you'll need each of these basic items.

*COUPLERS: Plastic couplers hold the metal decorating tube to the bag of icing, and allow you to change tubes while using the same bag of icing. A coupler has two parts, a base and a ring. It's helpful to have at least three of these.
*DECORATING BAGS: You'll need several of these to hold decorating tubes and icing. You can make them from parchment paper (and on page 69 we show how) or buy them. Beginners usually find the 10″ size most useful.
*DECORATING TUBES: These little metal tubes are available in many shapes and sizes, but there are six basic shapes: round, star, drop flower, leaf, rose and basket weave. Information on which sizes you'll find most useful follows in this chapter.
*FLOWER NAIL: This round, flat metal or plastic nailhead is really a miniature turntable, used to pipe roses and other flowers. Many

people prefer to use the bottom of a pint jar. Of the flower nails sold, the #7 size is the most versatile.
*FOOD COLORS: Paste food colors are used to tint icings for decorating because these creamy colorings don't affect the consistency of the icing. Most shades can be mixed from the three primary colors: red, blue and yellow.

Liquid food colors are fine for tinting cake batter, coconut, sugar, and basic cake frostings not used for decorating. You can buy the colors in sets of four: red, blue, yellow and green.
*PARCHMENT: You can use this white, medium-weight paper to make your own decorating bags (see page 69), and it can be purchased in rolls or in pre-cut triangles.
*TURNTABLE: A decorating turntable is a luxury, and a lazy Susan that turns smoothly is an excellent substitute. If you decide to buy a decorating turntable, many models are available. The best are heavy-duty metal and are at least 12″ in diameter and 4″ high.

In addition, you'll also need a few more common items: cardboard and florist's foil, or aluminum foil, for making sturdy, attractive bases for your cakes; a compass, for measuring circles of waxed paper and cardboard; a ruler, for planning designs and finding the center of a cake; toothpicks, for mixing small amounts of colored icing and for marking design points on frosted cakes; and boxes for any cakes that you plan to transport. Some kitchen shops and mail-order suppliers sell cake boxes in a variety of sizes, but you can usually improvise.

Decorating terms

These are some of the terms and techniques commonly used in cake decorating.

ATTACH: To secure flowers and other decorations to an iced cake, just pipe a dot of icing on each decoration and use it as glue. If you're using Royal Icing for your decorations, so much the better, because it hardens and is more stable than butter cream icings.
FIGURE PIPING: This technique is used to form figures from icing as in the Rag Dolls Cake on page 143.
FILLING IN: Use this method to cover an outlined area or design. A star tube is often used, but you can use a metal spatula if you want a smooth area.
FROSTING: This is the overall covering of a cake.
ICING: This refers to recipes used to create decorative, edible designs for cakes. Most of the icings in this book also can be used to frost a cake (except for Royal Icing and Chocolate Decorating Icing).
LEVELING: To make the top layer of a cake flat for frosting and decorating, slice away the crown with a serrated knife.
OUTLINING: A round tube is most often used to pipe icing over the design lines of a pattern.
PIPE: This means to squeeze icing through a decorating tube to form decorations.
SCORE: To mark design lines in icing, gently press a toothpick or the point of a knife against the surface.
STRIPING: This technique is used to create multicolored icing decorations by adding stripes of color to the inside of a decorating bag with either a brush or a spatula.

Frosting a layer cake for decorating

There's a real difference between just frosting a cake and frosting a cake that's to be decorated. A beautifully decorated cake begins with a smooth, even coat of basic decorating icing or butter cream frosting. Frosting a cake smoothly is easy if you follow these directions.

1. LEVEL THE CAKE AND PREPARE THE BASE. If your cake is lopsided or too rounded on top, trim the excess with a serrated knife.

If you place the bottom layer on a round of cardboard, you'll be able to easily move the cake to a serving plate after decorating. If you prefer to frost your cake right on the serving plate, slide four strips of waxed paper under the cake to keep the plate free of drips while you frost; then remove them before you start to decorate.
2. FILL THE LAYERS. Spread the bottom layer with frosting, preserves, pudding or your own favorite filling. Then add the second layer, top side down, so that the flat bottoms form a level base and top.
3. FROST THE TOP. Frosting needs to be the right consistency; it's right when a metal spatula glides easily over it. If it's too thick, thin it with a little milk. Heap a mound of frosting in the center of the cake and spread it across the top,

pushing excess frosting down the sides.

4. FROST THE SIDES. Start with the excess frosting from the top, adding more as needed. It's best to work from the top of the cake down, pushing loose crumbs to the cake base. Be sure the spatula touches only the frosting, or crumbs will mix with the frosting. Some cake decorators find that an angled metal spatula makes it easier to frost the sides.

5. SMOOTH THE SIDES. With a round cake, hold the spatula upright against the side of the cake and, pressing lightly, turn the cake slowly without lifting the spatula from the cake. (A lazy Susan or turntable makes this easy.) Return any excess frosting to the bowl and repeat the procedure until the sides are smooth.

With square and rectangular cakes, smooth each side separately, holding the spatula firmly.

Running your spatula under hot water will help smooth the frosting, but be sure to shake off excess water.

6. SMOOTH THE TOP. Placing the spatula flat on one edge of the cake top, sweep it across the cake to the center, removing excess frosting. Repeat until the top of the cake is smooth.

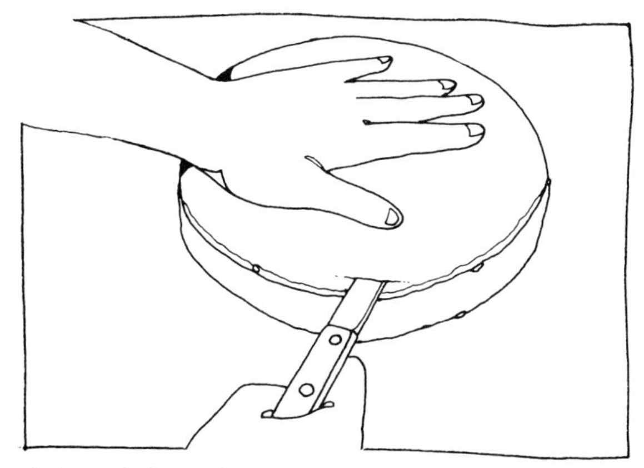

1. Level the cake

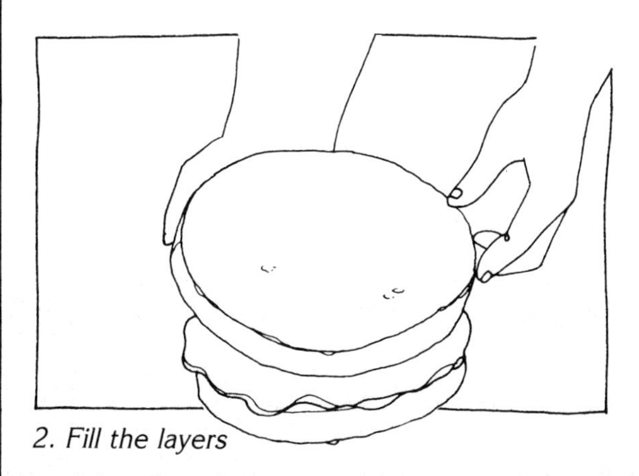

2. Fill the layers

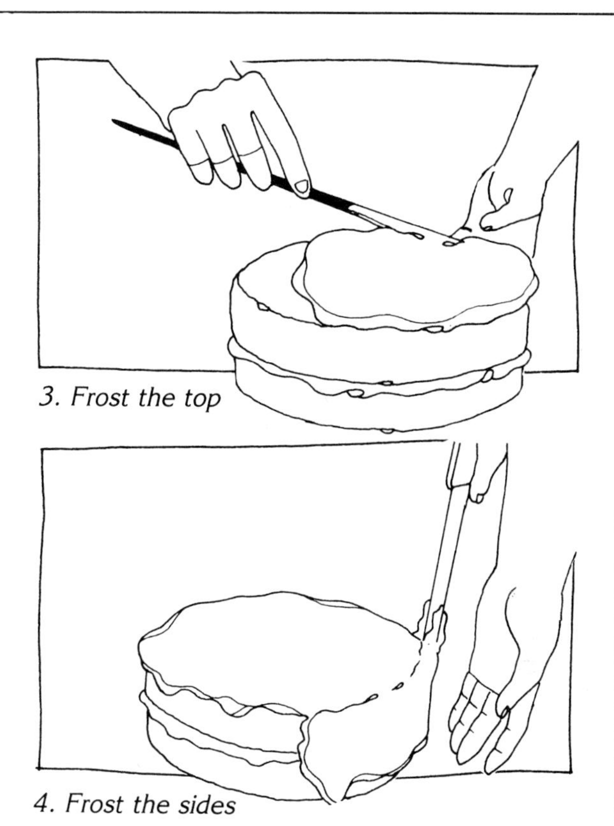

3. Frost the top

4. Frost the sides

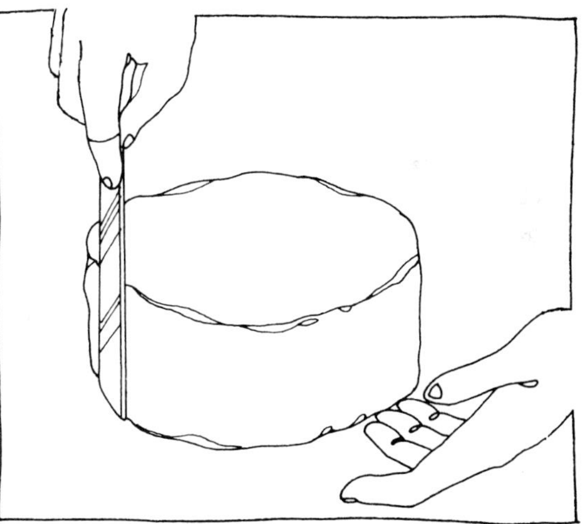

5. Smooth the sides

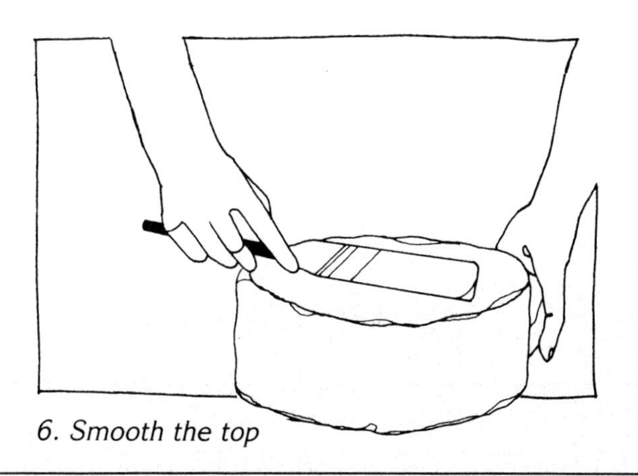

6. Smooth the top

Using the string method to mark design lines

Once you've added an even coat of frosting to your cake, you may want to mark guidelines for design lines.

Begin by marking the center of the top layer with a toothpick. Then cut a length of string about 18″ long and, holding it taut, use it to mark a line across the top of the cake, through the center point. Next, holding the string at a right angle to the first line, mark a second line across the cake, dividing the top into four equal sections. To mark the top in eight equal sections, add two more lines.

Using decorating bags

There are two types of decorating bags, plastic and parchment, and each has its advantages. Beginners usually find the 10″ bags to be most convenient.

PLASTIC BAGS: These convenient pliable plastic or plastic-coated polyester bags are readymade and reusable. After each use, wash in hot water and dry thoroughly before reusing.

You'll probably want to use a coupler with these bags so that you can change decorating tubes without changing bags; this saves lots of time when you want to pipe one color of icing with several different tubes.

Lightweight, disposable plastic bags also are available.

PARCHMENT BAGS: Made from paper triangles, these bags are grease-free and sanitary because they're used only once.

These disposable bags are almost impossible to refill. They're especially useful for piping small amounts of icing because a parchment triangle can be cut in half and used to form two small decorating bags. It's also practical to use these when you use the color striping method of tinting icing, because paste food colors can stain plastic bags.

Filling a plastic decorating bag

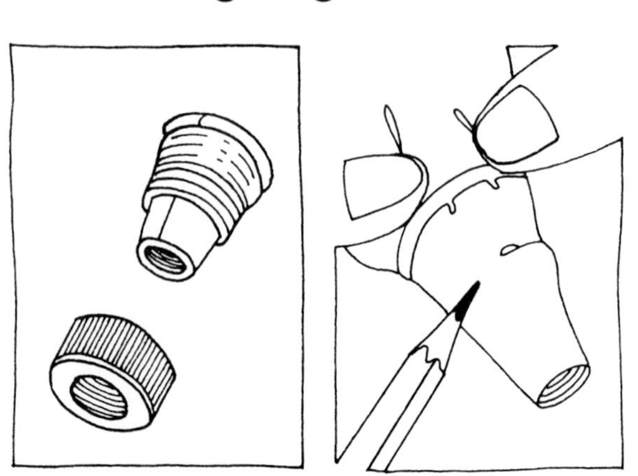

1. Screw the ring off the threaded coupler base.
2. Push the coupler base, narrow end first, down into the tip of the decorating bag, forcing it as far down into the bag as possible. Then mark the bottom thread of the coupler base on the outside of the bag with a pencil. Remove coupler base. Snip off bag at pencil mark.

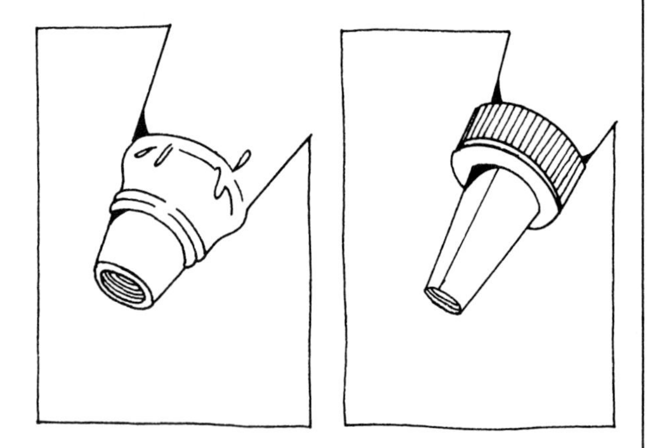

3. Return the coupler base to the bag so that the two bottom threads of the coupler base show through the open tip of the bag.
4. Slip the metal decorating tube of your choice onto the coupler base and screw the coupler ring over the tube to secure it.

To change tubes, unscrew the ring, remove the tube, replace it with another tube and screw on the ring again.

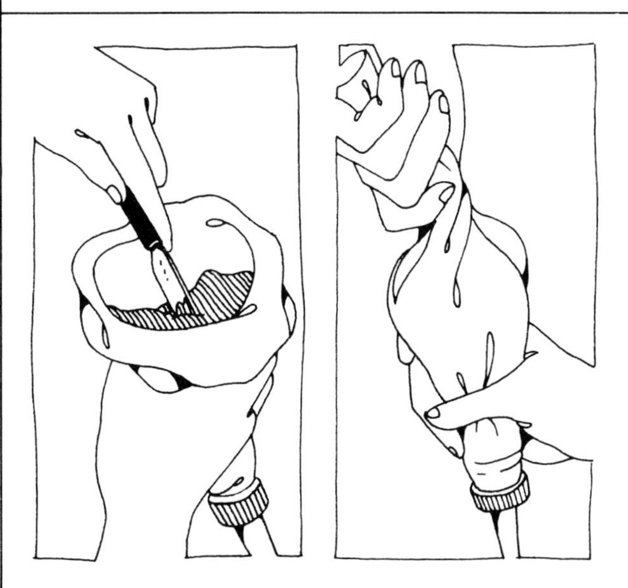

5. With the coupler and decorating tube in place, you're ready to add the icing.
   Fold down the top of the bag to form a cuff about 2″ wide and hold the bag below the cuff. Using a metal spatula, add the icing. Fill the bag no more than half full (or you may find yourself squeezing icing out the wrong end of the bag!).
6. To decorate, unfold the cuff and twist the end of the bag closed. Release air trapped in the bag by squeezing out some of the icing. As you decorate, continually twist the end of the bag to force icing into the tube.

Making a parchment cone

Once you've made a few of these, you'll be able to make one in less than a minute.

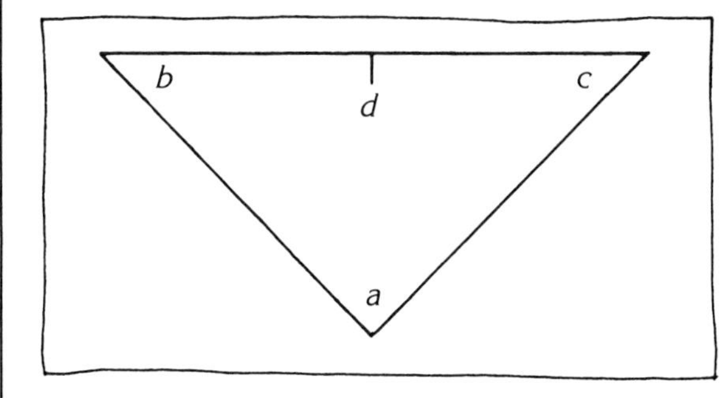

1. Mark the points of the triangle A, B and C as shown. To find D, bring C and B together and lightly crease the center with your index finger.

2. Place the triangle flat, with point A facing you. Hold point C between your right thumb and forefinger.

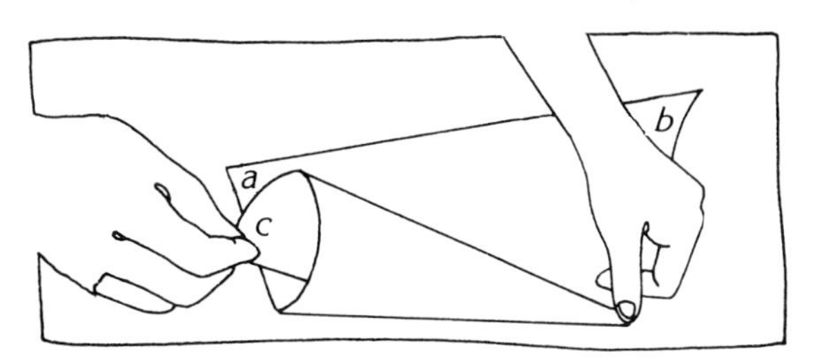

3. Roll corner C up and over to center base point A, holding your left thumb at D.

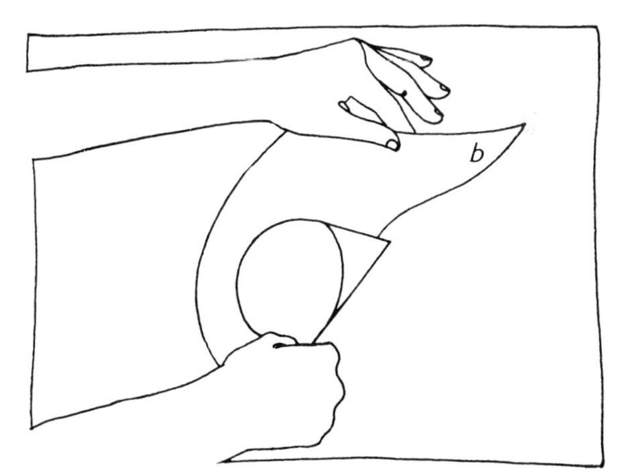

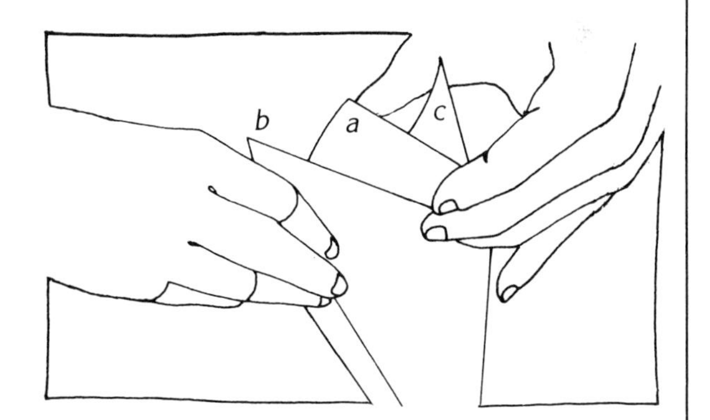

4. Holding points A and C together, roll corner B up and wrap it around to meet points A and C, forming a cone.

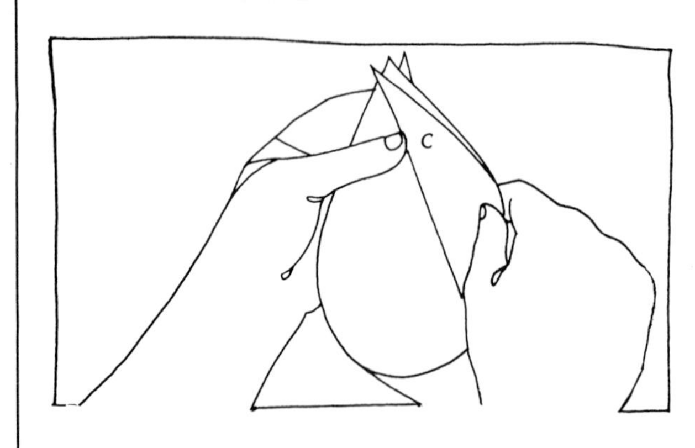

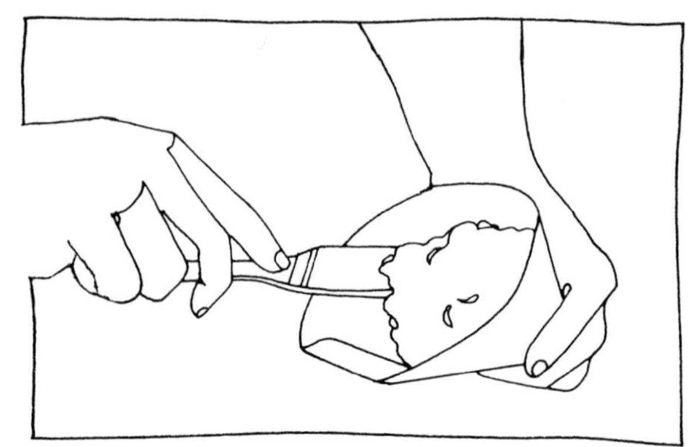

7. Holding the cone near the bottom, fill it half full with icing, using a spatula. Remember to fill only about halfway.

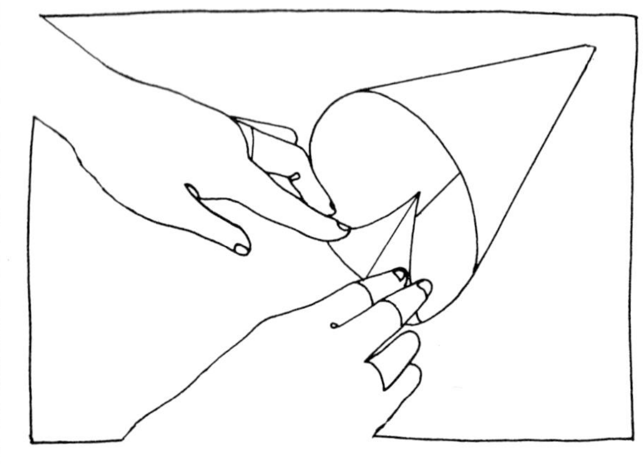

5. Adjust the outside seam where all points meet and make sure the tip of the cone is needle-sharp. Fold points A, B and C inside the bag. Tape the outside of the seam near the top to hold the cone together.

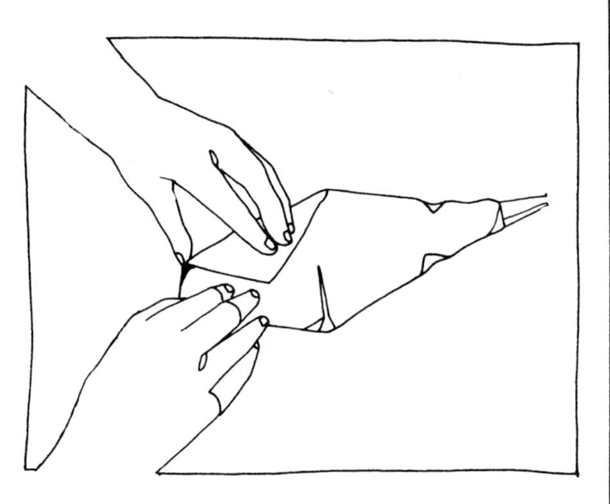

8. Fold down the top of the cone, using a diaper fold: press the top of the bag flat above the icing and fold in first one side, then the other, and finally the top. Continue to roll down the top to force the icing into the tube.

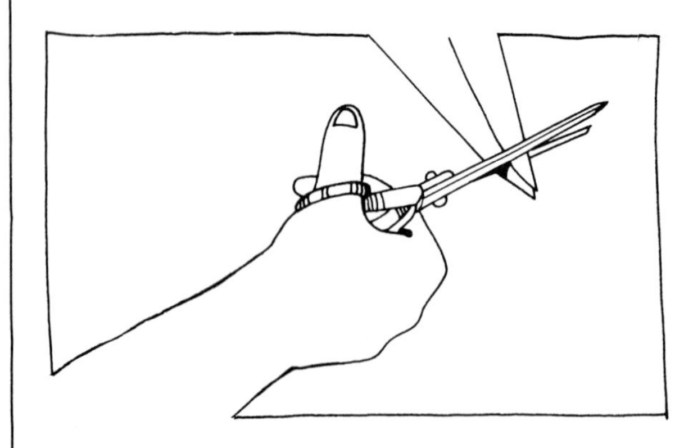

6. To make the opening for your decorating tube, snip ¾" off the tip of the bag. It's better to be cautious in cutting; the tube will drop through if the hole is too large.

Drop the decorating tube of your choice into the cone, narrow end first. Be sure the tube sticks out of the hole you've cut, but don't worry if it doesn't fit snugly—the icing will help hold it in place.

Guidelines for piping decorations

The only way to learn to make professional-looking decorations is to practice. Make a batch of either butter cream or royal icing and begin piping decorations on a baking sheet, the bottom of a baking pan or a sheet of waxed paper. After you've squeezed out some decorations, scrape them up, return the icing to the bag and try again.

Every decoration you make with a decorating bag and tube is the result of three things working together. You'll know when you have all three things right because you'll create perfect results. These are the three elements that produce those results.

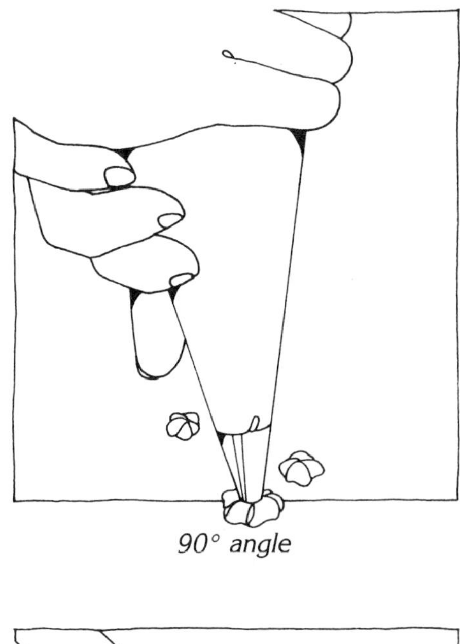

90° angle

*ICING CONSISTENCY: If your icing isn't just right, your decorations won't be right either, and just a few drops of liquid can make the difference.

If a butter or shortening-based icing isn't stiff enough, stir in a little sifted confectioners' sugar. (On hot, humid days, these icings will soften more quickly than Royal Icing.) To stiffen Royal Icing, continue beating until the mixture stands in peaks. Royal Icing is best for making flowers with upright petals.

To thin icing, blend in a little water. You'll want a thinner consistency for letters or script.

*HAND POSITION: The way you hold a decorating tube is important. Grasp it with your right hand and guide it with your left (unless you're left-handed).

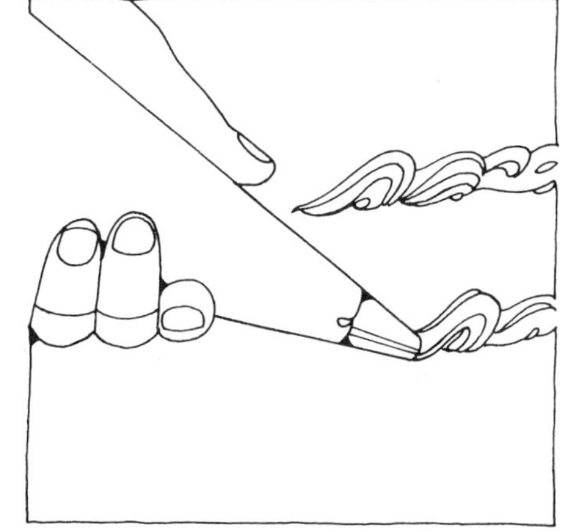

45° angle

Depending upon the type of decorations you're making, the bag should be held at either a 90° angle, perpendicular to your work surface, or at a 45° angle, halfway between vertical and horizontal. Our directions for making decorations tell which angle to use for each decoration.

*PRESSURE: The amount of pressure you apply to the decorating bag and the steadiness of that pressure will affect the size and uniformity of your decorations. Learn to apply pressure consistently so that you can move the bag in an easy glide.

Six basic decorating tubes

There are six basic shapes of decorating tubes—each available in a variety of sizes. The number of the tube determines the size of the decoration: a round tube #2 is smaller than a round tube #12. Both tubes can make the same shapes—for example, a dot—but the #2 tube makes a smaller dot than the #12.

On the pages that follow, we tell exactly how to make various decorations, including the bag position and amount of pressure needed. Most decorations are made with icing of medium consistency, but when another consistency is recommended, it's noted.

1. STAR TUBES: If you've never used a decorating tube, start with a star tube. Serrated-edge tubes called star tubes are the easiest to work with as well as the most versatile. They're used to make many popular decorations: stars, shells, zigzags and rosettes. The most often used sizes are #14, #16, #18, and #21. To start with, you'll find #16 and #21 most useful.

Pipe several stars (see page 74) until you can form a group of stars that are all the same size. Then try other star techniques such as a star border.

2. ROUND TUBES: Smooth round tubes—sometimes called plain tubes—are used to make dots, balls, lines and written messages. Round tubes #3 and #5 are most useful to beginners; and other sizes most often used are #1, #2, #4, #6, #8, #10 and #12.

3. LEAF TUBES: V-shaped openings in these tubes give icing leaves their characteristic points. You can use any leaf tube to make plain, ruffled or stand-up leaves. The most common leaf tubes are #65, #67 and #352. The one you'll use most often is #67.

4. DROP FLOWER TUBES: With these you can make dozens of pretty flowers quickly and easily even if you're a beginner. These tubes have star-shaped openings, and the number of points on the tube determines the number of petals a flower will have. Each tube can make two different kinds of flowers—plain and swirled. The most popular tubes are numbers #106, #2D, #129, #136, #190, #224 and #225. The one most beginners find useful is #225.

5. ROSE TUBES: Sometimes called ribbon tubes, these tubes have a tear-shaped opening and can make many kinds of decorations in addition to roses: flower petals, ribbon garlands, ribbon swags, bows and streamers. The most popular sizes are #101, #102, #103 and #104, and #104 is used most often by beginners.

6. BASKET WEAVE TUBES: Used for making ribbed icing stripes, these tubes have one smooth side and one serrated side. For the basket-weave effect, short horizontal stripes are interwoven over vertical rows of stripes. You'll find basket-weave tubes #46, #47 and #48; the one most commonly used is #47.

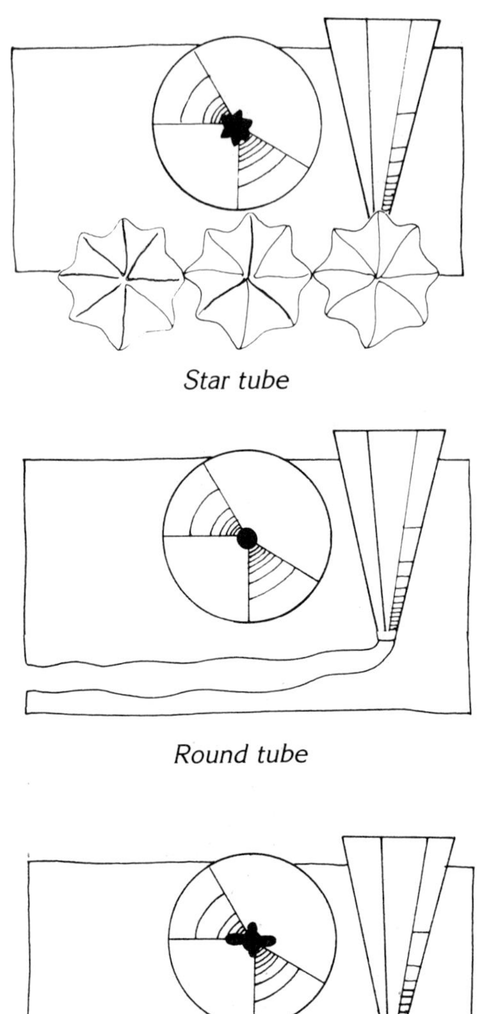

Star tube

Round tube

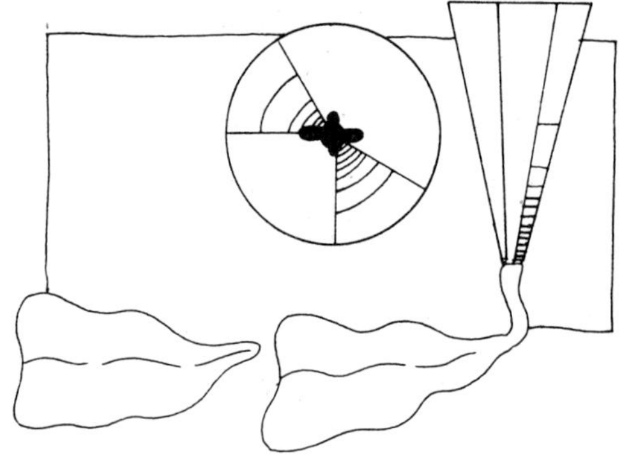

Leaf tube

Drop flower tube

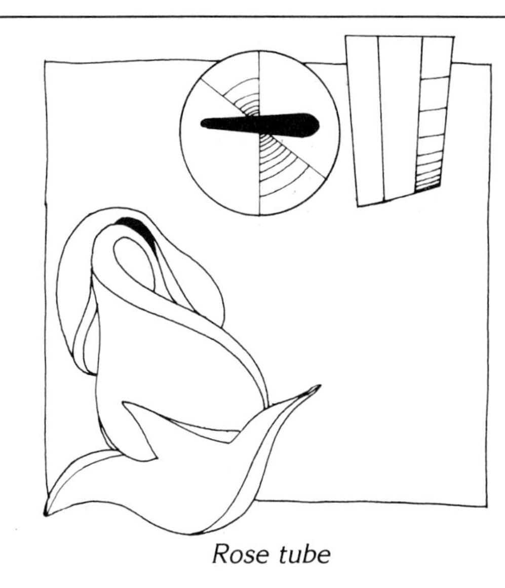

Rose tube

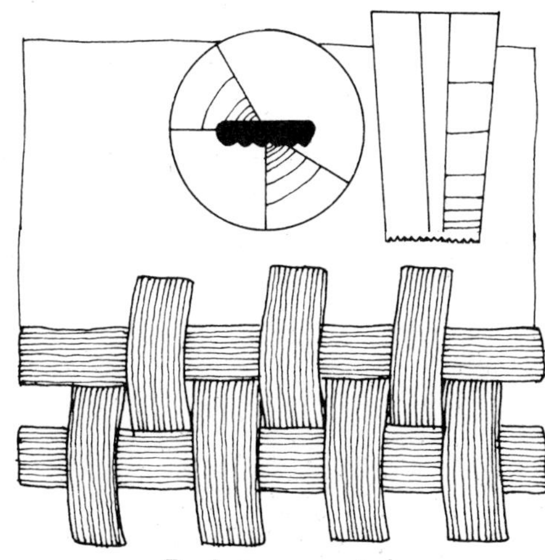

Basket weave tube

Creating special color effects

You can pipe borders and flowers in dramatic two-toned or even multiple color combinations just by painting a stripe of paste food color on the inside of the decorating bag.

We suggest using parchment decorating bags because paste colors can stain plastic bags. Here are two ways to use this technique.

*BRUSH STRIPING: Insert your decorating tube in a parchment bag and select the color or colors of icing you wish to use. Brush a stripe of paste food color 1/8" wide inside the bag, from the tube up to the halfway point of the bag. Then fill the bag halfway with white or pastel icing and squeeze out multicolored borders or flowers.

For a more dramatic effect, brush the entire inside of the bag with any paste food color and fill the bag with icing tinted a medium shade of the same color.

*SPATULA STRIPING: Using a metal spatula instead of a brush to apply paste food color to the inside of the bag produces subtle effects that are perfect for natural-looking flowers. Roses look especially pretty piped in two shades of the same color.

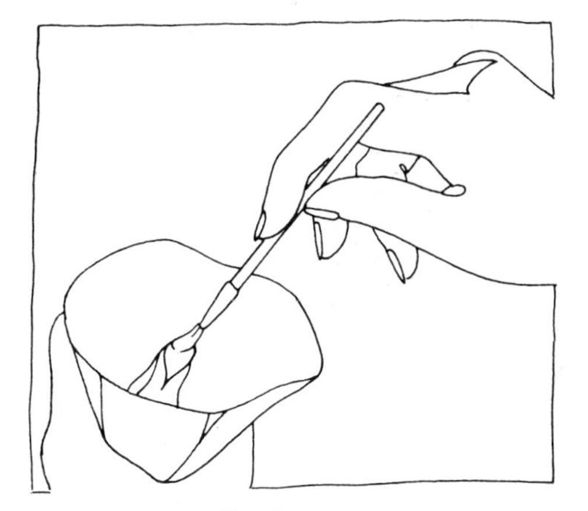

Brush striping

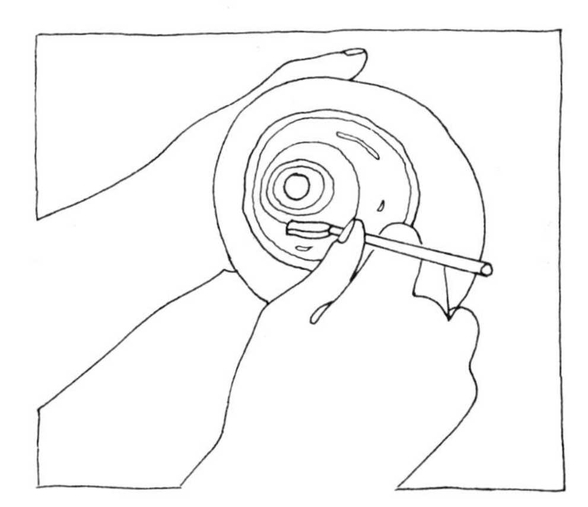

Brush striping for deep colors

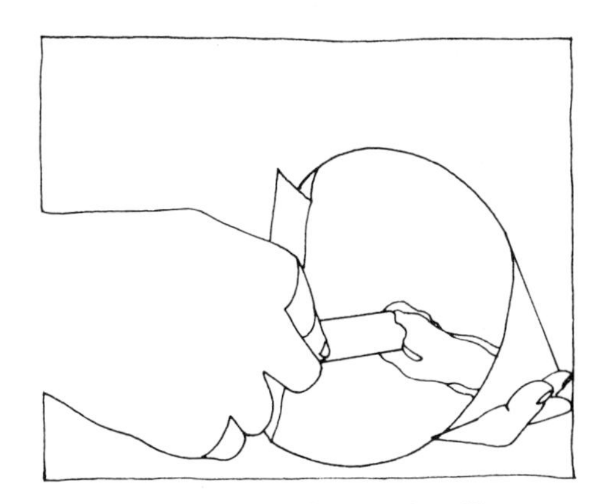

Spatula striping for subtle effects

Borders, garlands and other designs

The six basic shapes of decorating tubes can be used to make all the designs described below.

1. Star Tube Techniques

Use star tube #16 or #21, and for the best results use an icing of medium consistency.

*STARS: Holding the decorating bag at a 90° angle, perpendicular to the work surface, with the tube almost touching it, squeeze out icing to form a star. Then stop pressure and pull tube away.

Be sure to stop squeezing before lifting the tube, or the stars will have pointed centers. To make large stars, increase pressure; for smaller stars, reduce pressure.

*STAR FILL-IN: You can use this method to cover a section or the entire surface of a cake. Pipe stars evenly and close together, adjusting the position of the tube so that the points of the stars interlock and cover the entire area with no gaps. Keep the bag at a 90° angle.

If you use this method to decorate the entire surface of the cake, the cake needn't be frosted first.

*STAR BORDER: A row of stars makes a pretty trim around the edges of a cake. Keep the stars as uniform as possible and pipe them close together so there are no gaps. Continue to use a 90° angle.

*RIBBED BORDER: For this border, hold the decorating bag at a 45° angle, with the tube almost touching the surface. Squeeze out icing, moving the tube along the surface. Don't twist the bag. When finished, stop pressure and pull tube away.

*STAR PUFFS AND ROSETTES: The same basic method is used for both these decorations, with the decorating bag held at a 90° angle and with the tube slightly above the work surface.

To make a star puff, squeeze the bag and move your hand in a circular motion, continuing the motion past the starting point and into the center of the decoration. Stop pressure and pull tube away.

A rosette is made the same way until you reach the starting point of the decoration; then stop pressure and pull tube away.

*ROSETTE BORDER: Make this border by piping a line of rosettes.

*SHELL BORDER: This is the most often used cake border. Holding the bag at a 45° angle, with the tube slightly above your work surface and the end of the bag pointing toward you, squeeze with heavy pressure and lift the tube slightly as icing builds and fans out into a full base. Relax pressure as you pull the tube down and toward you to make a tail. Stop pressure and pull tube away.

When making shells, always work toward yourself, starting each new shell behind the tail of the previous shell.

*REVERSE SHELL BORDER: This border is a perfect choice when you need a formal look. Holding the bag at a 45° angle with the tube slightly above the work surface, squeeze to let icing fan out as if you were making a shell, then swing the tube around to the left in a curve as you relax pressure to form the tail of a shell. Stop pressure and pull tube away.

Repeat, but this time swing the tube to the right as you form the tail. Continue, alternating directions, for a series of reverse shells.

*FLEUR-DE-LIS: This decoration is used most often on the sides of cakes—especially wedding cakes. Holding the bag at a 45° angle, make a shell. Keeping the bag at a 45° angle, and to the left of the shell, squeeze bag to fan out icing into shell base. Then as you relax pressure to form the tail, move the tube slightly to the right and join the tail of this shell to the tail of the first shell. Repeat on the right side of the first shell.

*ZIGZAG BORDER: Hold the bag at a 45° angle, with the tube touching the surface. The end of the bag should point to the right, and your fingertips holding the bag should face you. Steadily squeeze out icing, moving your hand in a tight side-to-side motion, forming a zigzag line. To end, stop pressure and pull tube away.

*ZIGZAG GARLANDS: Use the zigzag method and increase the pressure as you form the center curve of the garland; then use less pressure to complete it. To end, stop pressure and pull tube away.

*PUFF BORDER: Holding the bag at a 45° angle, be sure your fingertips holding the bag face you. Touch tube to surface and use a zigzag motion with a light-to-heavy-to-light pressure so that the puff will be larger in the center. To end, stop pressure and pull away. Repeat to form a row of puffs.

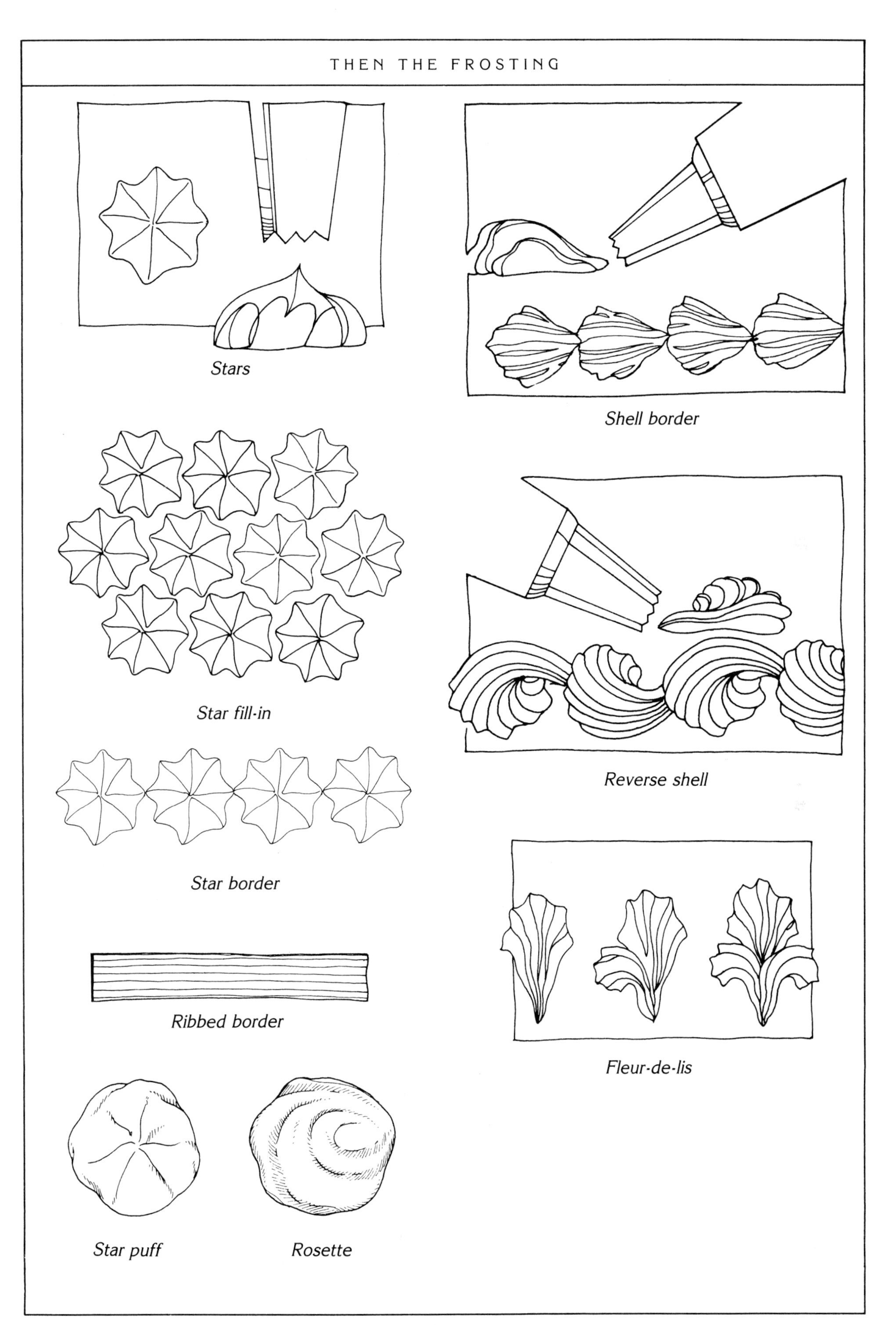
Stars
Shell border
Star fill-in
Reverse shell
Star border
Ribbed border
Fleur-de-lis
Star puff
Rosette

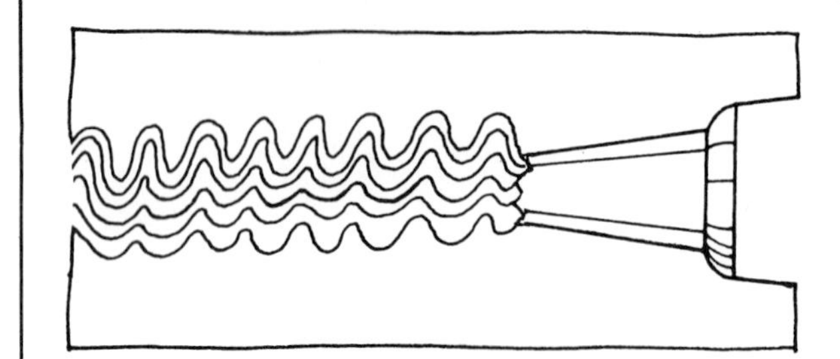

Zigzag border

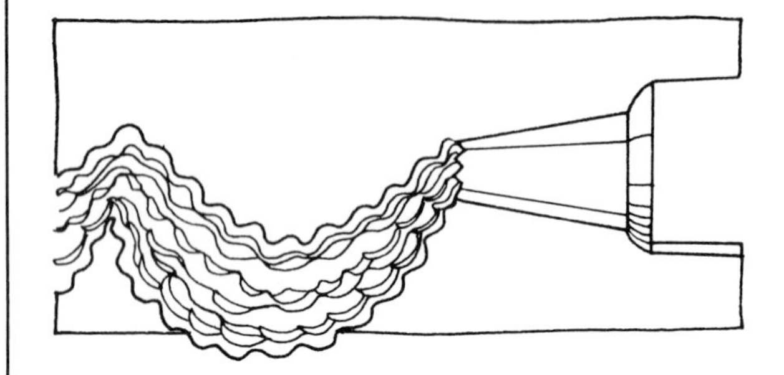

Zigzag garlands

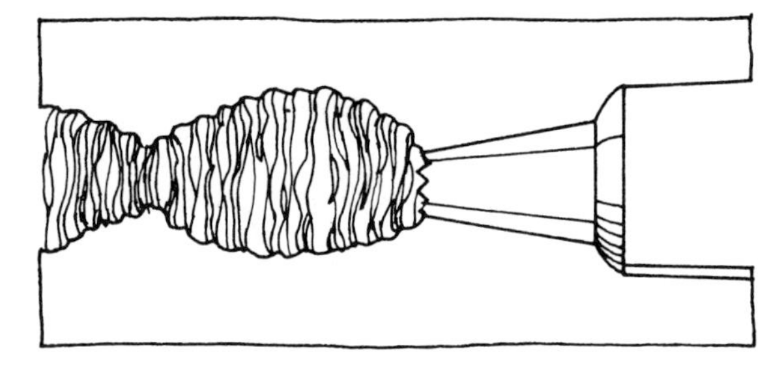

Puff border

2. Round Tube Techniques

For best results, use tube #3 and an icing of thin consistency.

*DOTS: Holding the bag at a 90° angle slightly above the work surface, steadily squeeze out a dot of icing until the dot is the size you want. Stop pressure and pull tube away.

For larger dots, lift the tube gently as the icing forms a mound, keeping the tip of the tube buried in the dot. When the dot is the size you want, stop pressure and pull away the tube.
*BEADS: Hold the bag at a 45° angle, with the tube slightly above the work surface and the end of the bag pointing toward you. Squeeze and lift the tube slightly so the icing fans out into a base. Relax pressure as you draw the tube down and bring the bead to a point, forming a teardrop.
*BEAD HEARTS: Pipe two beads side by side, joining them at the points.
*PRINTING AND WRITING: For most printing and writing, we recommend round tube #3. Letters are combinations of straight, curved and slanted lines, so it's important to practice these motions. Practice moving your whole arm, not just your fingers, to form the lines.

For an easy guide, mark your message in the icing with a toothpick. As you pipe the letters, hold the tube at a 45° angle and let it lightly touch the icing.
*OUTLINES: You can use a round tube to outline contours or cover guidelines when transferring a pattern to a cake. Hold the bag at a 45° angle and let the tube touch the work surface. Squeeze out some icing and be sure it sticks to the starting point; then raise the tube slightly and continue to squeeze. To end, stop squeezing, touch the tube to the surface and pull it away.
*PIPED LACE: Hold the bag at a 90° angle, with the tube slightly above the work surface. Pipe the icing in continuous lines, curving it up, down and around, but never let the lines cross. Then stop pressure and pull tube away.
*DROP STRINGS: This technique is usually used to decorate the sides of a cake.

To practice, mark an inverted baking pan with icing dots around the top edge, about 1½" apart. Hold the bag at a 90° angle, with the end of the bag pointing slightly to the right. Touch the tube to the first mark and squeeze until icing sticks to the surface. Then pull the tube straight out, away from the surface, allowing the icing to drop in an arc joining two dots. To end, stop pressure as you touch the tube to the second mark.

Repeat, attaching string to the third mark and so on, forming a row of drop strings. A hint for perfect stringwork is to let the string—not your hand—drop to form an arc. Keep the strings the same length.

To form a double row of drop strings, return to the first mark and squeeze the bag so that the icing drops into a smaller arc within the first arc. Join the end of each smaller arc to the end of the corresponding arc in the first row. Be sure to pipe the longest drop strings first.
*LATTICE: To practice this technique, tape a sheet of waxed paper over a design of any shape—for example, a circle.

Holding the bag at a 90° angle, begin by piping diagonal lines from one side of the circle to the other, through the center, working toward the edges. Then crisscross those lines with another series of diagonal lines in the opposite direction, keeping the lines evenly spaced. Cover the edges of the outline with any star border you choose.

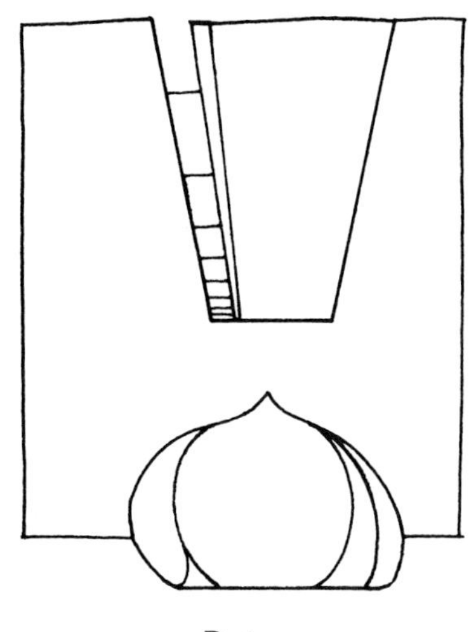

Dots

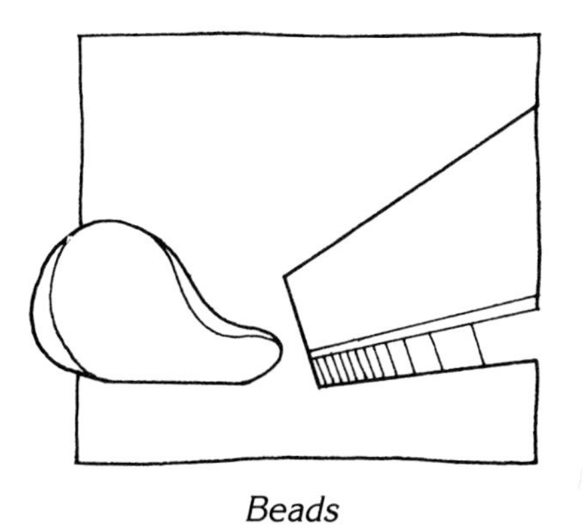

Beads

Bead hearts

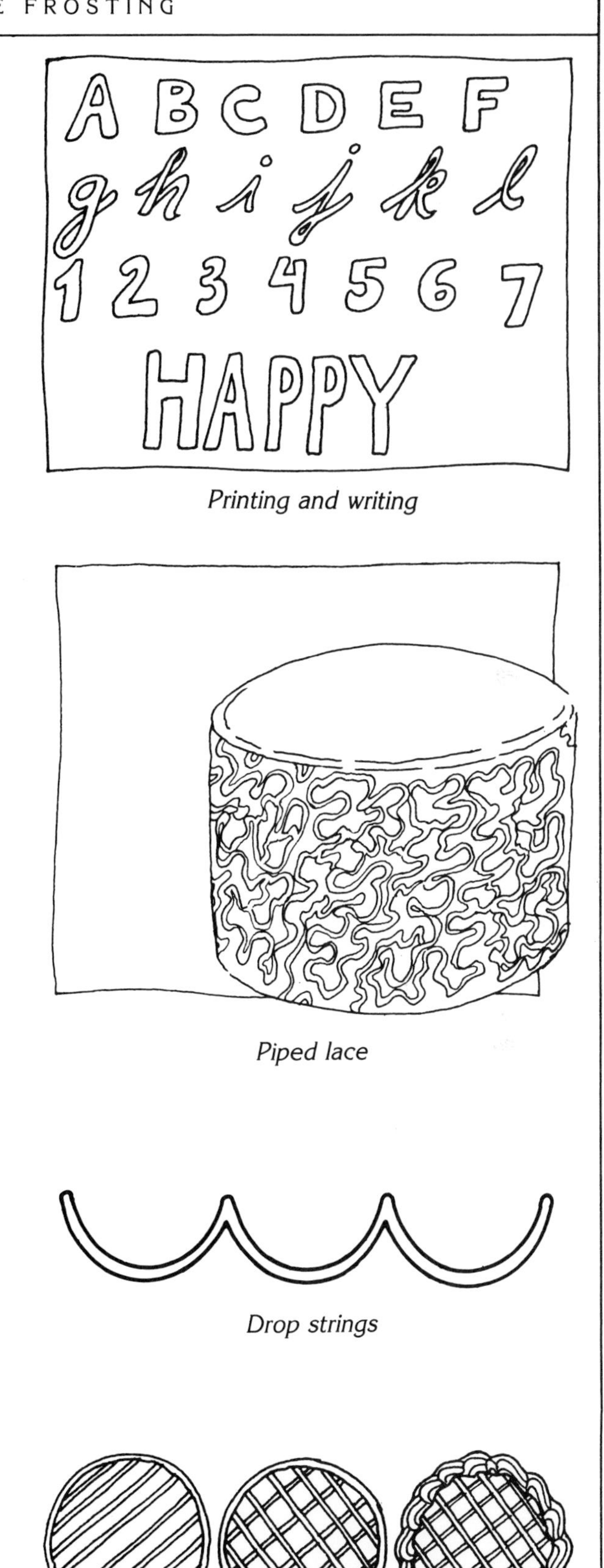

Printing and writing

Piped lace

Drop strings

Lattice

3. Drop Flower Tube Techniques

The easiest flowers for beginners to master are drop flowers. The icing should be slightly stiff so that the flowers will hold their shape. Tube #225 is the easiest to use; hold the bag at a 90° angle, with the tube touching the surface.

*STAR FLOWERS: Squeeze and keep the tip of the tube in the icing until star petals are formed. Stop pressure and pull away tube.
*SWIRLED FLOWERS: Curve your wrist to the left, and as you squeeze out icing, bring your hand around to the right. Stop pressure and pull tube away. To make centers for these flowers, use round tube #2 or #3.
Swirled drop flowers can't be made directly on a cake. If you use butter cream icing, pipe swirled flowers onto waxed paper and freeze overnight. Pipe royal icing swirled flowers on waxed paper and let dry.

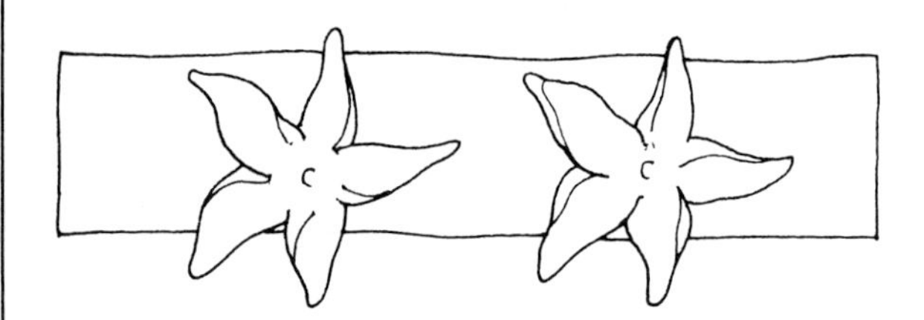

Star flowers

Swirled flowers

4. Leaf Tube Techniques

Use tube #67 and an icing of thin consistency.

*BASIC LEAF: With your fingertips on the bag pointing toward you, hold the bag at a 45° angle. Squeeze while holding tube in place so that the icing fans out into a base; then relax and stop pressure as you pull the tube away and draw the leaf to a point.
*RUFFLED LEAF: This is made just like the basic leaf, except that you move the tube back and forth slightly as you draw the leaf to a point.
*STAND-UP LEAF: Holding the bag at a 90° angle, squeeze and hold tube in place as the icing fans out to form a base. Relax and stop pressure as you pull the tube straight up and away to create a stand-up leaf.

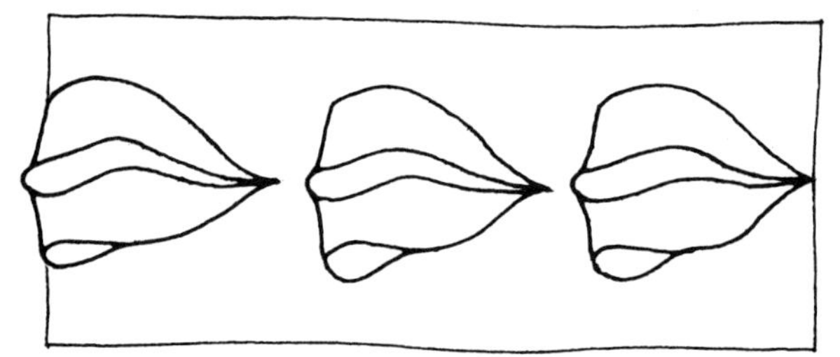

Basic leaves

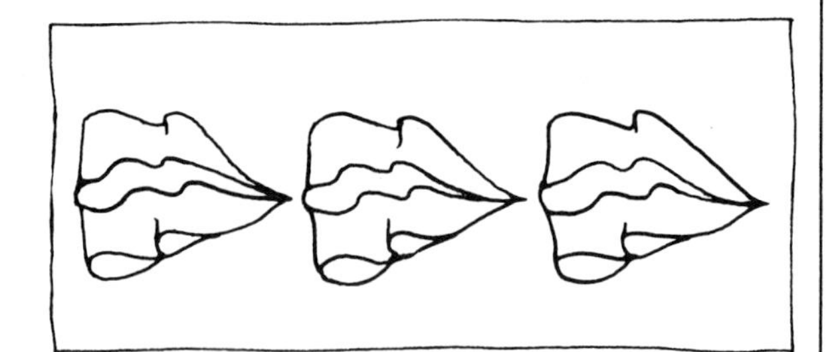

Ruffled leaves

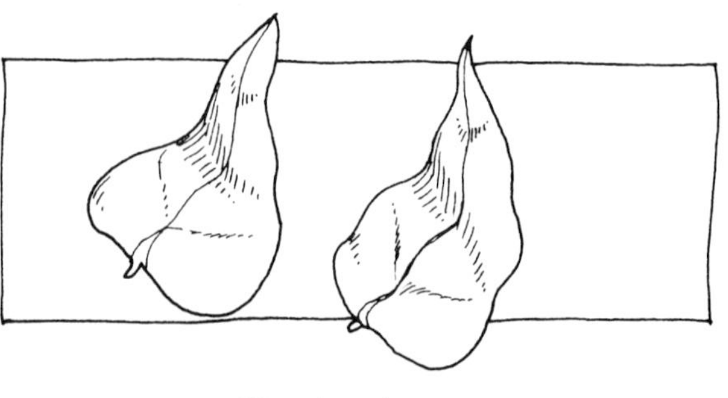

Stand-up leaves

5. Rose Tube Techniques

Use tube #104 and an icing of medium consistency.

*RIBBON GARLAND: Holding the bag at a 45° angle, touch the wide end of the tube to the surface, angling the narrow end of the tip out and about ¼″ away from work surface. As you squeeze, swing the tube down and up to the right.
*RIBBON SWAG: Make this the same way as a ribbon garland but as you finish each curve, move the tube up and down in three short strokes to form a swag.
*RUFFLE: Use the same method as for a ribbon garland, but as you form the curve, move your hand up and down slightly to form a ruffle.

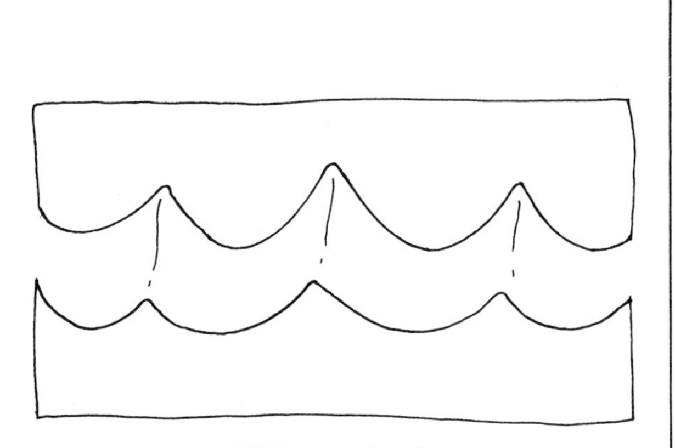

Ribbon garland

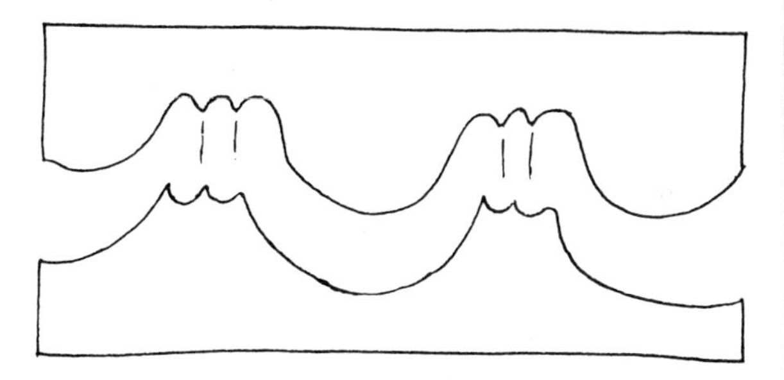

Ribbon swag

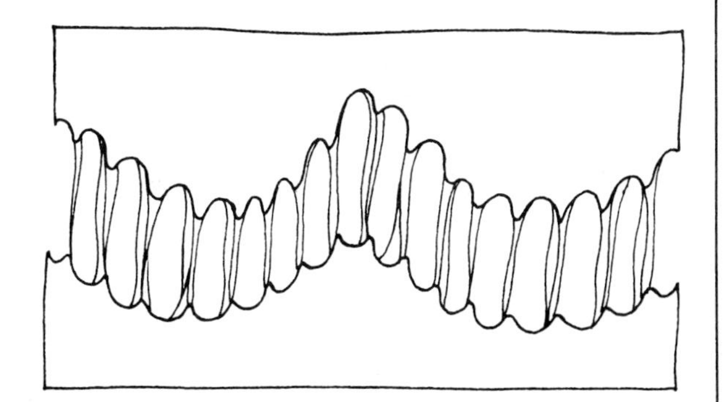

Ruffle

6. Basket Weave Tube Techniques

Use tube #47 and an icing of medium consistency.

*RIBBED STRIPE: Hold bag at a 45° angle, with the serrated side of the tube facing up. With the tube touching surface, use a steady pressure to squeeze out icing in a long stripe. When the stripe is long enough, stop pressure and pull tube away.
*SMOOTH STRIPE: Make this just like the ribbed stripe, but keep the smooth side of the tube facing up.
*BASKET WEAVE: Hold the bag at a 90° angle, with the serrated side of the tube facing up. Touch tube to surface and squeeze out a 3″ vertical line.

Change to a 45° angle, with your fingertips holding the bag pointing toward you. Touch tube to work surface, keeping the serrated side facing up, and hold the tube on the left side of the vertical line. Squeeze a short horizontal bar over the vertical line. Then add more horizontal bars, each about a tube-width apart, over the vertical line.

Change to a 90° angle and make another 3″ vertical line to the right of the first one, overlapping the ends of the horizontal bars. Then overlap this line with more horizontal bars, adding them between the spaces of the bars in first row.

Keep repeating this procedure, alternating vertical lines and horizontal bars, to create the basket-weave effect.

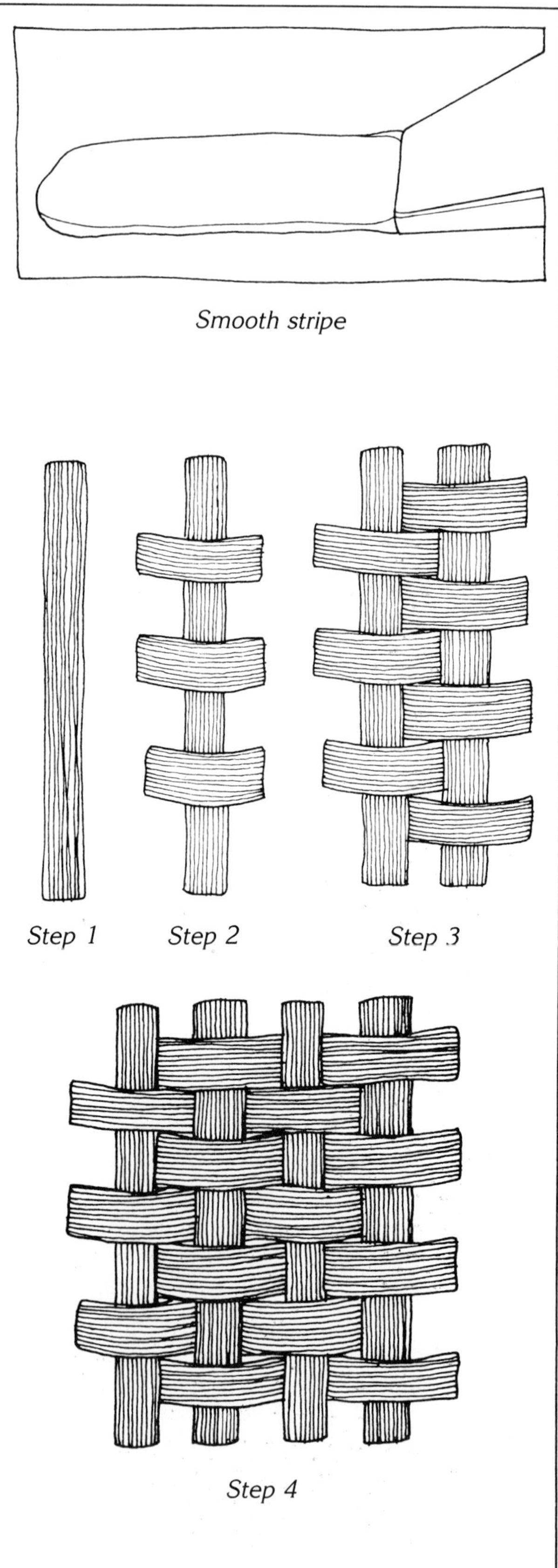
Smooth stripe

Step 1 Step 2 Step 3

Step 4

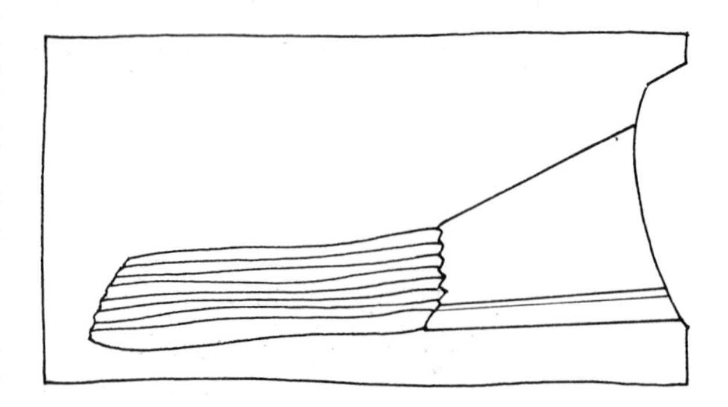
Ribbed stripe

Dolls holding candles will light up any child's birthday. The Ring-around-the-Rosy cake at right features a smiling circle of dolls that are simple to make (see page 142). Their heads are made from lollipops and candy mints, and their pretty bonnets are paper muffin-pan liners.

The Rag Dolls below take time, but they're made in advance with Royal Icing (see page 143). To honor a little boy, pipe short pants on each doll. These dolls make extra-special party favors for young guests to carry home.

Just one decorating tube was used to apply almost every bit of icing on these three cakes. Except for some outlining and the swirls of pink "ice cream" on the opposite page, all the icing was piped with star tube #21.

Uncle Sam's Hat, left, is stacked four layers high—an appropriate salute to either Presidents' Day or the Fourth of July (see page 147).

You needn't be an artist to recreate the Classic Car shown below (you'll find the pattern on page 144), and you can copy other designs by using the same technique.

To make the yummy-looking Strawberry Ice Cream Cone at right, see page 130.

Standard-sized baking pans are used to make this Sweetheart Cake and Heart Cupcakes. The large heart is made from one round and one square cake layer (page 146); muffin pans become heart-shaped cupcake molds when you insert a marble between each cup and paper liner (page 108).

A garden of flowers

You can create dozens of beautiful blossoms ranging from simple to elaborate using a variety of tubes. With these directions and some practice, even a novice can turn out pretty flowers.

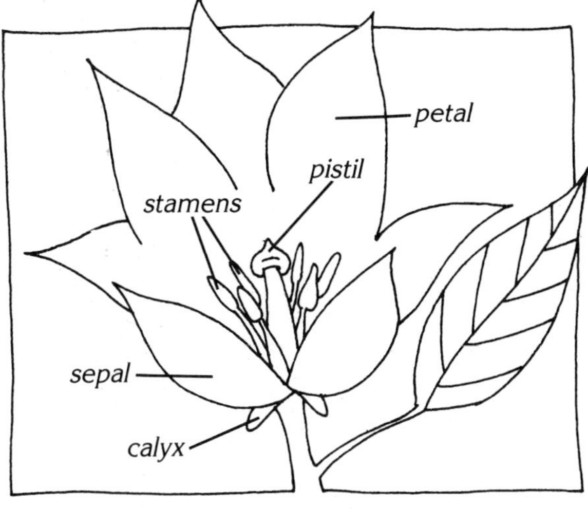

Parts of a flower

Rosebud

1. Using icing of stiff consistency and rose tube #104, hold the bag at a 45° angle so that the end of the bag points toward your right shoulder and your fingertips holding the bag point toward you.

To make the base petal, touch the wide end of the tube to the surface and point the narrow end toward the right. Squeeze and move the tube forward ¼"; then hesitate so that the icing fans out, and move back.

2. Keep the bag in same position, with the wide end of the tube touching the inside right edge of the base petal, and the narrow end of the tube pointing slightly above the base petal. Squeeze so icing catches the inside edge of the base petal, and roll it into an interlocking center bud. Stop pressure and pull tube away.

3. Using round tube #3, add sepals and calyx. Hold the bag at a 45° angle to the base of the bud, with the end of the bag pointing toward you. Touch tube to bud, squeeze and pull tube up and away, relaxing pressure to form a pointed sepal. Make 3 sepals in all and one rounded calyx.

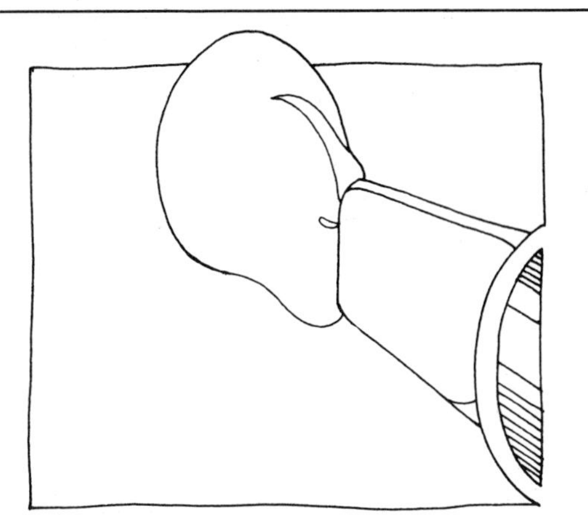

Forming the base petal of a rosebud

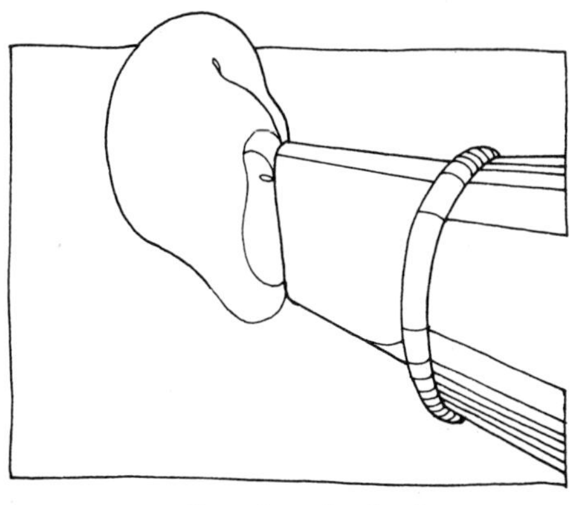

Forming the bud

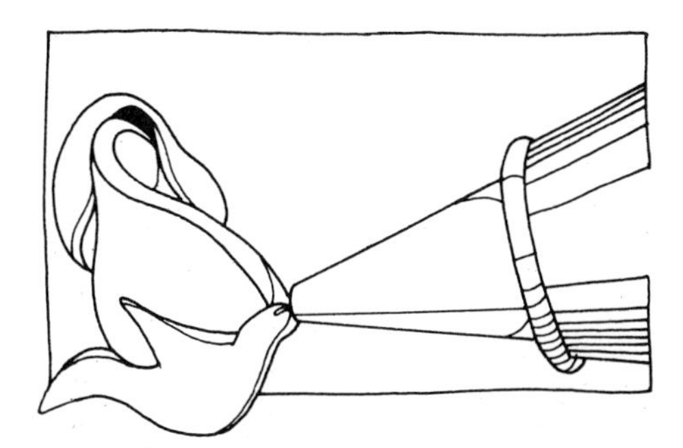

Adding sepals and calyx

Half-Rose

1. Start by making a rosebud according to the directions above, but omit sepals and calyx.

Then make the first petal. Holding the bag at a 45° angle so the end of the bag points to the right and your fingertips gripping the bag point toward you, place the wide end of the tube on the bottom left side of bud. Squeeze out icing and move tube up, around to the right and down, relaxing pressure.

2. Make second petal by using the same method in reverse, touching the wide end of the tube to bottom right of bud. Squeeze and move tube up, around to the left and down to center of bud base. Stop pressure and pull tube away.
3. Thin the icing and add sepals and calyx with round tube #3, using the same method as in step 3 of rosebud.

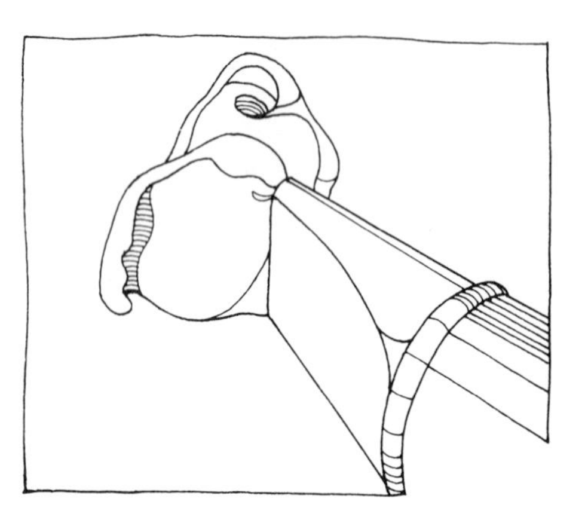

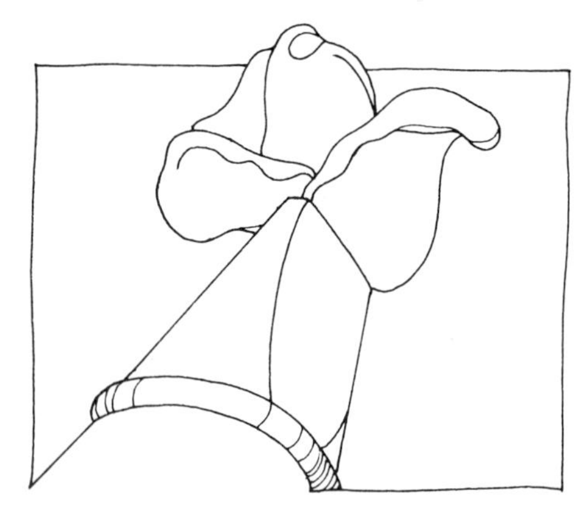

Shaping flowers evenly

You'll need a flower nail or some sort of turntable to make most other flowers.

Some people find a pint-jar easier to use than a flower nail; just put the lid on the jar and attach a square of waxed paper to the lid with a dab of icing. Then, resting the jar on your work surface, turn the jar slowly with your free hand as you pipe onto the waxed paper.

If you use a metal or plastic flower nail, use the same method to attach waxed paper to the top, and slowly rotate the nail as you pipe a flower, holding the nail with your thumb and index finger.

Whichever method you use, slide the waxed paper off the surface along with the flower and allow the flower to dry before you peel away the paper.

Sweet Pea I

1. Hold the bag at a 45° angle, with the wide end of rose tube #104 touching the paper and the narrow end at a slight angle. Turning the flower nail or jar in a half-circle, pipe the back petal, jiggling the tube slightly to create a ruffled edge.
2. Holding the narrow end of the tube straight up to create a cupped edge, pipe 2 smaller petals on top of the back petal.
3. Change to a 90° angle and squeeze out the center petal, lifting the tube slightly as you apply pressure. Let up on pressure, lower tube and pull away.

Sweet Pea II

1. Hold the bag at a 45° angle, with the wide end of rose tube #104 touching the paper and the narrow end up. Start by piping the center petal, lifting the tube slightly, then letting up on pressure as you lower the tube and pull it away.
2. Pipe side petals in the same way, tilting the tube sideways to pipe a petal at left and right.

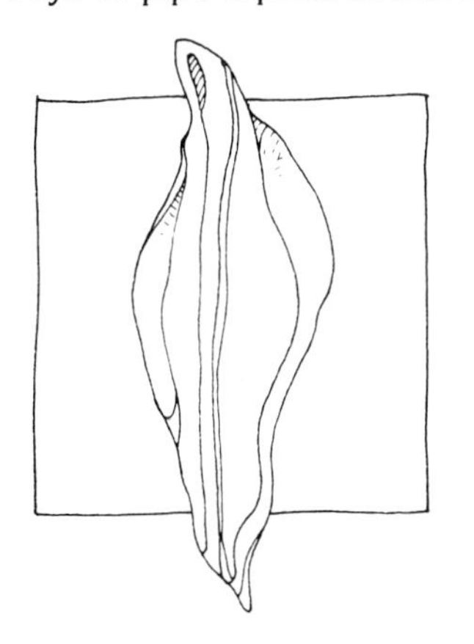

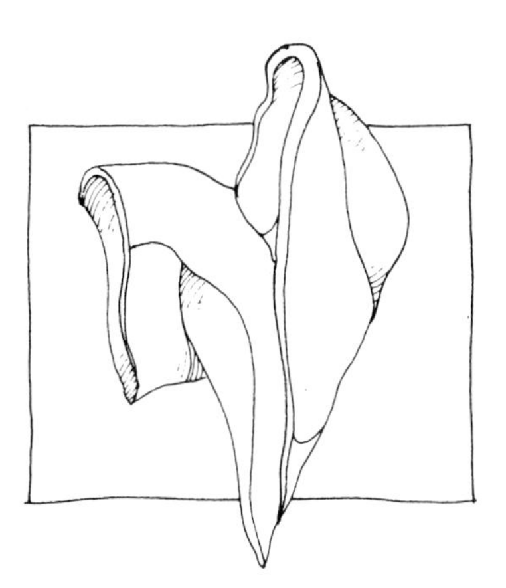

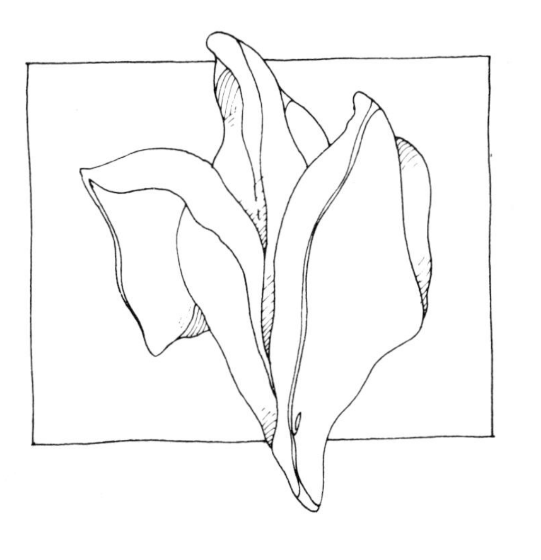

Violet

1. With wide end of rose tube #59° directly in the center of the paper, hold the tube at a 45° angle. To form the first petal, squeeze and move tube ½″ out toward edge and then back to center as you rotate the nail.
2. Pipe 4 more petals.
3. Use round tube #1 to pipe stamens on center.

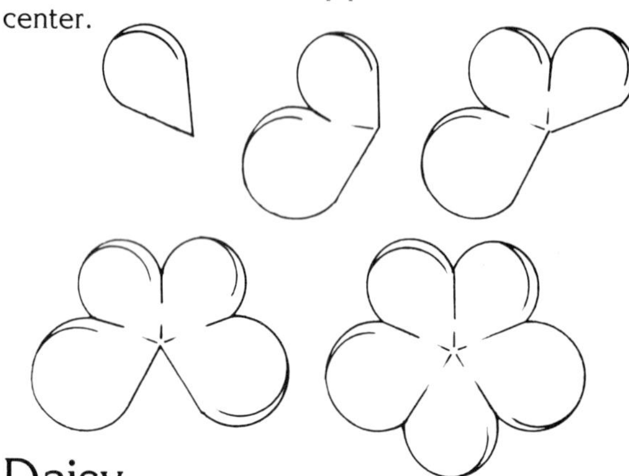

Daisy

1. Using rose tube #104 with the narrow end of the tube touching the outer edge of the paper, squeeze out a petal, moving to center of paper and easing up on pressure to stop. Rotate and repeat 10 or 11 times for remaining petals.
2. Use round tube #4 to pipe a large dot on the center. Moisten your finger and gently flatten the center.

Mum

1. Using specialty tube #79, #80 or #81, pipe a mound in center of the paper (the larger the mound, the larger the mum will be).
2. Holding the tube at a 45° angle at the outer edge of mound, with half-moon opening pointing up, make a series of ½″-long petals around the mound.
3. Make a second row of slightly shorter petals on top of the first row. Continue adding rows until mound is covered, making each row of petals shorter than the one before.
4. Use round tube #1 to pipe stamens on center.

Pansy

1. Holding bag at a 45° angle with wide end of rose tube #104 at center of paper, make 2 back petals, piping a wide curve for each, with the second petals slightly behind the first.
2. Pipe 2 slightly shorter petals on top of the first 2.
3. To make the bottom petal, pipe a large ruffled petal by jiggling your hand slightly as you pipe.
4. Use round tube #1 to pipe a yellow teardrop for the center.

Daffodil and Jonquil

1. Hold bag at a 45° angle, with the wide end of rose tube #104 touching center of paper and narrow end almost parallel to paper. Pipe 6 petals, starting each at the center and moving it out nearly an inch toward the edge of the paper; then curve the petal slightly and return it to the center as you turn the nail.
2. Dip your fingers in cornstarch and pinch the end of each petal to a point while the icing is still damp.
3. Use round tube #2 to pipe a coil in the center to form center tube of flower.

Half-Carnation

1. Using very stiff icing and holding rose tube #104 at a 45° angle, make a single petal by piping with a slightly jiggling motion, from center to edge, lifting the tube slightly as you reach the end of the petal. Return to center and let up on pressure. Repeat to form a fan of petals.
2. Pipe second row of shorter petals on top of the first.
3. Continue adding rows until you have 4 or 5 rows, creating a round half-flower.
4. Use round tube #3 to pipe calyx.

Rose

1. Holding the bag at a 45° angle with the wide end of rose tube #104 touching the paper and the narrow end up, pipe while turning the nail counterclockwise until you have formed a dome. Pipe a second dome right on top of the first.
2. With the wide end of the tube touching the base of the dome, pipe a petal by moving tube up and then back down to the base while turning the nail counterclockwise.
3. Pipe second petal in the same way, starting slightly over the end of the first petal.
4. Add a third petal, ending where the first petal began.
5. Starting at a point slightly below the center of any petal, pipe a second row of 4 or 5 petals.
6. Starting at a point slightly below the center of any petal in the second row, pipe a third row of 7 petals.

Step 1

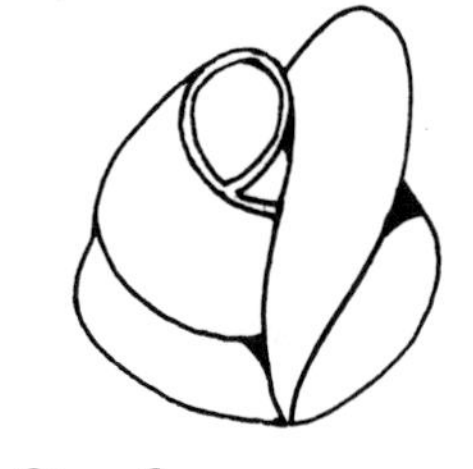
Step 2

Step 3

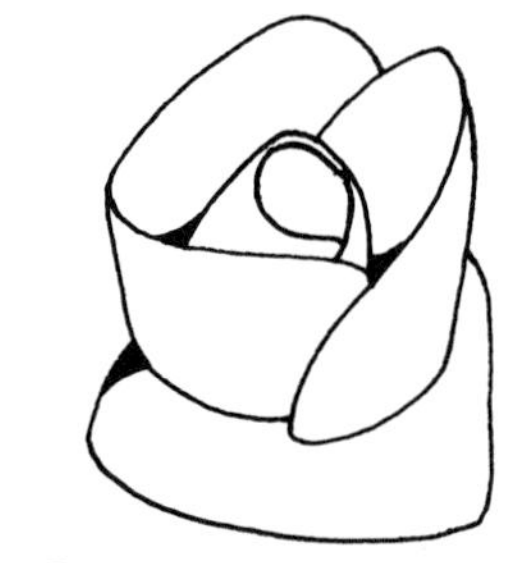
Step 4

Step 5

Step 6

Using Run Sugar

With this technique you can copy any picture or bring your own designs to life. Although it looks complicated, the Run Sugar technique is simple: first you outline your designs with Royal Icing, then thin the icing and fill in the outline. You'll find recipes for Royal Icing and Run Sugar on page 64.

1. MIX ROYAL ICING. As you prepare the icing, beat at low speed instead of the usual high speed so that you'll whip in less air; otherwise, bubbles will appear in your finished design.

Fill a decorating bag halfway. Keep remaining icing in a bowl covered with a damp paper towel. If you plan to cover a large area with one color, have a second decorating bag ready to use when the first batch of icing is used up, because Royal Icing hardens quickly and seams will show on your finished design.

2. OUTLINE THE DESIGN WITH ROYAL ICING. Begin by taping a pattern of your design to your countertop or any flat work surface. Then tape a sheet of waxed paper or clear plastic wrap over the pattern, making sure the paper is wrinkle-free.

Using Royal Icing and round tube #2 or #3, outline your design on the waxed paper, keeping the lines as smooth as possible.

3. LET THE OUTLINE DRY. If the color of the outline is similar to the color you plan to use within the design, a few minutes of drying time is enough—just until the icing forms a crust. But if the outline color is darker or lighter than the second color you plan to use, wait at least an hour or two; otherwise, the two colors will mix at the edges.

4. FILL IN THE DESIGN WITH RUN SUGAR. Before you fill in the design, Royal Icing must be thinned. Place the amount of icing you need in a bowl and add water a few drops at a time, stirring gently by hand. Don't beat the icing; this will introduce too much air.

To check the consistency, remove a spoonful of the thinned icing, drop it back into the same bowl, and begin counting to 10. If it takes a full count of 10 for the spoonful of Run Sugar to disappear, the icing is ready.

Fill a decorating bag about half full. If you are using a parchment bag, you won't need a decorating tube; just snip off the tip of the cone to make a small opening. If you are using a plastic decorating bag, use a round tube #2 or #3. Place the tip inside the outlined area, and press out icing gently. Don't press too hard, or the outline may break. Fill in the area quickly so that the icing will not begin to crust before you finish filling in the area. If air bubbles appear in the icing, prick them with a pin. It's best to fill in areas of the same color at the same time; for example, do all pinks first, then all greens.

5. LET DRY. After the entire design is filled in, let it dry thoroughly. Most designs will dry in about 48 hours.

6. PEEL OFF PAPER. When the design is completely dry, carefully peel away plastic wrap or waxed paper. Be gentle, because these designs are very fragile.

Place a few dabs of icing underneath the design to attach it to the cake. If you'd like to save the design as a keepsake or for reuse, place it on three or four sugar cubes or small mounds of hardened icing.

These decorations make it easy to serve the cake, too—just lift off the design before cutting the cake.

3 Simply Beautiful Cakes

Before you add a single thing to your grocery list, shop your kitchen shelves for decorating ideas. All the cakes in this chapter were made without using a decorating tube, and many are decorated with inexpensive, easily available ingredients.

Even confectioners' sugar or baking cocoa can create a delicate design on a plain pound cake when sifted over a paper doily. Here are more techniques for making cakes look extravagantly beautiful—including some ideas that won't make a dime's worth of difference in the actual cost of your cake.

Candies and cookies: In this book we've used lollipops, candy corn, jellybeans, mints, animal crackers, chocolate jimmies, marshmallows, cinnamon candies—and more.

Chocolate: Shred it, grate it, curl it, or melt and drizzle it! Morsels of semisweet chocolate can create geometric designs like the Wagon Wheel on page 96.

To add an initial, a greeting or a freehand design to the top of a cake, melt a 1-oz. square of semisweet chocolate with 1 tsp. butter over low heat; then drizzle it over the cake or swirl it with a small paintbrush.

Colored sugar and coconut: Place granulated sugar or shredded coconut in a plastic bag or glass jar and add a few drops of liquid food color; shake until tinted. A border of pale pink coconut or a sprinkling of tinted sugar makes a white frosting even prettier.

Flowers: Any tube cake such as the Daffodil Blossom Cake pictured on page 102 is perfect for fresh flowers because the hole in the center can hold a small glass of water.

You can crystallize fresh flowers by dipping them in egg white and sugar, and they'll keep several days. For directions, see page 166. Silk flowers are a simple way to dress up a cake, too.

Fruit: Fresh, candied, dried and even canned fruit offer abundant possibilities.

With a cup of fresh blueberries, a cup of fresh strawberries and a cup of heavy cream, you can turn a square cake into a dramatic red-white-and-blue Strawberry Star like the one on page 94. Glazed fruits make beautiful decorations, too. When fresh fruits aren't available, a glaze of melted peach preserves can transform canned apricots, pears and cherries into a beautiful topping, as for a Glazed Fruit Gateau (see page 99).

Raisins and other dried fruits are well suited for designs like the Fruit-and-Nut Flower pictured on page 30.

Nuts: Slivered, chopped, halved or toasted nuts can be used as garnishes, as borders, or to lavishly cover a cake on all sides.

Part of the fun of cake decorating is the chance to improvise, so don't overlook other decorating resources that may be just inside your cupboard or blooming outside your window.

Chocolate Lace Pound Cake

(12 servings)

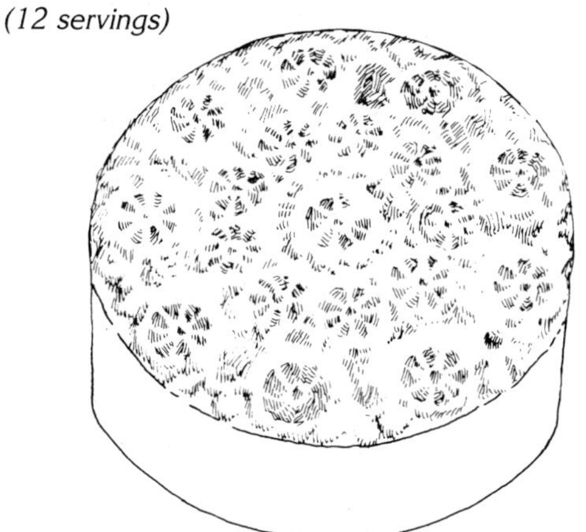

Grandma's Chocolate Pound Cake (see page 43), baked into 1 (12″) round layer
12″ round paper doily
¾ c. confectioners' sugar

Place doily on top of cool cake. Sift confectioners' sugar over the doily, covering all exposed areas of cake. Carefully lift doily.
Variation: On a yellow cake, substitute cocoa for the confectioners' sugar. Or use a combination of the two—sift cocoa over the cake first, covering the surface, then place the doily on top and sift confectioners' sugar over it.

Black and White Chiffon Cake

(12 servings)

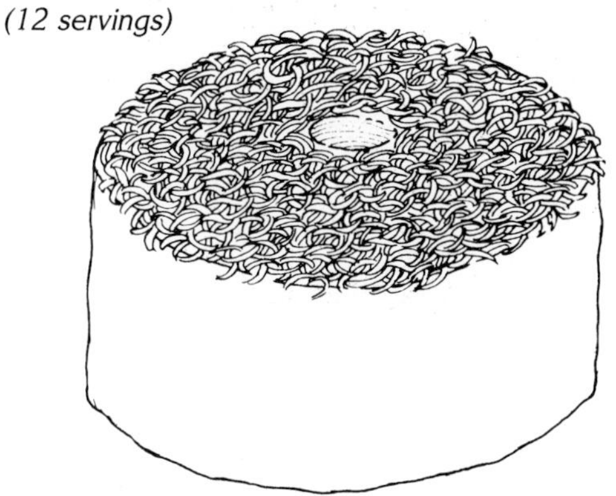

Chocolate Chip Chiffon Cake (see page 53)
or any 10″ chiffon cake
Creamy Vanilla Frosting (see page 53)
2 (2-oz.) milk chocolate bars, coarsely shredded

1. Cut cake horizontally into 3 equal layers.
2. Fill layers with Creamy Vanilla Frosting and sprinkle with some of the coarsely shredded chocolate.
3. Frost top and sides of cake with Creamy Vanilla Frosting.
4. Decorate top of cake with remaining chocolate.

Daffodil Blossom Cake

(12 servings; see photo, page 102)

1 small glass
Daffodil Cake (see page 47)
or any 10″ tube cake
Lemon Frosting (recipe follows)
daffodil blossoms and leaves

1. Insert a glass in the center of the cake.
2. Frost sides and top of cake with Lemon Frosting, swirling the frosting with a spatula (see photo, page 102). Refrigerate at least 2 hours.
3. Just before serving, add water to the glass in the center of the cake and arrange daffodils in the glass with a few leaves, sprigs of fern or other greenery.

Variation: In place of daffodils, substitute a cluster of roses, lilies-of-the-valley, daisies, pansies or any other fresh flowers.

Lemon Frosting

¾ c. sugar
3 tblsp. cornstarch
⅛ tsp. salt
⅔ c. water
3 egg yolks, beaten
¼ c. lemon juice
1½ tsp. grated lemon rind
1 c. heavy cream, whipped

Combine sugar, cornstarch, salt and water in 2-qt. saucepan. Stir well. Cook over medium heat, stirring constantly, until mixture comes to a boil. Boil 1 minute. Remove from heat.

Stir some of the hot mixture into beaten egg yolks. Stir egg yolk mixture back into hot mixture. Cook over low heat, stirring constantly, 2 minutes. Remove from heat.

Stir in lemon juice and lemon rind. Cool completely. Fold cooled mixture into whipped cream.

Strawberry Angel Cake

(12 servings)

2 pt. fresh strawberries
Super Angel Food Cake (see page 45)
or any 10″ angel food cake
Strawberry Fluff (recipe follows)

1. Select 20 whole strawberries for decoration and set aside. Hull remaining strawberries. Slice enough of the hulled strawberries to make 1 c. and set aside for Strawberry Fluff.
2. Cut cake horizontally into 3 equal layers.
3. Fill layers with Strawberry Fluff. Frost sides and top of cake with Strawberry Fluff, swirling the frosting with a spatula as illustrated.
4. Just before serving, cut 8 of the reserved whole strawberries in half. Decorate cake with halved and whole strawberries as shown.

Strawberry Fluff

1 c. sugar
1 egg white
1 c. sliced strawberries (reserved from recipe for Strawberry Angel Cake)

Combine ingredients in bowl and beat 3 to 5 minutes, or until stiff peaks form, using an electric mixer at high speed. Makes 5 c.

Strawberry Star

(8 servings)

Feather-light Yellow Cake (see page 7)
or any 8″ square cake layer
Sweetened Whipped Cream I (see page 63)
1 c. fresh strawberries, hulled and sliced
1 c. fresh blueberries

1. Frost top and sides of cake with Sweetened Whipped Cream I.
2. Use a toothpick to mark a 5-pointed star on top of the cake as illustrated.
3. Arrange sliced strawberries inside design lines of star.
4. Arrange blueberries around the strawberry star to cover the remaining areas on top of the cake.

Apricot-glazed Sponge Cake

(12 servings)

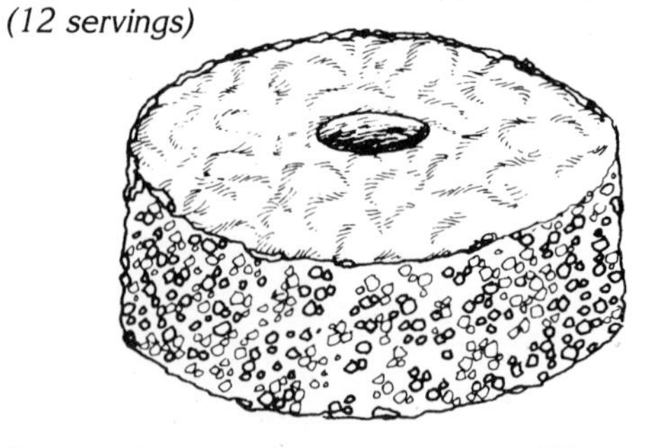

Golden Sponge Cake (see page 47)
or any 10″ sponge cake
Coffee Butter Cream Filling (recipe follows)
1 (12-oz.) jar apricot preserves (1 c.)
⅔ c. finely chopped walnuts

1. Cut cake horizontally into 3 equal layers.
2. Fill layers with Coffee Butter Cream Filling and reassemble cake.
3. Spread apricot preserves over sides and top of cake. Sprinkle sides with walnuts.

Coffee Butter Cream Filling

1 tblsp. instant coffee powder
1 tblsp. warm water
½ c. butter or regular margarine
2 c. sifted confectioners' sugar
1 tsp. vanilla

Dissolve coffee powder in warm water in bowl. Add butter, confectioners' sugar and vanilla. Beat until smooth, using an electric mixer at medium speed.

Chocolate-Cherry Cake Roll

(10 servings; see photo, page 138)

batter for Bûche de Noel (cake only; see page 52) or for any chocolate sponge cake roll
sifted baking cocoa
1 (24-oz.) jar cherry pie filling
Cocoa Cream (recipe follows)
2 (2.2-oz.) milk chocolate candy bars, shredded

1. Bake cake as directed. Turn out on dish towel and roll up as directed. Cool slightly.
2. Unroll cake and spread with cherry filling. Reroll cake, using towel to help make a tight roll. Place seam side down.
3. Frost cake roll with Cocoa Cream.
4. Sprinkle with shredded milk chocolate as illustrated (see photo, page 138).

Cocoa Cream

1 c. heavy cream
2 tblsp. baking cocoa
½ c. sifted confectioners' sugar

Combine all ingredients in a chilled bowl. Beat until soft peaks form, using an electric mixer at high speed.

Chocolate-Cherry Heart

(12 servings)

Chocolate Velvet Cake (see page 15) or any chocolate cake, baked into 1 (9″) round cake layer and 1 (9″) square cake layer
2 (21-oz.) cans cherry pie filling
1 c. heavy cream
½ c. sifted confectioners' sugar
2 tblsp. baking cocoa
chocolate jimmies

Assembling the cake

1. Cut round cake layer in half to form 2 semicircles and arrange them next to the square cake as illustrated to form a heart.
2. Using the pie filling, arrange the cherries on top of the heart as shown. Add enough of the remaining filling to cover the surface of the heart.
3. Whip heavy cream in chilled bowl until it begins to thicken, using an electric mixer at high speed. Gradually beat in confectioners' sugar and baking cocoa. Beat until soft peaks form.
4. Frost sides of heart with cocoa whipped cream, extending cream to form a ridge about ½″ over top edge of cake.
5. Sprinkle chocolate jimmies on sides of heart.

Wagon Wheel

(12 servings)

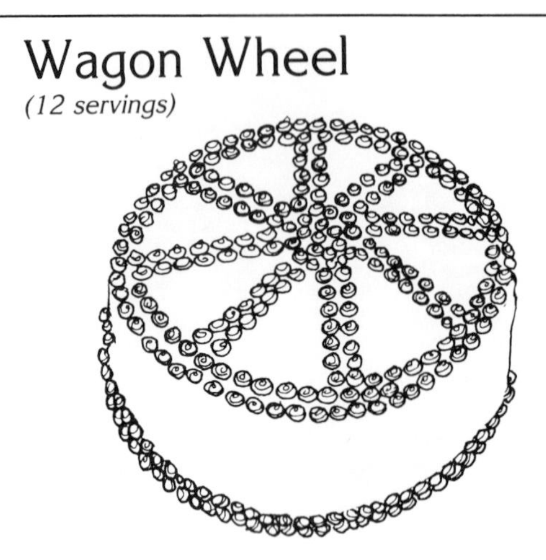

2 c. butter cream frosting (see Index)
¼ c. baking cocoa
Blue Ribbon Yellow Cake (see page 6)
  or any 2 (9″) round cake layers
1 (6-oz.) pkg. semisweet chocolate pieces

1. Combine butter cream frosting and baking cocoa in bowl. Beat until smooth and creamy, using an electric mixer at low speed.
2. Fill and frost cake with cocoa-butter cream frosting. Smooth frosting, using a metal spatula.
3. Use a toothpick to mark a cross on top of the cake. Then mark a second cross to form 8 intersecting lines as illustrated, and mark a small circle in the center as shown. Cover the circle with chocolate pieces and place 2 rows of chocolate pieces over the lines to form spokes.
4. Use remaining chocolate pieces to make 2 rows around top and bottom edges of cake as shown.

Summer Garden Cake

(16 servings; see photo, page 31)

Never-Fail White Cake (see page 6)
  or any 13x9x2″ cake
1¾ c. butter cream frosting, tinted yellow
  (see Index)
7 small chocolate-covered mints
2 (36″) strands black shoestring licorice
12 orange and 9 yellow fruit pectin
  jelly candies
13 green spearmint leaf candies

1. Frost top and sides of cake with yellow butter cream frosting.
2. Use a toothpick to mark 7 points equally spaced across top of cake, between 2 and 4″ below the long edge, for centers of flowers as illustrated (see photo, page 31). Place a mint over each point.
3. Cut licorice into 7 strands, making each strand long enough to extend from the center of a flower to opposite edge of cake. Place licorice on cake as shown to form stems.
4. Cut orange and yellow candies in half. Starting at one side of the cake, arrange 6 orange halves around a mint to form petals. Arrange 6 yellow halves around the adjoining mint. Repeat with remaining candies, alternating orange and yellow flowers.
5. To make leaves, cut leaf candies in half lengthwise. Arrange leaves along stems. Then arrange a pair of leaves on the side of cake below each stem as shown.

Cupcake Flower Baskets

(24 servings)

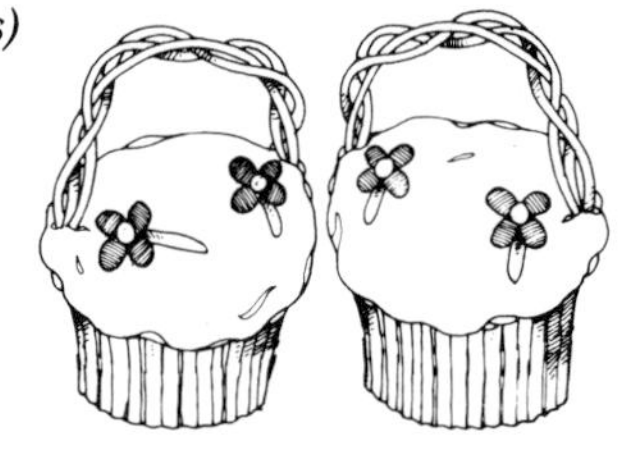

Light Chocolate Brownie Cupcakes (see page
  21) or any 24 cupcakes
3¼ c. butter cream frosting (see Index)
48 small gumdrops in assorted colors
  (red, orange, purple, yellow)
6 small yellow gumdrops
12 small green gumdrops
24 red licorice twists

1. Frost tops of cupcakes with butter cream frosting.
2. Cut each of the 48 assorted gumdrops into quarters. Form 2 flowers on each cupcake, using 4 red, orange, yellow or purple gumdrop slices for the petals of each flower.
   Cut the 6 yellow gumdrops into eighths. Place a yellow gumdrop slice in center of each flower.
   Cut the green gumdrops lengthwise into eighths. Place 2 green gumdrop slices on each flower for leaves.
3. Insert the ends of a licorice twist in each cupcake, about ¼″ from the edge, pushing the ends down until secure.

Flower Bowl Cake

(12 servings)

batter for Silver White Cake (see page 6)
  or 1 (18½-oz.) pkg. cake mix
7-Minute Frosting (see page 62)
7 small purple gumdrops
14 red, orange and yellow fruit slice candies
9 green fruit slice candies

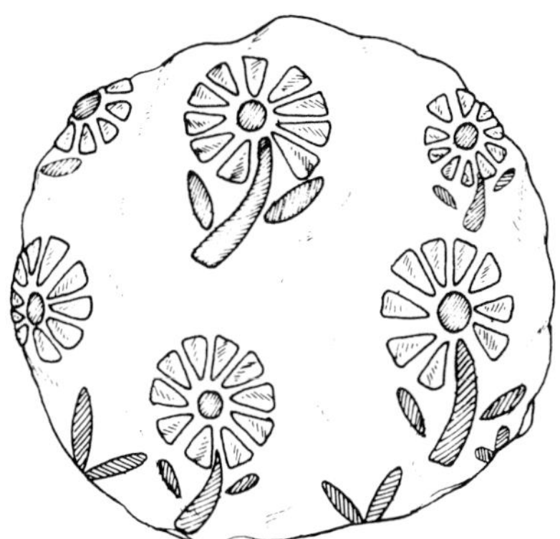

Prepare cake batter as directed.

Pour batter into well-greased and floured 2½-qt. glass oven-proof bowl.

Bake in 325° oven 50 minutes, or until a cake tester or toothpick inserted in center comes out clean. Cool in bowl on rack 10 minutes. Remove from bowl; cool on rack.

To assemble:

1. Frost cake, round side up, with 7-Minute Frosting.
2. Use a toothpick to mark 6 points equally spaced around the cake, about 3″ from the bottom. Place a gumdrop on each point and one on top of the cake.
3. Trim the white strips and the outer colored edges from the red, orange and yellow candies, dipping scissors or knife into a bowl of cool water as needed to prevent sticking.

   Cut each semicircle into 5 triangles. Arrange 10 triangles around each gumdrop center as shown.
4. Trim the white strips and outer colored edges from the green fruit slices. Cut green strips into desired lengths to make flower stems.

   Cut each green semicircle into 5 leaf shapes. Arrange stems and leaves on flowers. Use remaining leaves to form a border around the bottom of the cake.

Marshmallow Rose Cake

(16 servings)

1 (10-oz.) pkg. large marshmallows
sugar
1 egg white, slightly beaten
pink decorating sugar
Hurry-Up Cake (see page 7)
  or any 13x9x2″ cake
7-Minute Frosting (see page 62), tinted pink
12 green spearmint leaf candies

1. Roll 3 marshmallows on a well-sugared surface into ovals about ⅛″ thick. Sprinkle with sugar to prevent sticking. Cut ovals in half crosswise.
2. To form the center of a rose, tightly roll a marshmallow half. Place several more halves around the center, overlapping slightly and pressing together at the base. Add as many halves as necessary to obtain desired size. Repeat to form about 13 more roses. Set aside.
3. Brush edges of rose petals with egg white. Sprinkle edges with colored sugar, shaking off excess. Set aside.
4. Frost top and sides of cake with 7-Minute Frosting.
5. Arrange roses diagonally on top of cake as illustrated. Decorate with spearmint leaves.

Yellow Shadow Cake

(12 servings)

Party Angel Food Cake (see page 46)
or any 10″ angel food cake
2 c. butter cream frosting (see Index)
Lemon Glaze I (see page 39)
7 large white gumdrops
2 large green gumdrops
sugar

1. Frost top and sides of cake with butter cream frosting. Set cake aside for about 15 minutes.
2. Spoon Lemon Glaze I over cake, letting it drizzle over the side to create shadow effect as illustrated.
3. Roll gumdrops into long strips on a well-sugared surface. Cut white strips in half lengthwise.

To make a rose, roll up and arrange 2 white gumdrop strips. Repeat to form 6 more roses.

Use a toothpick to mark 7 points equally spaced on top of cake. Place one rose on each point.

4. Cut green gumdrop strips into various lengths. Arrange them around roses as shown.

Individual Fruitcakes

(10 servings)

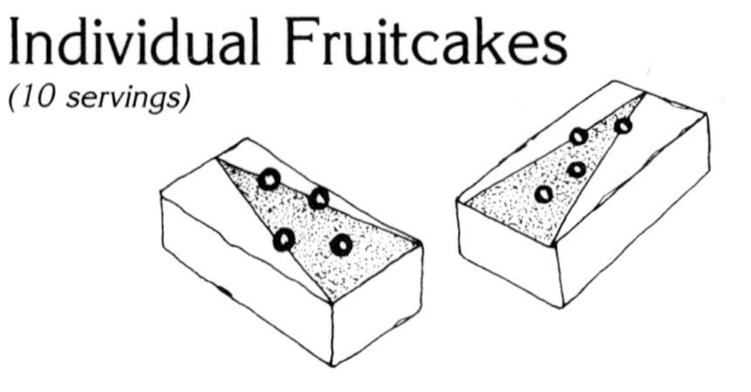

3 (36″) strands red shoestring licorice
⅔ c. sugar
green food coloring
10 Miniature Fruitcakes (see page 40)
1 c. Apple-Lemon Glaze (see page 41)
20 red candied cherries, halved

1. Cut licorice into 20 (4¼″) lengths and 10 (2″) lengths. Set aside.
2. Tint sugar with green food coloring. Set aside.
3. Frost tops of fruitcakes with Apple-Lemon Glaze.
4. Place 2 (4¼″) lengths of licorice on top of each fruitcake, bringing the ends together in a point at the top of the cake as illustrated.

Add a (2″) length of licorice across the bottom of each cake to complete the triangles.

5. Sprinkle green sugar inside each licorice triangle, filling the triangles to resemble trees.
6. Decorate each tree with 4 red candied cherry halves, randomly spaced.

Fruitcake Packages

(10 servings)

10 Miniature Fruitcakes (see page 40)
1 c. Apple-Lemon Glaze (see page 41)
10 (36″) strands red shoestring licorice
10 green spearmint leaves, halved
15 red candied cherries, halved

1. Frost tops of fruitcakes with Apple-Lemon Glaze.
2. Wrap a strand of licorice around each fruitcake and tie a bow as illustrated.
3. Arrange 3 candied cherry halves and 2 spearmint leaves beside each bow.

Marzipan Carrot Cake

(12 servings)

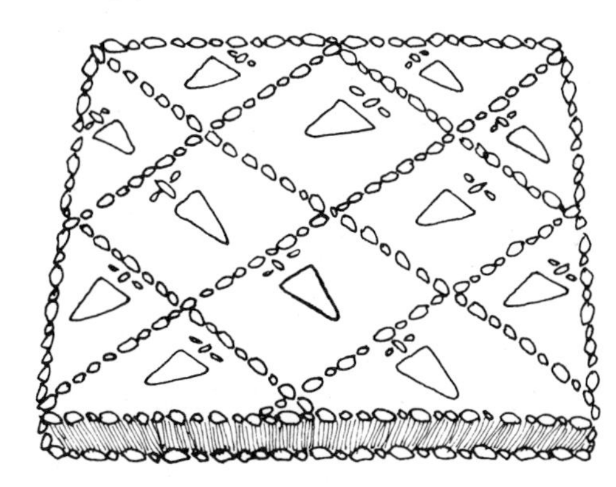

Carrot Cake (see page 36)
 or any 13x9x2" cake
1 ¼ c. butter cream frosting (see Index), tinted yellow
1 ½ oz. marzipan (see page 159):
 tint 1 oz. orange;
 tint ½ oz. green
¾ c. chopped walnuts

1. Frost top and sides of cake with yellow butter cream frosting. Smooth frosting, using a metal spatula.
2. Use a toothpick and a ruler to mark 6 intersecting diagonal lines on top of the cake as illustrated.
3. To make 12 carrots, divide orange marzipan into 12 equal pieces. Roll each piece into a 1" cylinder. Pinch one end to form a point and round the other end. Place a carrot in the center of each section on top of cake.
4. To make 12 stems and leaves, divide green marzipan into 12 equal pieces. Roll part of each piece into a ½" cylinder to form a stem, and shape the remainder of each piece into two smaller, flatter pieces to form leaves. Place a stem and 2 leaves at the top of each carrot.
5. Arrange some of the chopped walnuts along the diagonal lines on top of cake and around the top edge of the cake to form a border. Sprinkle remaining walnuts on sides of cake.

Fruit-and-Nut Flower

(10 servings; see photo, page 30)

Old-fashioned Spice Cake (see page 56)
 or any 2 (8") round cake layers
2 c. butter cream frosting (see Index)
3 dried apricots
1 (5-oz.) pkg. blanched, slivered almonds
1 ½ c. raisins

1. Fill and frost sides and top of cake with butter cream frosting.
2. Place an apricot half in the center of the cake. Use a toothpick to mark 8 points equally spaced around the top edge of cake.
3. Then mark 8 petal shapes from points to center of cake. Cover each petal shape with almonds as illustrated (see photo, page 30).
4. Fill the spaces between the petals with raisins. Then add a border of raisins along the top and bottom edges of the cake.
5. Use a toothpick to mark 8 points on the side of the cake, marking each point halfway between two of the petals above it.

Cut 2 apricot halves into fourths. Place an apricot section over each point. Arrange 8 almonds around each apricot center as shown to form petals.

Glazed Fruit Gâteau

(12 servings)

1 (3 ¼-oz.) pkg. lemon pudding and pie filling mix
1 ½ tsp. grated lemon rind
1 (29-oz.) can pear halves, drained
1 (8 ¾-oz.) can apricot halves, drained
14 maraschino cherries, cut in half
Festive Layer Cake (see page 11)
 or any 2 (9") round yellow cake layers
¾ c. peach or apricot preserves
1 c. heavy cream

1 tblsp. sugar
1 tsp. vanilla
1 drop yellow food coloring
½ c. toasted sliced almonds

1. Prepare lemon pudding and pie filling according to package directions. Stir lemon rind into hot mixture; cool well.
2. Reserve 4 pear halves, 5 apricot halves and 8 maraschino cherry halves. Chop remaining fruit and fold into cooled filling.
3. Cut each cake layer in half horizontally, making 4 layers. Spread filling between layers.
4. Arrange pears, apricots and cherries on top of cake as illustrated.
5. Melt preserves in a small saucepan over low heat and press through sieve. Quickly spoon over fruit.
6. Combine cream, sugar, vanilla and food coloring in chilled bowl. Beat until soft peaks form, using an electric mixer at high speed. Frost sides of cake with whipped cream mixture and decorate with almonds as shown. Refrigerate until serving time.
Variation: It's easy to vary this cake by substituting other canned fruits such as plums, peaches or sliced pineapple.

Strawberries and Cream Spectacular
(12 servings)

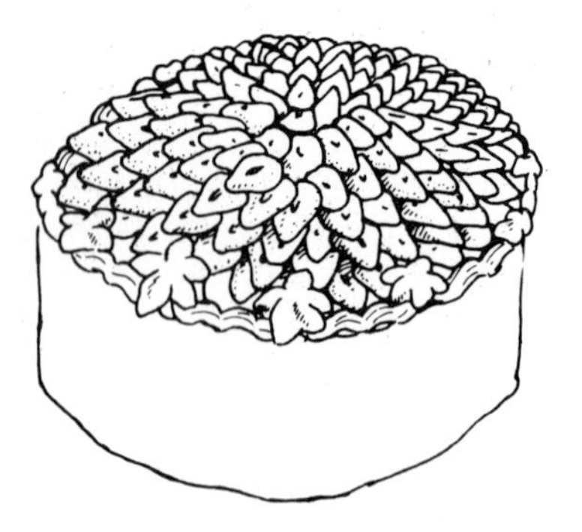

Blue Ribbon Yellow Cake (see page 6)
or any 2 (9") round yellow cake layers
Strawberry Cream Filling (recipe follows)
¾ c. red currant jelly

1. Fill cake layers with Strawberry Cream Filling.
2. Arrange sliced strawberries reserved from recipe for Strawberry Cream Filling in a circle around the top of cake, placing points toward the edge as illustrated.
Make another circle of berries within this circle and continue in the same way until top is covered. Refrigerate 10 minutes.
3. Melt currant jelly in a small saucepan over low heat, stirring constantly. Carefully spoon or brush jelly over strawberries.
4. Frost sides of cake, using some of the whipped cream reserved from recipe for Strawberry Cream Filling. Spoon remaining whipped cream mixture in puffs around the top edge of cake. Refrigerate until serving time.

Strawberry Cream Filling

2 pt. fresh strawberries, hulled
2 c. heavy cream
¼ c. sugar
1 tsp. vanilla

Chop enough strawberries to make 1 c. Slice remaining strawberries and reserve to decorate cake.
Combine cream, sugar and vanilla in chilled bowl. Beat until soft peaks form, using an electric mixer at high speed.
Remove 1 c. of the whipped cream; refrigerate remaining cream to decorate cake. Fold 1 c. chopped strawberries into 1 c. whipped cream.

Ice Cream Cake
(14 servings)

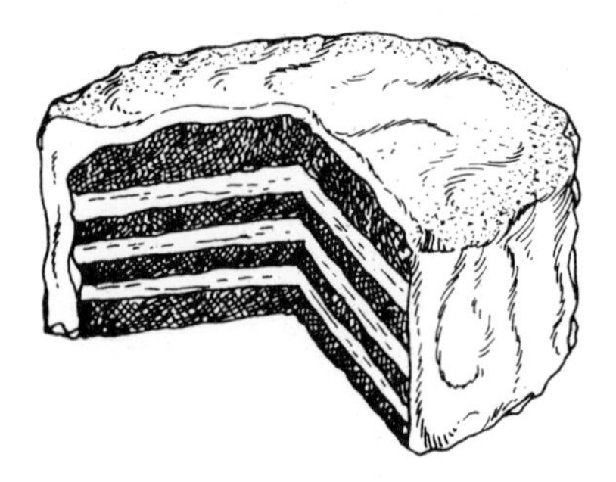

Anna Marie's Chocolate Cake (see page 17)
or any 2 (9") round chocolate cake layers
1 pt. mocha fudge ice cream, softened
1 pt. cherry vanilla ice cream, softened
1 pt. pistachio ice cream, softened
⅔ c. chocolate-flavored syrup
1½ c. heavy cream, whipped
baking cocoa

A drift of silk flowers creates a delicate effect, and a look that will last throughout the day, even during the most unseasonable weather. The intricate lacework that decorates this Wedding Cake with Silk Flowers (page 165) is meant to be piped randomly, so you can't make a mistake.

The frosting on the cake can be enough decoration in itself, especially when it's piped in a fanciful pattern or spread in graceful swirls. All the decorations for the Whipped Cream Fantasy at left are made with one decorating tube (see page 109), and there's no need to tint the icing (although you could!).

The Daffodil Blossom Cake below is decorated with lemon frosting that's swirled with a spatula, and the cake is crowned with a cluster of fresh blossoms (see page 93).

Pink and white and unabashedly pretty, these two cakes can celebrate a multitude of special occasions. The latticework circles and drop flowers on the Pink and White Party Cake at right are piped in advance with Royal Icing, then arranged on the cake and outlined with butter cream frosting (see page 124).

The challenging Candy Box below is a square layer cake topped with real chocolates, and the Run Sugar lid blooms with Royal Icing pansies (for directions, see page 151).

More than 150 guests can enjoy a slice of this multi-tiered Wedding Cake with Crystallized Flower (page 166). The decorations are made by dipping fresh, thin-petaled blossoms such as alstroemer in egg white and dusting them with sugar, a technique that could be used for any cake.

1. Cut each cake layer horizontally into 2 equal layers.
2. Spread one cake layer with mocha fudge ice cream; top with second layer. Repeat with remaining ice cream and cake layers.
3. Freeze overnight, or until firm. Trim away any uneven edges.
4. Fold chocolate syrup into whipped cream. Frost cake with chocolate cream, swirling the cream with a spatula as illustrated. Freeze until frosting is frozen.
5. Ten minutes before serving, remove cake from freezer. Place a little baking cocoa in a small sieve and dust the top edge of the cake with the cocoa as shown.

Pecan Torte

(10 servings)

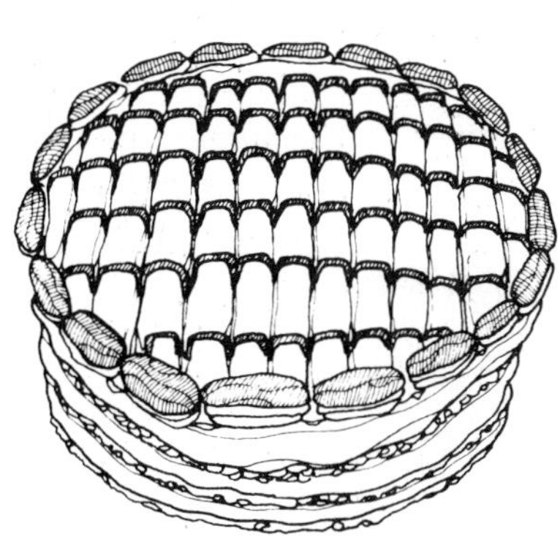

3¾ c. pecan halves
3 tblsp. flour
1 tsp. baking powder
¼ tsp. salt
6 eggs, separated
1 c. sugar
3½ (1-oz.) squares unsweetened chocolate
2 c. heavy cream
2 tblsp. confectioners' sugar

Set aside 18 uniform pecan halves. Finely grind remaining pecans.

Combine ground pecans, flour, baking powder and salt in bowl.

In another bowl, beat egg whites until soft peaks form, using an electric mixer at high speed.

In a small bowl, beat egg yolks and sugar at high speed until thick and lemon-colored.

Gently fold egg yolk mixture into pecan mixture. Fold egg yolk-pecan mixture into beaten egg whites.

Pour batter into 2 greased and waxed paper-lined 8″ round cake pans.

Bake in 350° oven 25 minutes, or until cake springs back when touched. Cool in pans on racks 5 minutes. Remove from pans; cool on racks.

Meanwhile, melt unsweetened chocolate in top of double boiler over simmering (not boiling) water. Holding pecan halves lengthwise, coat half of each pecan with chocolate. Place on waxed paper and refrigerate until firm. Keep remaining chocolate warm.

To assemble:

1. Whip heavy cream in chilled bowl until it begins to thicken, using an electric mixer at high speed. Gradually beat in 2 tblsp. confectioners' sugar. Beat until soft peaks form.
2. Cut each cake layer horizontally into 2 equal layers. Fill layers and frost top of cake with whipped cream.
3. Drizzle remaining chocolate in horizontal lines across the top of cake as illustrated. Gently pull a spatula lengthwise through the strips to form design as shown.
4. Arrange chocolate-coated pecans around top of cake, rounded side facing up. Refrigerate until ready to serve.

Himmel Torte

(12 servings; see photo, page 139)

1 c. chopped, pitted dates
1 c. boiling water
1⅔ c. sifted cake flour
1 tsp. baking soda
¼ tsp. salt
½ c. shortening
1 c. sugar
1 egg
1 tsp. vanilla
½ c. chopped walnuts
1 (20-oz.) can crushed pineapple, drained
Snowflake Cream (recipe follows)
red candied cherries
holly leaves

Combine dates and boiling water in bowl; cool to lukewarm.

Sift together cake flour, baking soda and salt; set aside.

Cream together shortening and sugar in bowl

until light and fluffy, using an electric mixer at medium speed. Beat in egg and vanilla.

Stir in date mixture and dry ingredients, mixing well. Add walnuts. Pour batter into greased and waxed paper-lined 9″ square baking pan.

Bake in 350° oven 50 minutes, or until sides pull away from pan. Cool in pan on rack 10 minutes. Remove from pan; cool on rack.

Snowflake Cream

3 c. heavy cream
3 tblsp. sugar
1 tsp. vanilla

Combine all ingredients in chilled bowl and beat until soft peaks form, using an electric mixer at high speed.

To assemble:

1. Tear cake into bite-sized pieces. Begin to shape torte by making a layer of cake pieces, 8″ in diameter, on a round cake plate as illustrated. Add a layer of pineapple, then spread with a layer of Snowflake Cream. Repeat layers twice more, decreasing diameter each time. Gently shape into a mound, using both hands.
2. Frost cake with remaining Snowflake Cream, swirling the cream with a spatula as shown (see photo, page 139). Decorate with candied cherries and holly leaves or as you wish.

To serve, slice or spoon torte onto dishes.

Chocolate Torte

(20 servings)

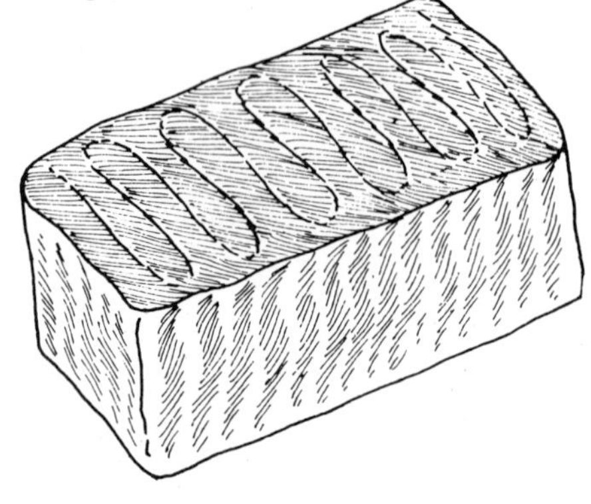

1¾ c. sifted flour
2 c. sugar
¾ c. baking cocoa
1½ tsp. baking soda
1½ tsp. baking powder
1 tsp. salt
2 eggs
1 c. milk
½ c. cooking oil
2 tsp. vanilla
1 c. boiling water
Rich Chocolate Filling (recipe follows)
¾ c. toasted, slivered almonds
Vanilla Whipped Cream (recipe follows)

Sift together flour, sugar, baking cocoa, baking soda, baking powder and salt into bowl.

Add eggs, milk, oil and vanilla. Beat 2 minutes, using an electric mixer at medium speed. Blend in boiling water at low speed.

Pour batter into 15½x10½x1″ waxed paper-lined jelly roll pan.

Bake in 350° oven 22 minutes, or until a toothpick inserted in center comes out clean. Cool in pan on rack 10 minutes. Remove from pan and cool on rack.

Rich Chocolate Filling

1 c. butter, softened
2 (4-oz.) pkg. sweet chocolate, melted and cooled

Beat butter into cooled chocolate in bowl until fluffy, using an electric mixer at medium speed.

Vanilla Whipped Cream

1½ c. heavy cream
4 tsp. sugar
¾ tsp. vanilla

Combine all ingredients in chilled bowl. Whip until soft peaks form, using an electric mixer at high speed.

To assemble:

1. Cut cake crosswise into thirds. Cut each third horizontally into 2 equal layers.
2. Spread one layer with Rich Chocolate Filling. Sprinkle with some of the almonds. Repeat with remaining layers, stacking layers to make a 6-layer torte and ending with Chocolate Filling.
3. Frost sides of torte with Vanilla Whipped Cream, swirling the cream with a spatula as shown. Chill 2 hours before serving.

4

Decorated Cakes for Celebrations

Remember how proud you were when you passed your first driver's test? "Our teenagers can get their driver's licenses at 16," an Ohio dairy farmer's wife told us, "so a 16th birthday is an important one." To dramatize the event for some of her young friends, she presents them with a 13x9" Driver's License cake decorated with information about the recipient.

Cakes like those are the ones that people enjoy most, because they're so personal. Do you have friends who are about to pack for a well-earned vacation? Treat them to a big send-off with a Bon Voyage cake by arranging and decorating two round cake layers to resemble a colorful hot-air balloon.

Are you planning a shower for someone who's expecting a baby? In this chapter you'll find ideas for decorated cakes that resemble alphabet blocks and a baby carriage, as well as a full-size stork pattern for a sheet cake that's designed for easy transport.

Many farm and ranch cooks design personalized birthday cakes for family members every year. One Indiana woman created the cake we call Harvest Celebration for her husband's birthday two years ago. "That was the summer when planting tried the very souls of Indiana farmers," she remembers. Decorated with a ring of cornstalks around the side and topped with a golden sunburst, the cake is a tribute to her partner's determination and to nature's bounty.

Many designs in this chapter can easily be personalized, including the All-occasion Cake. The Book cake can become a book of knowledge to honor a graduate, or a Bible to celebrate confirmations or bar and bas mitzvahs.

Of course, not all celebrations are so personal, and sometimes the flavors or the colors of the cake aren't important—as long as the cake is absolutely beautiful and utterly irresistible. The white-on-white Whipped Cream Fantasy cake pictured on page 102 would suit almost any occasion, and its pretty design is made with just one decorating tube.

Because springtime brings such a resurgence of social events, we've included several decorating ideas with spring flowers, including a Tulip cake, a Flowered Loaf Cake, and Flowered Cupcakes made with Royal Icing. For a spectacular centerpiece for any spring celebration, create your own version of the Spring Flower Basket with Royal Icing flowers pictured on page 31. This decorating idea won first place at a local fair for the Kansas woman who developed it.

Once you've worked with Royal Icing you'll want to try Run Sugar, and we've used this technique in the Pinwheel Quilt cake (see photo, page 30) and the Black-eyed Susans cake at the end of this chapter.

With the Run Sugar technique you can outline and fill in almost any design you like—the choice is yours.

Jelly-Topped Cake
(24 servings)

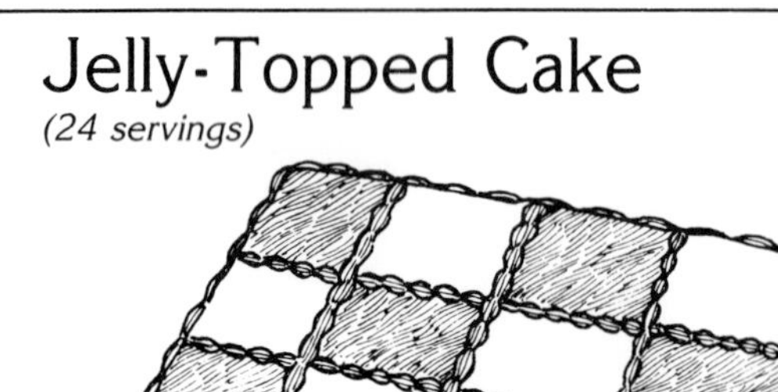

Hurry-Up Cake (see page 7)
or any 13x9x2" cake
Basic Vanilla Butter Cream Icing (see page 60)
1 c. chopped walnuts
½ c. raspberry preserves
½ c. apricot preserves
decorating tube: star #16

1. Frost sides of cake with some of the Basic Vanilla Butter Cream Icing. Press walnuts into sides of cake.
2. Mark top of cake into 12 equal squares, using the string method.
3. Alternating raspberry and apricot preserves, frost each square with preserves.
4. Using the remaining Basic Vanilla Butter Cream Icing and star tube #16, pipe shell borders between squares of raspberry and apricot preserves as illustrated.
Then pipe a shell border around bottom and top edges of cake.

Heart Cupcakes
(24 servings; see photo, page 84)

batter for Silver White Cake (see page 6)
or for any 24 cupcakes
2¼ c. decorating icing (see Index):
tint ¾ c. light pink;
tint ¾ c. dark pink
colored sugar, silver dragées or any other
cake decorations
decorating tubes: round #2; star #17; leaf #65

1. Place paper liners in 24 muffin-pan cups. Place a glass marble or small ball of aluminum foil between each paper liner and muffin-pan cup. (This makes a heart-shaped mold.)
2. Fill paper liners ⅔ full of batter. Bake in 350° oven 15 minutes, or until a cake tester or toothpick inserted in center comes out clean. Cool on racks.
3. Frost tops of cupcakes with some of the decorating icing in the colors of your choice.
4. Decorate some of the cupcakes with colored sugar, dragées or other decorations as illustrated (see photo, page 84).
5. Using remaining decorating icing and decorating tubes, pipe decorations on cupcakes as follows.
Use round tube #2 to pipe lace, written messages and bead borders.
Use star tube #17 to pipe shell borders.
Use leaf tube #65 to pipe ruffled borders.

Straw Hat
(12 servings)

Old-Fashioned Peppermint Fudge Cake (see page 21) or any 2 (9") round cake layers
4½ c. decorating icing (see Index), tinted yellow
1 (14") cardboard round
decorating tube: basket weave #47
29" red ribbon, 1" wide

1. Fill cake with yellow decorating icing. Center cake on cardboard round and place on a sturdy base.
2. Using yellow decorating icing and basket weave tube #47, pipe a basket weave pattern on sides and top of cake and over cardboard rim as illustrated.
3. Place ribbon around hat to form the hatband.

Driver's License
(16 servings)

Spicy Applesauce Cake (see page 27)
or any 13x9x2" cake
3½ c. decorating icing (see Index):
tint ¾ c. brown;
tint ½ c. blue
decorating tubes: round #1; star #17

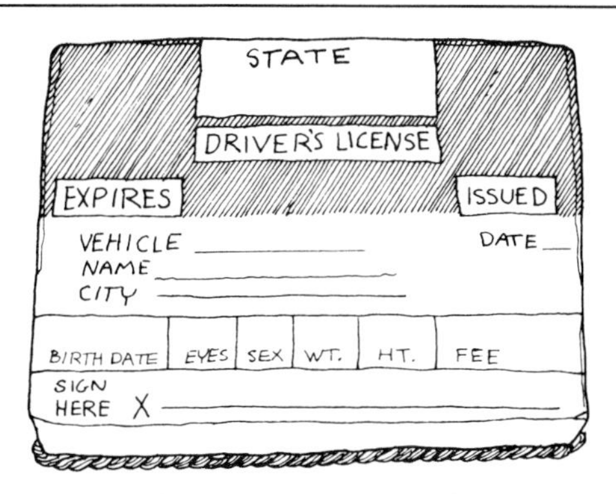

1. Frost top of cake with some of the white decorating icing, leaving a strip about 4″ wide across the top of the cake unfrosted. Then frost 4 white rectangles across the top of the cake as illustrated. Frost sides of cake with more of the white decorating icing.

Then frost the remaining areas across the top of the cake with some of the brown decorating icing.

Smooth frosting, using a metal spatula.

2. Use a toothpick to mark lines and printing on top of cake as illustrated, writing in the correct state, year and other information.

3. Using remaining brown decorating icing and round tube #1, pipe lines and boxes for birth date and other vital statistics and driver's signature at the bottom of the cake; then fill in the boxes with information to personalize the cake.

4. Using blue decorating icing and round tube #1, pipe type of vehicle, driver's name, city and other appropriate information in the white rectangles at the top of the cake.

Change to star tube #17 and pipe a rosette border around bottom edges of cake. (To personalize this cake even more, wrap plastic wrap around a snapshot of the person being honored and place the photo in the upper right corner of the cake.)

Birthday Bunch

(12 servings)

Waldorf Spice Cake (see page 25)
  or any 2 (9″) round cake layers
2¾ c. decorating icing (see Index):
  tint 1 c. yellow
decorating tubes: round #3; star #21
1 (36″) strand black shoestring licorice
14 small purple gumdrops, cut in half
2 green spearmint leaf candies

1. Fill and frost top and sides of cake, using white decorating icing. Smooth icing, using a metal spatula.

2. Use a toothpick to mark the words *Happy Birthday from the Bunch* on top of cake, around the outer edge as illustrated.

3. Using yellow decorating icing and round tube #3, pipe the words over the design lines.

Change to star tube #21 and pipe a star border around bottom edge of cake.

4. Cut licorice into lengths of 7″, 2½″ and 2″ and arrange on top of cake as shown to form stems.

5. Arrange gumdrops around stems to form the bunch of grapes.

6. Place spearmint candies at the top of the stems to form leaves.

Whipped Cream Fantasy

(12 servings; see photo, page 102)

Basic White Layer Cake (see page 5)
  or any 2 (9″) round cake layers
Whipped Cream Icing (see page 64)
decorating tube: star #21

1. Fill and frost top and sides of cake with some of the Whipped Cream Icing. Smooth icing, using a metal spatula.

2. Use a toothpick to mark the center of the top of the cake. Mark 8 equal triangles on top of the cake, using the string method.

3. Using more of the Whipped Cream Icing and star tube #21, pipe a shell border around the top edge of the cake. Pipe a star border over the marked lines on top of the cake. Then pipe a star in the center of each triangle (see photo, page 102).

4. Mark 8 points equally spaced around the bottom edge of the cake, centering each point between 2 lines on top of the cake. Then use a toothpick to draw a line from each point to a line on top of the cake, marking 8 triangles

around the side of the cake as shown.
5. Pipe a star border over the marked lines on the sides of the cake. Pipe a star in the center of each triangle. Pipe a shell border around the bottom edge of the cake.

Sunshine Cake
(12 servings)

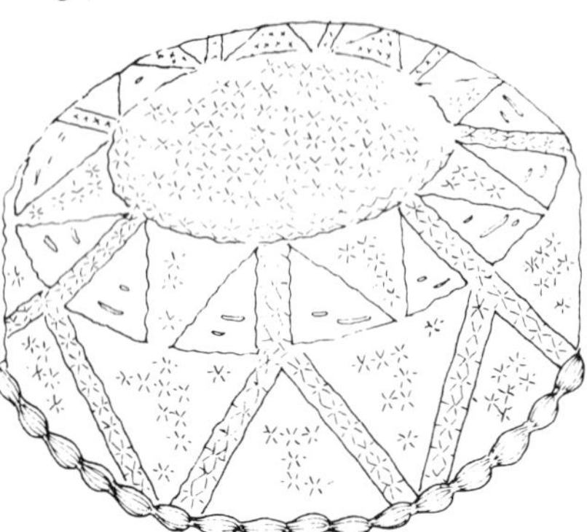

Basic White Layer Cake (see page 5)
 or any 2 (9″) round cake layers
4 c. decorating icing (see Index):
 tint 1 c. orange;
 tint 1 c. yellow
decorating tube: star #21

1. Fill and frost top and sides of cake with white decorating icing. Smooth icing, using a metal spatula.

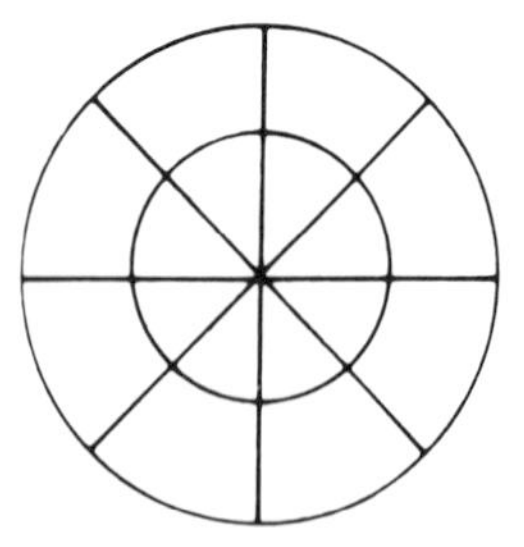

Marking the cake

2. Use a toothpick to mark center of top of cake. Then mark 8 equal triangles on top of cake as illustrated, using the string method.
3. Use a toothpick to mark a point on each of the 8 lines on top of the cake, 2″ from the edge. Connect points, pulling toothpick through icing, to form a 5″ circle in the center.
4. Using orange icing and star tube #21, pipe stars evenly and close together to fill the circle. Then pipe stars over lines from circle to edge of cake.
5. Use a toothpick to mark 8 points equally spaced around the bottom edge of cake, centering each point between 2 of the orange lines on top of cake. Then mark lines to connect these points with the orange lines.
 Pipe orange stars over the lines on the side of the cake.
6. To form small triangles on top of cake, use yellow icing and star tube #21 to pipe a row of 4 stars beside one section of the orange circle, between 2 lines as shown. Then pipe a row of 3 stars below it. Pipe 2 more stars below that row, and add 1 star at the edge to form a ray of the sun.
 Repeat 7 times around the remaining sections of the circle.
7. Continuing with yellow icing and star tube #21, pipe stars evenly and close together to fill each downward-pointing triangle on the side of the cake.
8. Pipe a shell border around the bottom.

Bon Voyage Balloon
(12 servings)

Festive Layer Cake (see page 11), baked into 1 (8″) round cake layer and 1 (9″) round cake layer
4 c. decorating icing (see Index):
tint 1 c. yellow;
tint 1 c. pink;
tint 1½ c. green
decorating tubes: star #17; basket weave #47; round #4
2 wooden skewers
4 (36″) strands black shoestring licorice
30x15″ cardboard rectangle

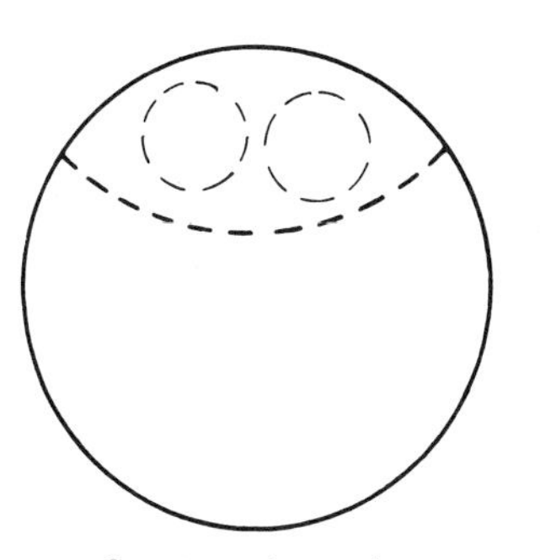

Cutting the cake

1. To form gondola, cut 8″ layer as illustrated. Using a cookie cutter, cut 2 (2½″) circles from excess cake; set aside.
2. Place 9″ round cake layer at top of cardboard base; this cake will become the balloon. Use a toothpick to mark 4 curved lines on top of cake as illustrated.
3. Using some of the white decorating icing and star tube #17, pipe a row of stars over all 4 marked lines.
4. Using yellow decorating icing and star tube #17, pipe stars evenly and close together to fill the center stripe of the balloon.
5. Reserve 2 tblsp. of the pink decorating icing. Using remaining pink icing and star tube #17, pipe stars on the 2 stripes at the outer edges of the balloon.
6. Using some of the green decorating icing and star tube #17, pipe stars to fill the 2 remaining stripes on the balloon.
7. Place gondola several inches below decorated balloon. Change to basket weave tube #47 and use remaining green icing to pipe a basket weave pattern on top and side of gondola.
8. Arrange cake circles above gondola as shown; secure with wooden skewers.
9. Frost cake circles with remaining white decorating icing.
10. Using reserved pink decorating icing and round tube #4, pipe faces on frosted circles.
Using yellow decorating icing and star tube #17, pipe hair.
11. Connect balloon and gondola with licorice as shown, inserting one end of each strand in the bottom of the balloon and the other end in the top of the gondola.

Tennis Set

(16 servings)

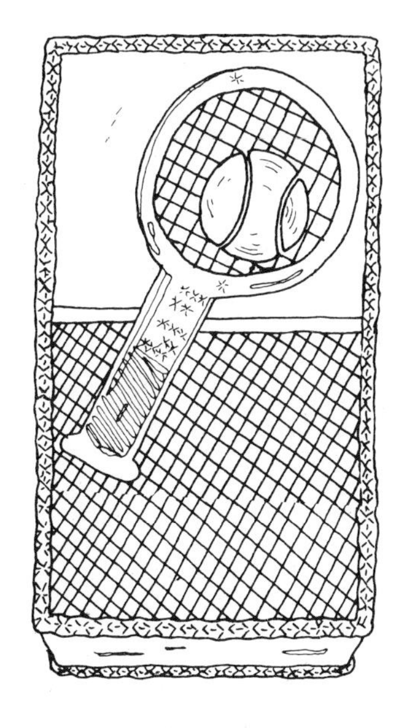

Hummingbird Cake (see page 37) or any 13x9x2″ cake
3¾ c. decorating icing (see Index):
tint ½ c. brown;
tint ¼ c. black;
tint ¾ c. green
decorating tubes: star #21; round #3

1. Frost top and sides of cake with some of the white decorating icing. Smooth icing, using a metal spatula.
2. Use a toothpick to draw tennis racket on top of cake as illustrated.
3. Using brown decorating icing and star tube #21, pipe stars evenly and close together to fill upper half of racket handle. Then pipe stars around rim of racket.
4. Change to round tube #3 and use remaining brown icing to pipe a series of vertical and horizontal lines for strings on racket as shown.
5. Using black decorating icing and star tube

#21, pipe a row of zigzag lines over the lower half of handle to form grip.
6. Using some of the green decorating icing and star tube #21, pipe a circle on top of tennis racket as shown to form the ball. Fill circle with more of the green icing.
7. To make the net, change to round tube #3 and use more of the green icing to pipe a horizontal line about 5″ from bottom of cake.

Working from left to right, pipe a series of diagonal lines, evenly spaced, below the horizontal line. Repeat, working from right to left.
8. Using remaining white decorating icing and round tube #3, pipe 2 semicircles over tennis ball as shown.

Change to star tube #21 and pipe a white star border along bottom and top edges of cake.

It's In The Cards

(10 servings)

Lime Cake (see page 10)
  or any 2 (8″) round cake layers
2¾ c. decorating icing (see Index):
  tint 1½ c. red
1 (6-oz.) pkg. miniature semisweet chocolate
  pieces
¼ c. light corn syrup
decorating tubes: plain #4; star #16

1. Fill and frost cake layers, using the white decorating icing. Smooth icing, using a metal spatula.
2. Use a toothpick to draw a cross on top of the cake, marking the top into 4 equal sections.

Draw a spade, heart, club and diamond in the 4 sections as illustrated.
3. Melt ½ c. of the chocolate pieces in top of double boiler over hot (not boiling) water. Slowly stir in corn syrup.

Remove double boiler from heat. Allow mixture to cool slightly, but keep it over the warm water.
4. Spoon chocolate mixture inside the design lines on top of the cake and smooth with a spatula.
5. To decorate sides of cake, use a toothpick to draw a spade, heart, club and diamond below each corresponding shape on top. Outline each shape, using more of the chocolate pieces.
6. Using some of the red decorating icing and star tube #16, pipe a puff border around bottom edge of cake. Place a chocolate piece between each pair of puffs.
7. Change to plain tube #4 and pipe a bead border along lines on top of cake, extending each line down to the bottom border.

Use remaining red decorating icing to pipe a bead border around top edge of cake.

Chocolate Mousse Cake

(16 servings; see photo, page 138)

1 c. butter or regular margarine
4 (1-oz.) squares unsweetened chocolate
1 c. sugar
1 c. packed brown sugar
3 eggs
2 tsp. vanilla
½ tsp. salt
1 c. sifted flour
½ c. semisweet chocolate pieces
Chocolate Mousse Filling (recipe follows)
2 c. heavy cream, whipped
decorating tube: drop flower #2D

Melt ½ c. of the butter and unsweetened chocolate in 2-qt. saucepan over low heat. Remove from heat and cool to room temperature.

Cream together remaining ½ c. butter, sugar and brown sugar in bowl until light and fluffy, using an electric mixer at medium speed.

Add eggs, 1 at a time, beating well after each addition. Blend in vanilla, salt and chocolate mixture. Beat 2 minutes more until fluffy.

Blend in flour at low speed.

Pour batter into 3 greased, floured and waxed paper-lined 9″ round cake pans. Build batter about ½″ up edges of pans.

Bake in 350° oven 20 minutes, or until

edges pull away from sides of pans. Cool on racks 10 minutes.

Remove cakes from pans. Cool on racks.

Draw an 8″ circle on waxed paper. Melt semisweet chocolate pieces in top of double boiler over hot (not boiling) water. Spread melted chocolate on waxed paper, filling the circle. Refrigerate until set.

Remove from refrigerator. Let stand 10 minutes at room temperature.

Cut chocolate into 16 wedges. Return to refrigerator until ready to use.

To assemble:

1. Spread top of each cake layer with Chocolate Mousse Filling. Stack layers.
2. Frost sides and top with some of the whipped cream. Using remaining whipped cream and drop flower tube #2D, pipe a drop flower border around bottom and top edges of cake.
3. Decorate top of cake with chocolate wedges as illustrated (see photo, page 138). Pipe a drop flower in center of cake.

Chocolate Mousse Filling

1½ c. semisweet chocolate pieces
3 egg yolks
⅓ c. water
¾ tsp. vanilla
1½ c. heavy cream, whipped

Melt chocolate in top of double boiler over hot (not boiling) water.

Beat egg yolks, water and vanilla in bowl.

Stir egg yolk mixture into melted chocolate over hot water, using a wire whisk. Mix until smooth and thick, 1 to 2 minutes.

Remove from hot water and cool to room temperature.

Fold chocolate mixture into whipped cream.

Tulip Cake

(16 servings)

2 recipes for Original Chocolate Mayonnaise Cake (see page 20) or any 2 (9″) square cake layers
4 c. decorating icing (see Index):
  tint ¾ c. pink;
  tint ¾ c. green
decorating tubes: basket weave #47; star #21, #16; round #3; leaf #67

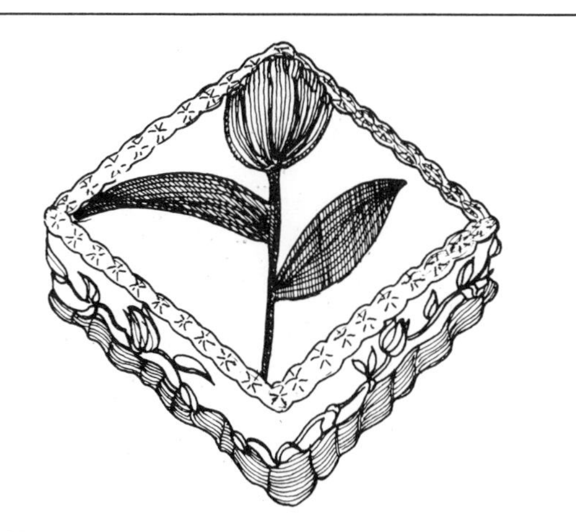

1. Fill and frost top and sides of cake, using some of the white decorating icing. Smooth icing, using a metal spatula.
2. Use a toothpick to draw tulip design on top of cake as illustrated.
3. Using some of the pink decorating icing and basket weave tube #47, pipe a ribbed stripe around the outline of tulip. Then fill in tulip with more ribbed stripes. Add 4 more ribbed stripes on top as shown.
4. Using some of the green decorating icing and star tube #16, pipe a ribbed stripe for stem. Outline leaves with a ribbed stripe and then fill as for tulip.
5. Use a toothpick to mark the center of each side of cake. Using more of the pink decorating icing and basket weave tube #47, pipe a small tulip above each point.
6. Use a toothpick to mark lines for vines on each side of the cake. Using green decorating icing and round tube #3, pipe vines as shown.

   Change to leaf tube #67 and randomly pipe leaves.
7. Using remaining pink decorating icing and basket weave tube #47, pipe a shell border around bottom edges of cake.

   Using remaining white decorating icing and star tube #21, pipe a star border around top edges of cake.

Posie Sheet Cakelets

(16 servings)

Fluffy Gold Cake (see page 8)
  or any 13x9x2″ cake
3 c. decorating icing (see Index):
  tint 1¾ c. light blue;
  tint ¼ c. yellow;
  tint ¼ c. green;

tint ¼ c. dark blue
decorating tubes: star #24; drop flower #225, #191; round #3; leaf #67

1. Frost top and sides of cake with light blue decorating icing. Smooth icing, using a metal spatula.
2. Mark 32 squares on top of the cake as illustrated, using the string method.
3. Using white decorating icing and star tube #24, pipe a shell border along marked lines on top of cake. Then pipe a shell border around top edges of cake as shown.
4. Using yellow decorating icing and drop flower tube #191, pipe a yellow drop flower in alternate squares.
5. Using some of the green decorating icing and round tube #3, pipe a green stem diagonally in each remaining square.
Change to leaf tube #67 and pipe a green leaf at the bottom of each stem. Then pipe a leaf at the top and bottom of each yellow flower.
6. Using dark blue decorating icing and drop flower tube #225, pipe a small drop flower at the top of each stem.

Harvest Celebration

(12 servings)

Party Angel Food Cake (see page 46)
or any 10″ angel food cake
2½ c. decorating icing (see Index):
tint ¾ c. light blue;
tint 1 c. green;
tint ¾ c. yellow
Chocolate Frosting (see page 61)
decorating tubes: leaf #67; star #17

1. Frost top of cake with light blue decorating icing. Smooth icing, using a metal spatula.
2. Frost sides of cake with Chocolate Frosting.
3. Trace sun pattern (see page 116) on a folded sheet of paper and cut out. Use a toothpick to trace the pattern on top of the cake. Then mark designs for 10 cornstalks evenly spaced around the side of the cake as shown.
4. Using green decorating icing and leaf tube #67, pipe cornstalks and leaves.
Change to star tube #17 and pipe a star border around bottom and top edges of cake.
5. Using yellow decorating icing and star tube #17, pipe a series of vertical zigzag lines over the sun outline on top of the cake; then fill in the outline with more zigzag lines.
To form ears of corn, pipe 3 stars at the top of each cornstalk.

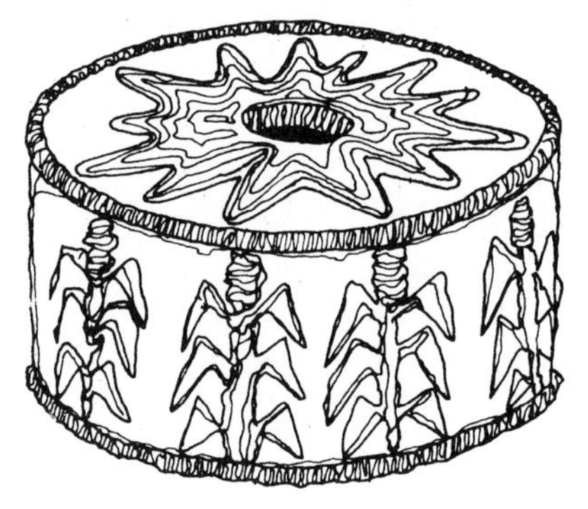

Forget-me-not Cake

(16 servings)

One-Bowl Cocoa Cake (see page 20)
or any 13x9x2″ cake
4 c. decorating icing (see Index):
tint ¾ c. yellow;
tint ¾ c. blue;
tint ½ c. green
decorating tubes: star #21, #16; round #3; drop flower #2D; leaf #67

1. Frost top and sides of cake with white decorating icing. Smooth icing, using a metal spatula.
2. Use a toothpick to draw a 9x6″ oval on top of cake as illustrated. Using yellow decorating icing and star tube #16, pipe a scalloped border over the oval by making small "u" shapes over design lines.

3. Using blue decorating icing and drop flower tube #2D, pipe forget-me-nots in center of oval and at each corner of cake top as shown.
Then pipe 3 flowers on each short side of cake and 6 flowers on each long side.
4. Using some of the green decorating icing and round tube #3, pipe stems below flowers in center of cake as shown.
Change to leaf tube #67 and randomly pipe leaves on stems and around flowers. Then add leaves to remaining flowers on top and sides of cake.
5. Using yellow decorating icing and star tube #16, pipe a star center on each flower.
Change to star tube #21 and pipe a shell border along top edges of cake. Then pipe a ribbed border along bottom edges of cake.
At 1″ intervals along ribbed border, pipe star flowers as shown.
6. Using remaining green decorating icing and leaf tube #67, pipe a leaf on each star flower.

Bridesmaid

(12 servings)

batter for Lime Cake (see page 10)
or any 2 (8″) cake layers
4″ circle of aluminum foil
1 (7½″) plastic doll
4¼ c. decorating icing (see Index):
tint 3½ c. yellow
decorating tubes: star #17; rose #104; drop flower #225; round #2

1. Prepare batter as directed. Pour batter into a 9-c. Turk's head tube pan and bake in 350° oven 40 minutes, or until cake springs back when touched. Cool in pan on rack 10 minutes. Remove from pan and cool on rack.
2. Center cake on a sturdy base.
3. To make foil apron for doll, cut a hole in the middle of 4″ circle, large enough to fit around doll's waist. Place doll in center of cake. Put foil apron in place.
4. Using some of the white decorating icing and star tube #17, pipe a rosette border around bottom edge of cake.
5. Using some of the yellow decorating icing and rose tube #104, pipe continuous rows of ribbon swags, working from the bottom to the top of cake as illustrated.
Change to star tube #17 and pipe stars evenly and close together, covering apron and forming bodice of dress.
6. Using remaining white decorating icing and drop flower tube #225, pipe white drop flowers randomly over skirt of dress.
7. Using remaining yellow decorating icing and round tube #2, pipe centers in flowers.

Alphabet Blocks

(12 servings; see photo, page 29)

Devil's Food Cake (see page 15)
or any 2 (8″) square cake layers
3⅔ c. decorating icing (see Index):
tint ⅓ c. green;
tint ⅓ c. yellow;
tint ⅓ c. red;
tint ⅓ c. blue;
tint ⅓ c. orange
decorating tube: round #8

1. Fill cake layers with some of the white decorating icing.

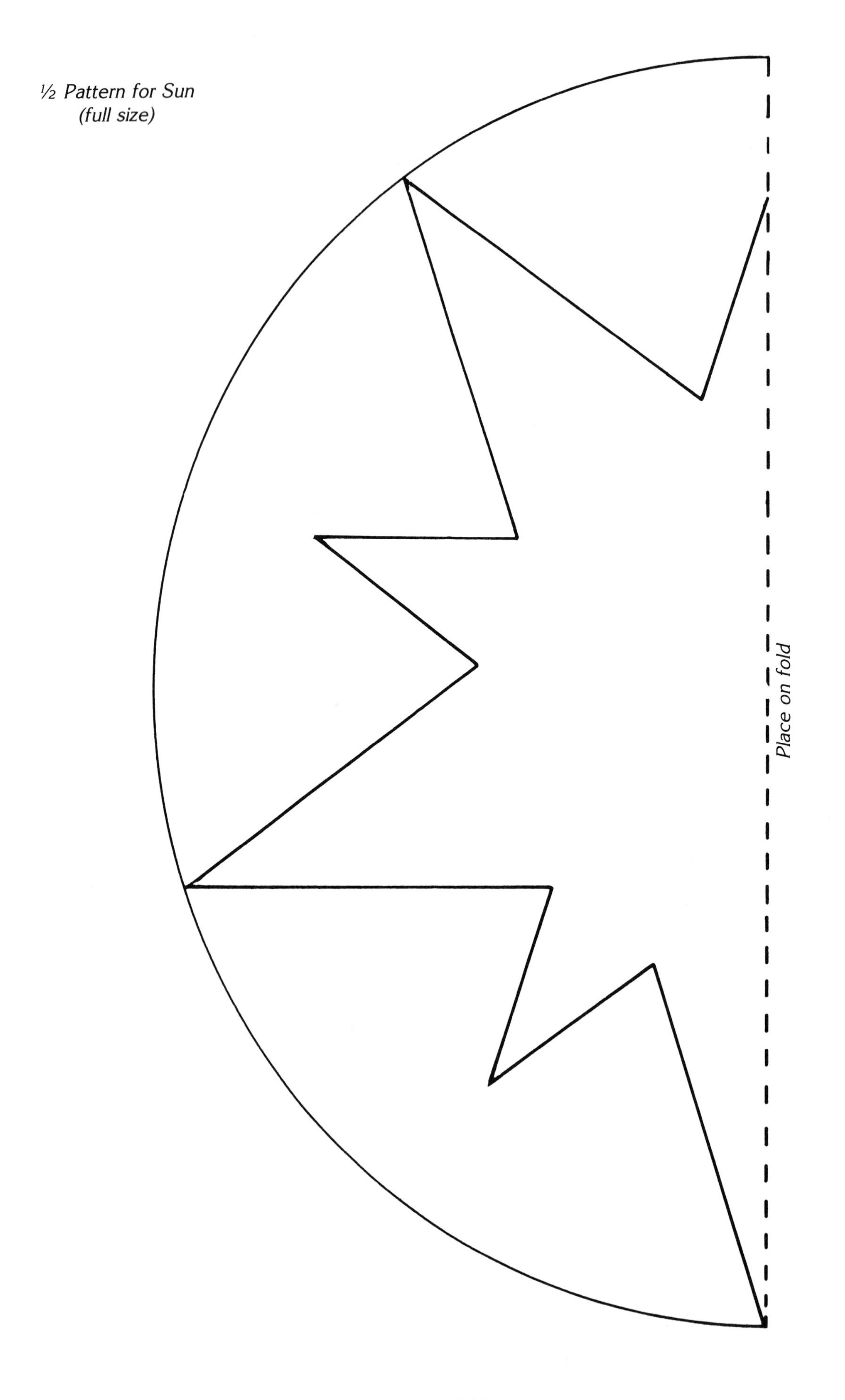
½ Pattern for Sun
(full size)
Place on fold

Cut cake into quarters, forming 4 (4″) square blocks. Frost sides and top of blocks with remaining white decorating icing.
2. Using some of the green decorating icing and round tube #8, outline the top of 1 block and 1 side of each of the other blocks. Pipe a small dot at the corners of each outline as illustrated (see page 29).
Repeat with yellow, red and blue decorating icing. Outline the remaining sides in orange.
3. Use a toothpick to mark a letter on top and sides of each block.
4. Continuing with orange decorating icing and round tube #8, pipe a letter over the outline on top of 1 block and 1 side of each of the other blocks. Then pipe another outline around each letter to make it larger.
Repeat for remaining blocks, choosing a contrasting color of icing for the top of each block.

Baby Carriage

(24 servings)

batter for Lemon Coconut Cake (see page 11) or for any 2 (13x9x2″) cakes
4¾ c. decorating icing (see Index):
tint 3½ c. pale yellow;
tint ¾ c. pale green
decorating tubes: star #21, #17; round #3; drop flower #190; leaf #67
12″ chenille stems: 1 green; 1 yellow (or 8 pipe cleaners)

In advance:

1. Prepare batter as directed. Pour batter into 1 (12″) round and 2 (5″) round cake pans, greased and lined with waxed paper.
2. Bake small layers in 350° oven 20 minutes and bake large layer 45 minutes, or until a cake tester or toothpick inserted in center comes out clean.
3. Cool in pans on racks 10 minutes. Remove from pans. Cool on racks.

To assemble:

1. Use a toothpick to draw a line across the middle of the 12″ round cake. Then cut a large wedge from the upper half of the cake as illustrated; the remainder of the upper half will form the hood of the carriage. The lower half will form the body of the carriage.
Place this cake on a sturdy base, 20 to 24″ square. (Set aside wedge for snacks.)
2. Frost sides and top of carriage with some of the yellow decorating icing, but do not frost the hood section on top. Smooth icing, using a metal spatula.

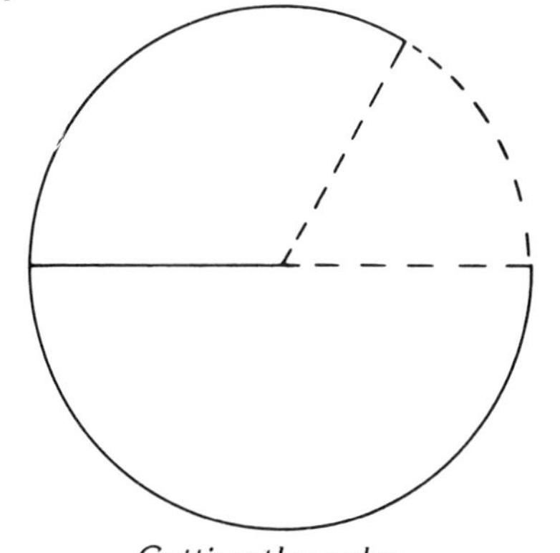

Cutting the cake

3. Frost each 5″ cake with more of the yellow decorating icing; these will form the wheels.
4. Use a knife to lightly mark 6 equal triangles on the hood as shown.
5. Using some of the white decorating icing and star tube #17, pipe rows of zigzag lines to fill 3 of the triangles on the hood, starting at one side and filling every other triangle.
6. Using some of the yellow decorating icing and star tube #17, pipe rows of zigzag lines to fill the remaining triangles.
Continuing with yellow icing and star tube #17, pipe a rosette border around all bottom edges of the carriage, using a continuous circular motion. Repeat this same motion on top of the carriage to outline the semicircle that forms the body of the carriage.
Then pipe a shell border straight across the top to divide the body of the carriage from the hood and around the top edge of the hood.

7. Place wheels at bottom of carriage as shown. Use more of the yellow icing and star tube #17 to pipe a star border around the bottom of each wheel.
8. Using some of the green decorating icing and round tube #3, pipe 5 straight lines between the yellow and white triangles on the hood. Then pipe spokes on each wheel as shown.
   Change to star tube #21 and pipe a rosette border around the top edge of each wheel.
9. Using more of the green decorating icing and round tube #3, pipe small green dots inside the semicircular border outlining the body of the carriage.
10. Using remaining white decorating icing and drop flower tube #190, pipe a white drop flower at the point where the triangles on hood meet. Then pipe a white drop flower in the center of each wheel.
   Change to yellow decorating icing and star tube #17 and pipe a yellow center in each white flower.
11. Using remaining green decorating icing and leaf tube #67, pipe 3 leaves around each flower.
12. Twist chenille stems together and insert in carriage as shown to form handle.

Stork
(24 servings)

2 c. Royal Icing (see page 64):
  tint 1 c. yellow
decorating tubes: rose #104; leaf #67;
  round #4, #2; star #17
Dolores' Pound Cake (see page 43) or any
  17x2x1″ sheet cake
4¾ c. decorating icing (see Index):
  tint 1 c. yellow;
  tint ⅓ c. blue;
  tint 1 tblsp. pink;
  tint 1 tsp. red;
  tint ¼ c. green

In advance:
1. Using yellow and white Royal Icing and rose tube #104, pipe 6 yellow roses with white centers and 6 white roses with yellow centers.
2. Allow roses to dry overnight.

To assemble:
1. Frost top of cake in pan with some of the white decorating icing. Smooth icing, using a metal spatula.
2. Trace the oval pattern to a sheet of paper and cut out. Then use a toothpick to trace pattern on top of cake as illustrated. Reserve a small amount of blue decorating icing for eyes of baby and stork. Use remaining blue decorating icing to frost oval.
3. Trace the stork pattern to a sheet of paper and cut out. Then use a toothpick to trace pattern on top of cake. Using more of the white decorating icing and leaf tube #67, fill outline of stork.
4. Change to star tube #17 and fill outline of baby's blanket with remaining white decorating icing.
5. Using pink decorating icing and star tube #17, fill design of baby's face.
6. Using blue decorating icing and round tube #4, pipe eyes for baby and stork.
7. Using red decorating icing and round tube #2, pipe baby's mouth.
8. Using some of the yellow decorating icing and round tube #4, pipe stork's beak, legs and feet.
   Change to star tube #17 and fill design outline for baby's bonnet. Then pipe a reverse shell border around top edges of cake. Continuing with yellow decorating icing, pipe a plain shell border around the blue oval.
9. Arrange 3 Royal Icing roses in each corner of the cake. Using green decorating icing and leaf tube #67, pipe leaves between roses.

Sweet Pea Cake
(12 servings)

1 c. Royal Icing (see page 64), tinted pink
decorating tubes: rose #104; round #3
Applesauce Layer Cake (see page 27)
  or any 2 (9″) round cake layers
3 c. decorating icing (see Index):
  tint ½ c. green
7″ circle of waxed paper

Pattern for Stork
(full size)

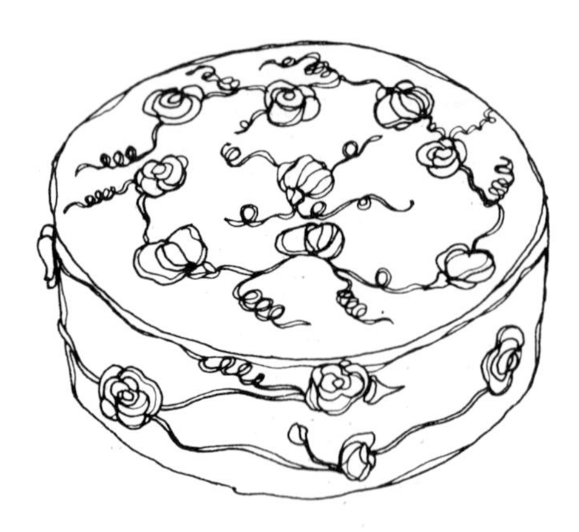

In advance:
1. Using pink Royal Icing and rose tube #104, pipe 21 sweet peas.
2. Allow sweet peas to dry overnight.

To assemble:
1. Fill and frost cake with white decorating icing. Smooth icing, using a metal spatula.
2. To make a pattern for the design on top of the cake, fold the waxed paper circle into eighths, forming a wedge. Cut a small notch ¼″ from the top on one side of the wedge as illustrated; cut another small notch 1½″ from the top on the opposite side. Then cut off the pointed end.

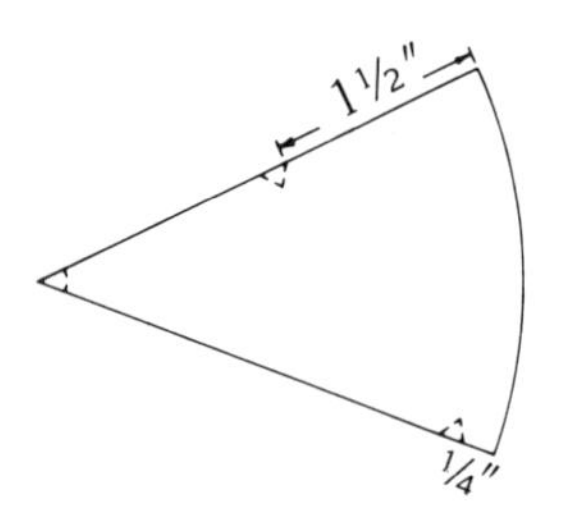

Making the pattern

3. Unfold the pattern and place it on top of the cake. Use a toothpick to mark a point through each hole.

Then use a toothpick to mark 4 points equally spaced around the side of the cake, just below the top. Mark another point at the bottom of the cake directly below each of these points. Finally, mark 4 more points halfway up the side of the cake and halfway between two pairs of points already marked.

4. Using green decorating icing and round tube #3, pipe curved lines around the side of the cake, connecting the marks as shown. Then connect all marks on top of cake, except center mark, with curved lines.
5. Place a Royal Icing sweet pea on each marked point on top and sides of cake.
6. Continuing with green decorating icing and star tube #3, pipe a calyx at the base of each sweet pea. Then pipe tendrils along green lines on sides and top of cake and around the center sweet pea.

Speedy Recovery
(12 servings)

1¾ c. Royal Icing (see page 64):
- tint ½ c. yellow;
- tint ½ c. peach;
- tint ¾ c. green

decorating tubes: rose #104; drop flower #225; star #32; leaf #67; round #2

2 Feather-light Yellow Cakes (see page 7) or any 2 (8″) square cake layers

2¾ c. decorating icing (see Index)

In advance:
1. Using yellow Royal Icing and rose tube #104, pipe 3 roses and 5 sweet peas.
2. Using peach Royal Icing and drop flower tube #225, pipe 30 drop flowers.
3. Allow flowers to dry overnight.

To assemble:
1. Frost top and sides of cake with some of the white decorating icing. Smooth icing, using a metal spatula.
2. Using remaining white decorating icing and star tube #32, pipe 4 scrolls along each top and bottom edge as illustrated to form borders.
3. Using some of the green Royal Icing and round tube #2, pipe several stems on top of

cake as shown. Then pipe a "get well" message of your choice.
4. Arrange roses, sweet peas and drop flowers on top of cake.
5. Using remaining green Royal Icing and leaf tube #67, pipe leaves around flowers and stems on top of cake. Then pipe 2 leaves to join each pair of scrolls on the bottom edges.
6. Place a drop flower between each pair of leaves on the bottom edges.

Cross

(16 servings)

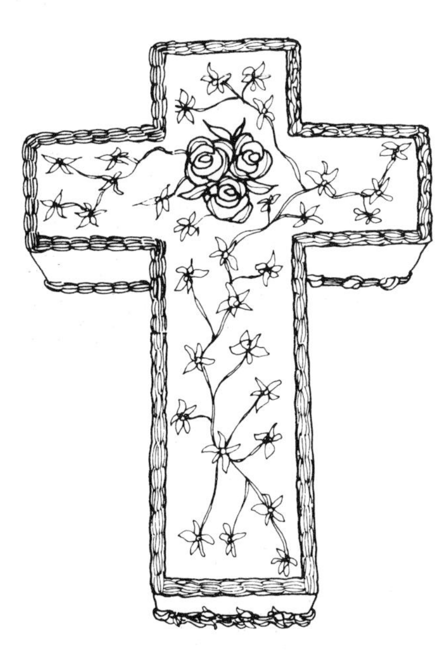

½ c. Royal Icing (see page 64), tinted gold
decorating tubes: rose #104; star #24, #17; drop flower #224; round #2; leaf #67
Never-Fail White Cake (see page 6) or any 13x9x2" cake
5¼ c. decorating icing (see Index):
tint 3 c. light yellow;
tint 1 c. gold;
tint ½ c. lavender;
tint ½ c. light green

In advance:

1. Using gold Royal Icing and rose tube #104, pipe 3 roses.
2. Allow roses to dry overnight.

To assemble:

1. Cut cake as illustrated and join sections with some of the yellow decorating icing.
2. Frost top and sides of cross with more of the yellow decorating icing. Smooth icing, using a metal spatula.
3. Using gold decorating icing and star tube #17, pipe a shell border around bottom and top edges of cross.
4. Using lavender decorating icing and drop flower tube #224, randomly pipe flowers over top of cross. Then pipe a row of flowers over bottom border, leaving ½" space between flowers.
5. Using white decorating icing and star tube #24, pipe centers on flowers on top of cake.
6. Using green decorating icing and round tube #2, pipe vines connecting flowers on top of cross.

Change to leaf tube #67 and randomly pipe leaves on top of cake. Then add a leaf to alternate flowers on bottom border.
7. Arrange 3 Royal Icing roses in center of cross as shown.

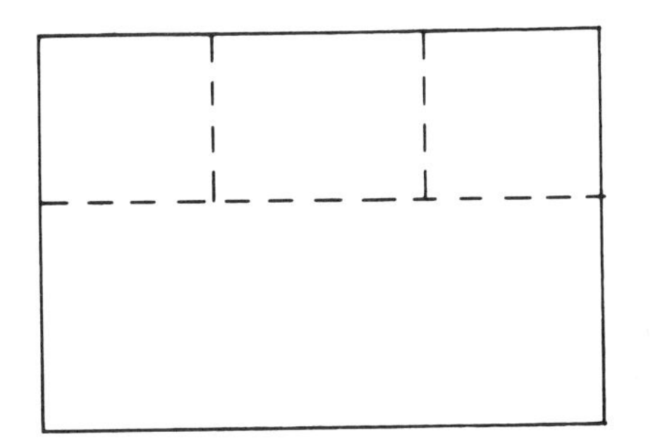

Cutting the cake

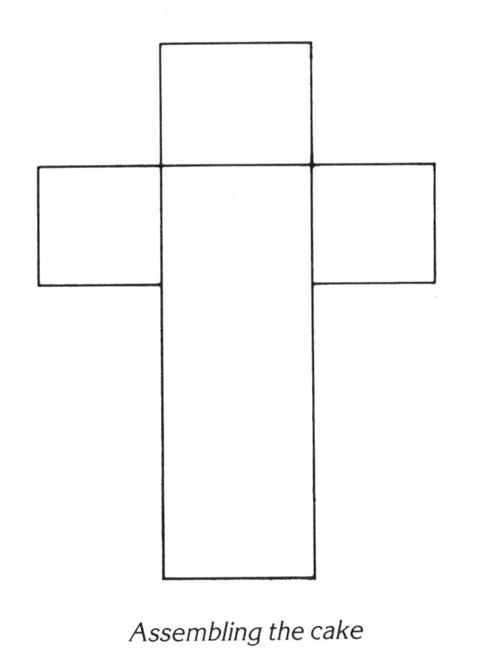

Assembling the cake

Rose Ring Cake

(8 servings)

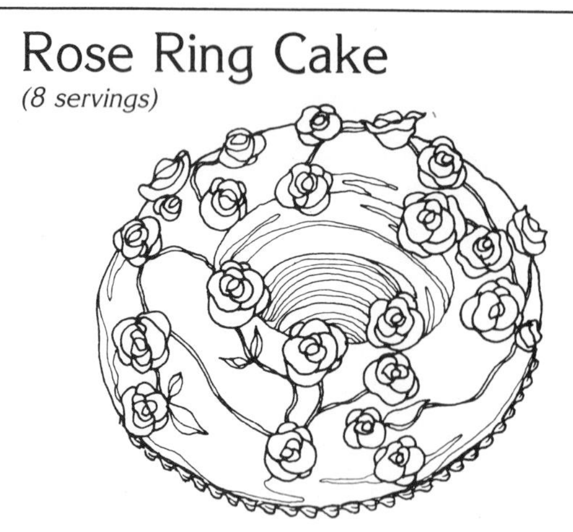

2 c. Royal Icing (see page 64):
tint 1 c. red;
tint 1 c. green
decorating tubes: rose #102; round #4;
leaf #65
Yellow Cake Ring (see page 7)
1¼ c. butter cream frosting (see Index)

In advance:

1. Using red Royal Icing and rose tube #102, pipe 20 small roses and 10 rosebuds.
2. Allow flowers to dry overnight.

To assemble:

1. Frost cake with the white butter cream frosting. Smooth frosting, using a metal spatula.
2. Use a toothpick to draw 4 clusters of stems and branches evenly spaced around top and sides of cake as illustrated.
3. Using some of the green Royal Icing and round tube #4, pipe stems and branches over design lines.
4. Randomly place Royal Icing roses on branches and stems around cake.
5. Using remaining green Royal Icing and leaf tube #65, pipe leaves around roses and rosebuds.

Pipe a leaf border around bottom edge of cake.

Sweet Sixteen

(12 servings)

2½ c. Royal Icing (see page 64), tinted pink
decorating tubes: rose large #125; round #2,
#1; star #16; leaf #67
Grandma's Chocolate Cake (see page 17)
or any 2 (9″) round cake layers
2¾ c. decorating icing (see Index):
tint 1¾ c. light green;
tint ¼ c. dark green

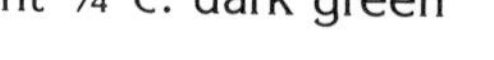

In advance:

1. Using pink Royal Icing and rose tube #125, pipe 10 roses.
2. Allow roses to dry overnight.

To assemble:

1. Fill cake with some of the white decorating icing.

Frost top and sides with some of the light green decorating icing.

Smooth icing, using a metal spatula.

2. Use a toothpick to mark a heart about 3½″ wide on top of the cake. Then mark the number 16 in the center.
3. Using more of the white decorating icing and round tube #1, pipe lace around the side of the cake as illustrated. Then pipe the number 16 in the center of the heart.

Change to star tube #16 and pipe a zigzag border around bottom and top edges of cake. Then outline the heart with a zigzag border.

4. Using remaining light green decorating icing and round tube #2, overpipe a row of beads in the center of top and bottom borders, around the heart and on top of the number 16.
5. Arrange Royal Icing roses around heart.
6. Using dark green decorating icing and leaf tube #67, pipe leaves around the roses.

All-occasion Cake

(12 servings)

2 c. Royal Icing (see page 64), tinted yellow
decorating tubes: rose #125, #104; star #32,
#17; leaf #67; round #3
Mahogany Cake (see page 19) or any

2 (9″) round cake layers
3 c. decorating icing (see Index):
tint 1¼ c. yellow;
tint ¼ c. green

In advance:

1. Using yellow Royal Icing and rose tube #125, pipe 4 roses.
   Change to rose tube #104 and pipe 12 rosebuds.
2. Allow flowers to dry overnight.

To assemble:

1. Fill cake with some of the white decorating icing. Frost top of cake with more of the white decorating icing.
   Frost sides of cake with yellow decorating icing.
   Smooth icing, using a metal spatula.
2. Using remaining white decorating icing and star tube #32, pipe a shell border around bottom edge of cake. Change to star tube #17 and pipe a border of 12 garlands equally spaced around top edge as illustrated.
   Change to round tube #3 and pipe a beaded arch over each shell of bottom border as shown.
3. Arrange Royal Icing roses on top of cake. Place rosebuds between garlands on top border as shown.
4. Using green decorating icing and leaf tube #67, pipe leaves around roses. Then pipe a leaf beside each rosebud.
   Change to round tube #3 and pipe an inscription of your choice. (This cake can carry almost any cheerful message, including congratulations, a welcome, or a salute saying "Enjoy your leisure!")

Book

(26 to 30 servings)

2¼ c. Royal Icing (see page 64):
tint 2 c. red;
tint ¼ c. green
decorating tubes: rose large #125; star #17; round #4; leaf #67
Lemon-Coconut Cake (see page 11) or any 2 (13x9x2″) cakes
5⅓ c. decorating icing (see Index):
tint ⅓ c. red
12″ red ribbon, 1″ wide

In advance:

1. Using red Royal Icing and rose tube #125, pipe 6 roses and 10 rosebuds. Cover remaining Royal Icing tightly and refrigerate for later use.
2. Allow flowers to dry overnight.

Assembling the cake

To assemble:

1. Arrange cakes on a sturdy base as illustrated, long sides together.
2. Measure 1″ from all 4 edges of each cake and insert a row of toothpicks as illustrated to mark a rectangle. Using a long, sharp knife, make a diagonal cut along the outside edges of both cakes, cutting from the row of toothpicks to the bottom of the cake. (Do not cut center of cake.) Set aside the 6 wedges of cake for snacks.

3. Then make a shallow cut from the inside edge of each cake toward the center, cutting diagonally and leaving about ½" of cake in the center. Remove toothpicks and both wedges of cake.

Flatten wedges of cake with your hands and replace them along the cut center edges to create a curved effect.

4. Frost book with a thin coat of white decorating icing; let dry. Then frost generously with more of the white decorating icing, keeping curved effect of pages. Smooth icing, using a metal spatula.

5. Draw a 4-tined fork horizontally across the edges of the book to make them represent pages.

6. Using more of the white decorating icing and star tube #17, pipe a zigzag border around bottom and top edges of book and down the corners of the pages.

7. Use a toothpick to draw a scalloped line around the edges of each page on the top of the book as shown. Using remaining white decorating icing and round tube #4, pipe beads over the scalloped lines.

8. Using red decorating icing and round tube #4, pipe a bead border in the center of the zigzag border around the bottom edge.

9. Arrange 3 Royal Icing roses and 4 rosebuds in the top left and lower right corners.

10. Place red ribbon down the center of the book. Arrange 2 rosebuds on top of ribbon.

11. Using green Royal Icing and leaf tube #67, pipe leaves around the roses and rosebuds.

Variations: This cake can represent a memory book, a book of knowledge to honor a graduate or a Bible to celebrate a confirmation, a bar mitzvah or a bas mitzvah.

Pink and White Party Cake

(12 servings; see photo, page 103)

1 c. Royal Icing (see page 64):
  tint ¼ c. pink;
  tint 3 tblsp. green
decorating tubes: round #2; star #17;
  drop flower #191; leaf #67
Basic White Layer Cake (see page 5)
  or any 2 (9") round cake layers
3½ c. decorating icing (see Index):
  tint 1 c. pink

In advance:

1. Draw 7 (2") circles on waxed paper. Cut out 1 circle and set it aside. Using white Royal Icing and round tube #2, pipe lattice over the 6 remaining circles.

Change to star tube #17 and pipe a shell border around each lattice circle.

2. Using pink Royal Icing and drop flower tube #191, pipe 7 drop flowers on another sheet of waxed paper.

3. Using green Royal Icing and leaf tube #67, pipe leaves on 2 sides of each flower.

4. Allow Royal Icing decorations to dry overnight.

To assemble:

1. Fill and frost top and sides of cake with some of the white decorating icing. Smooth icing, using a metal spatula.

2. Mark top of cake into 6 equal triangles, using the string method.

3. Using pink decorating icing and star tube #17, fill 3 alternate triangles as shown (see page 103), using a horizontal zigzag motion. Then pipe a pink rectangle on the side of the cake just below each white triangle, using an up-and-down zigzag motion.

4. Use the waxed paper circle as a pattern to mark a 2" circle on each white triangle on top of the cake. Then mark a circle in the center of each white section on the side of the cake.

5. Using remaining white decorating icing and star tube #17, outline each circle. Then pipe a second circle on top of the first.

6. Center a pink Royal Icing drop flower with leaves on top of the cake. Then place a flower in the center of each circle.

7. Remove Royal Icing lattice circles from waxed paper and place them over the flowers and circles on top and sides of cake.

Petit Fours

(32 servings)

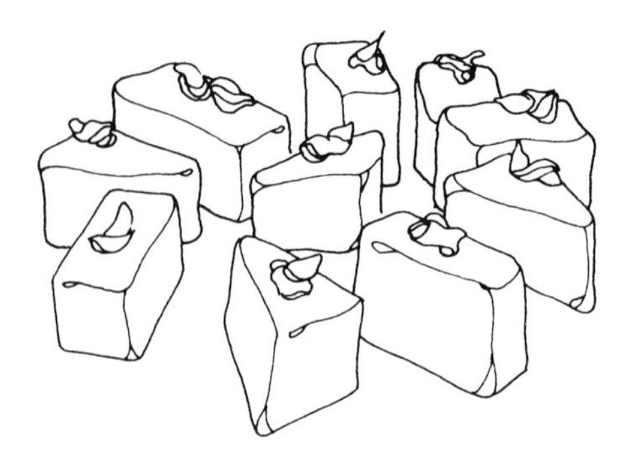

6 eggs
1 c. sugar
1½ tsp. vanilla
1 c. sifted cake flour
¼ c. melted butter or regular margarine
¼ c. apricot preserves
Fondant Frosting (recipe follows)
½ c. decorating icing (see Index):
tint 2 tblsp. pink;
tint 2 tblsp. yellow;
tint 2 tblsp. lavender;
tint 2 tblsp. green
decorating tubes: rose #102; leaf #67

1. Break eggs into large bowl. Set this bowl inside another bowl filled with hot (not boiling) water. Stir eggs until lukewarm.
2. Remove bowl of eggs from water. Add sugar and beat 8 minutes or until lemon-colored and very thick, using an electric mixer at high speed.
3. Reduce speed to low and blend in vanilla.
4. Fold in cake flour by hand. Stir in melted butter.
5. Pour batter into a greased and waxed paper-lined 15½x10½x1″ jelly roll pan.
6. Bake in 350°oven 20 minutes, or until cake springs back when touched.
7. Remove cake immediately from pan and cool on rack.
8. Trim crisp edges of cake. Cut cake in half crosswise to form 2 rectangles, about 7x9″ each. Spread half of the cake with preserves. Top with remaining half, bottom side up.
9. Cut cake into 16 equal rectangles, about 2¼x1¾″ each.
Cut 8 of the rectangles in half crosswise to make smaller rectangles; cut remaining rectangles in half diagonally to make triangles.
10. Place cake sections on a wire rack in a jelly roll pan. Spoon Fondant Frosting over cakes, spreading evenly over tops and sides with a small metal spatula. Scrape excess fondant from jelly roll pan and reuse. (If needed, rewarm fondant slightly.)
11. Using tinted decorating icing and rose tube #102, pipe a pink, yellow or lavender rosebud on top of each Petit Four.
12. Using green decorating icing and leaf tube #67, pipe a green leaf on each rosebud.

Fondant Frosting

2 c. sugar
⅔ c. light corn syrup
1⅓ c. water
1 tsp. vanilla
4 c. sifted confectioners' sugar

Combine sugar, corn syrup and water in 2-qt. saucepan. Cook over medium heat, stirring constantly, until mixture comes to a boil. Continue to cook, but do not stir, until mixture reaches 226° on a candy thermometer.
Remove from heat. Cool to 110°.
Stir in vanilla and confectioners' sugar until frosting is thick, but not too thick to pour.

Flowered Loaf Cake

(9 servings)

⅓ c. Royal Icing (see page 64)
decorating tubes: rose #104; round #5, #3; star #21; leaf #65
½ recipe for Rich Pound Cake (see page 42) or any 9x5x3″ loaf cake
2¼ c. decorating icing (see Index):
tint 1 c. yellow;
tint ¼ c. green;
tint ¼ c. orange;
tint 2 tblsp. red;
tint 2 tblsp. yellow

In advance:

1. Using white Royal Icing and rose tube #104, pipe 5 daisies.
2. Allow daisies to dry overnight.

To assemble:
1. Frost top and sides of cake with some of the yellow decorating icing. Smooth icing, using a metal spatula.
2. Use a toothpick to mark patterns for stems on top and sides of cake as illustrated.
Using some of the green decorating icing and round tube #3, pipe the stems.
3. Arrange 3 Royal Icing daisies on top of the cake and center another daisy on each long side of the cake as shown. Using remaining yellow decorating icing and round tube #3, pipe centers on daisies.
4. Using orange decorating icing and star tube #21, pipe a star flower on top of the cake at each corner and on each side of the center daisy. Then randomly pipe more star flowers over the stems on the sides of the cake.
5. Using red decorating icing and round tube #3, pipe centers on orange flowers.
6. Using remaining green decorating icing and leaf tube #65, pipe 1 or 2 leaves around each star flower.
7. Using white decorating icing and leaf tube #65, pipe a ribbon border around bottom edges of cake.
Change to round tube #5 and pipe a bead border around the top edges of cake.

Black-eyed Susans
(12 servings)

Run Sugar Icing (see page 64):
tint ⅓ c. orange;
tint 2 tblsp. dark brown;
tint ¼ c. medium green;
tint ⅓ c. light green
decorating tubes: round #3; star #17
2 recipes for Lazy Daisy Cake (see page 48)
or any 2 (9″) square cake layers
3 c. decorating icing (see Index):
tint ½ c. yellow

In advance:
1. Draw an 8″ square on a sheet of paper. Then copy black-eyed Susan design (see illustration) inside square.
2. Place sheet of lightly greased waxed paper over the pattern. Using orange Royal Icing and round tube #3, pipe flower petals, keeping lines as smooth as possible.
3. Using dark brown Royal Icing and round tube #3, outline centers of flowers.
4. Using medium-green Royal Icing and round tube #3, outline leaves and stems of flowers.
5. Using white Royal Icing and round tube #3, outline the white square background.
6. Thin Royal Icing with a little water (see page 64) and fill in outlines, using light green for leaves, orange for petals, dark brown for centers of flowers and white for background.
7. Allow run sugar square to dry at least 12 hours.

To assemble:
1. Fill and frost top and sides of cake with white decorating icing. Carefully peel waxed paper from back of run sugar square and place square on top of cake.
2. Using yellow decorating icing and star tube #17, pipe a shell border around bottom and top edges of cake and down each corner.

Spring Flower Basket

(12 servings; see photo, page 31)

3½ c. Royal Icing (see page 64)
paste food colors
decorating tubes: rose large #125, #104, #59°; round #8, #3, #2; specialty #79; leaf #67; basket weave #47; star #17
Waldorf Spice Cake (see page 25) or any 2 (9″) cake layers
2½ c. Rich Chocolate Icing (see page 61)
½ c. butter cream frosting (see Index), tinted green

In advance:

1. You'll need about 50 Royal Icing flowers to cover the top of this cake. Tint Royal Icing in an assortment of spring colors (see photo, page 31).

(We used rose tube #125 to pipe 5 roses, 7 half-roses, 3 daffodils, 3 jonquils and 13 daisies; rose tube #59° to pipe 9 violets; rose tube #104 for 7 pansies; and specialty tube #79 to pipe 3 chrysanthemums.)

Use round tube #8 for centers of daisies; round tube #3 for centers of daffodils and jonquils; and round tube #2 for centers of violets, pansies and chrysanthemums.

Use leaf tube #67 to pipe leaves.

2. Allow flowers to dry overnight.

To assemble:

1. Fill cake with some of the Rich Chocolate Icing.

Frost top of cake with green butter cream frosting.

Then frost sides of cake with a thin coat of Rich Chocolate Icing.

2. Using Rich Chocolate Icing and basket weave tube #47, pipe basket weave around sides of cake.

Change to star tube #17 and pipe a rosette border around top edge of cake, using a continuous circular motion.

3. Arrange Royal Icing flowers on top of cake (see photo, page 31). Using green Royal Icing and leaf tube #67, pipe leaves around flowers.

Variation: To simplify this cake and transform it into an autumn bouquet, substitute about 30 chrysanthemums for the spring blossoms.

Tint ¾ c. of the Royal Icing deep orange, ¾ c. gold, ¾ c. yellow and ½ c. green.

Use specialty tube #79 to pipe 7 white chrysanthemums, 8 deep orange chrysanthemums, 6 gold chrysanthemums and 8 yellow chrysanthemums.

Use round tube #2 to pipe an orange center in each yellow flower and a yellow center in each remaining flower.

Use leaf tube #67 to pipe leaves.

Allow flowers to dry overnight, and assemble as above.

Flowered Cupcakes

(24 servings; see photo, page 32)

2½ c. Royal Icing (see page 64)
paste food colors
decorating tubes: rose large #125, #104; specialty #79; leaf #67; round #8, #2
Light Chocolate Brownie Cupcakes (see page 21) or any 24 cupcakes
1½ c. decorating icing (see Index): tint ¼ c. green

In advance:

1. You'll need 24 large Royal Icing flowers (chrysanthemums, carnations or roses), or 48 small flowers (pansies or black-eyed Susans), or any similar combination of Royal Icing flowers to cover the tops of 24 cupcakes. Tint Royal Icing according to the flowers and colors you like best.

Use rose tube #125 to pipe black-eyed Susans and roses.

Use rose tube #104 to pipe pansies and half-carnations.

Use specialty tube #79 to pipe chrysanthemums.

Use round tube #8 for centers of black-eyed Susans, and round tube #2 for centers of pansies and chrysanthemums and stems of half-carnations.

2. Allow flowers to dry overnight.

To assemble:

1. Frost cupcakes with white decorating icing.
2. Arrange Royal Icing flowers on top of cupcakes as shown (see photo, page 32).
3. Using green decorating icing and leaf tube #67, pipe leaves around flowers as you wish.

Pinwheel Quilt

(12 servings; see photo, page 30)

1 c. Royal Icing (see page 64):
  tint ½ c. pale yellow;
  tint ¼ c. tan;
  tint ¼ c. brown
decorating tubes: round #2; basket weave #48
Peanut Butter Chocolate Chip Cake (see page 14) or any 13x9x2" cake
¾ c. Chocolate Butter Cream Icing (see page 61)
1½ c. decorating icing (see Index):
  tint 1¼ c. pale yellow;
  tint ¼ c. tan

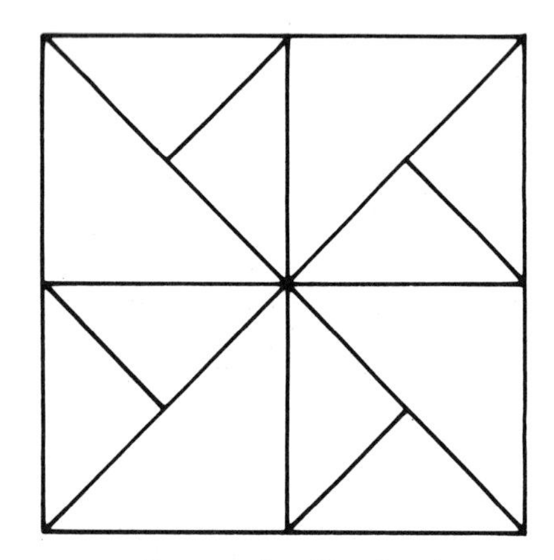

Pattern for Pinwheel (full size)

In advance:

1. Trace pinwheel pattern on a sheet of paper. Place a sheet of waxed paper over the pattern.
2. Using some of the pale yellow Royal Icing and round tube #2, outline the entire design, keeping lines as straight as possible. Repeat 11 times to form 12 squares.
3. Thin Royal Icing with a little water (see page 64). Continuing with round tube #2, fill in outlines, using yellow to fill the 4 small outer triangles, tan to fill the 4 large outer triangles and brown to fill the 4 small inner triangles of each square as illustrated.
4. Allow squares to dry at least 12 hours.

To assemble:

1. Frost sides of cake with Chocolate Butter Cream Icing. Frost top of cake with 1 c. of the pale yellow decorating icing.
2. Arrange Royal Icing squares on top of cake as shown (see photo, page 30).
3. Using pale yellow decorating icing and basket weave tube #48, pipe a ribbed border around the edges of the cake and between the squares.
4. Using tan decorating icing and basket weave tube #48, pipe a square over the ribbed border at each corner of the Royal Icing squares.

5

Cakes Just for Children

Birthdays mean more to children than any other holiday, and in this chapter you'll find 17 decorating ideas to light up a child's eyes.

None of these cakes requires a special pan. An Iowa farm woman's Clown cake is made from a round cake layer and 10 cupcakes. The Gum Ball Machine starts with two cake layers, one round and one square; frosted with red icing and decorated with candy-coated peanuts, it's a treat for any youngster.

The yummy-looking Strawberry Ice Cream Cone pictured on page 83 is easy to do. The cone is cut from a 13x9x2″ cake and the frosting is piped with a star tube to give it texture. Deep swirls of 7-Minute Frosting atop two round cake layers give the scoop of ice cream its rich, creamy look.

Cut-out cakes are a favorite of one Texas homemaker who sent us the idea for a cake that's popular in her family—a big green alligator with candy corn teeth.

In Montana, a rancher's wife first learned from a friend how to cut a boot-shaped cake. She changes the colors and design on the boot each time she makes it. "Living in Montana, we have plenty of reasons for making Cowboy Boot cakes," she wrote.

You can surprise your child with a special cake featuring his or her favorite sport, as one Ohio farm woman does. We've adapted her idea into a Baseball and Glove—a super-simple cake topped with a cupcake.

You can even make a five-car train from two square layers, as does one farm woman. The engine puffs marshmallow smoke and runs on a licorice track as it pulls four cars, including a coal car filled with chocolate morsels.

While growing up on an Illinois farm, the children in one family looked forward to seeing their mom invent a different cake each year. Now that they're grown, the cake that they remember best is the one called Ring-around-the-Rosy—and no wonder! Little girls wearing fluted bonnets ring this pretty cake, holding candles in their hands (see photo, page 81).

The adorable blue dolls that hold the candles on the Rag Dolls cake, also pictured on page 81, are made in advance, and you can change them into boy dolls just by piping on short pants and perhaps a hat. Best of all, you can use these cake decorations again; they'll keep indefinitely without refrigeration.

If your children like to draw, let them design their own cakes. One mother transfers her son's original design to a thinly frosted cake with a toothpick and fills in the colors with a star tube. Her son enjoys seeing his drawing come alive with color, and both of them look forward to working on this special project.

Let your child choose the flavor and the theme of the cake. Children who are old enough will enjoy stirring up the batter, mixing the icing and helping with the decorating—as well as licking the bowls.

Gum Ball Machine

(14 servings)

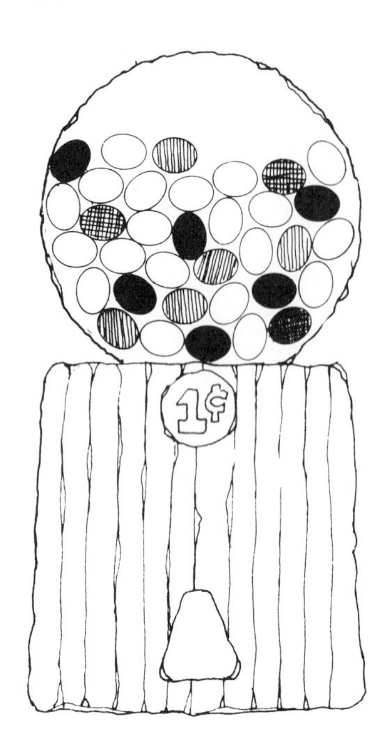

Silver White Cake (see page 6), baked into 1 (9″) round and 1 (9″) square cake layer (or any 9″ round and 9″ square cake layers)
2 c. decorating icing (See Index):
tint ¾ c. red;
tint 2 tblsp. black
decorating tube: round #2
1 lb. candy-coated peanuts

1. Arrange cakes as illustrated.
2. Frost sides and top of square cake with red decorating icing. To create a ribbed effect on the gum ball stand, gently draw a metal spatula across the cake, lengthwise from top to bottom.
3. Use a toothpick to draw coin slot and gum return on the stand.
4. Frost sides and top of round cake layer with white decorating icing, reserving 3 tblsp. for coin slot and gum return. Frost coin slot and gum return with white decorating icing.
5. Using black decorating icing and round tube #2, pipe "1¢" on coin slot.
6. Arrange candy-coated peanuts on top of round cake as shown.

Strawberry Ice Cream Cone

(24 servings; see photo, page 83)

2 recipes for Fluffy Gold Cake (see page 8), baked into 1 (13x9x2″) cake and 2 (9″) round layers (or any 13x9x2″ cake and two 9″ round layers)
2½ c. decorating icing (see Index), tinted yellow
decorating tube: star #21
3½ c. Boiled Frosting (see page 62), tinted pink

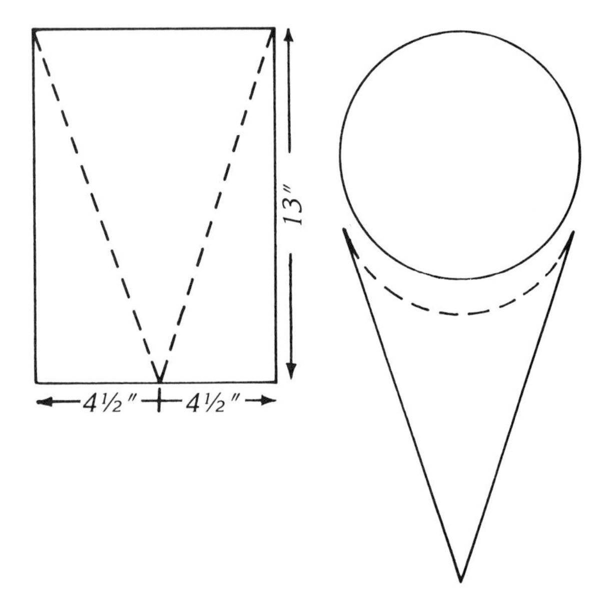

Cutting and assembling the cake

1. Cut 13x9x2″ cake into 3 triangles as illustrated. Arrange the 2 smaller triangles to form 1 large triangle, joining with some of the yellow decorating icing.

Frost the top of this triangle with more of the yellow decorating icing and top with large triangle to form a 2-layer triangle. Cut away a semicircle from the short side of triangle to form cone as shown.

2. Using remaining yellow decorating icing and star tube #21, pipe stars evenly and close together over sides and top of cone as shown (see photo, page 83).
3. Fill round cake layers with pink Boiled Frosting. Place at top of cone. Frost top and sides of round layers with pink Boiled Frosting, swirling the frosting with a spatula.

Baseball and Glove

(12 servings)

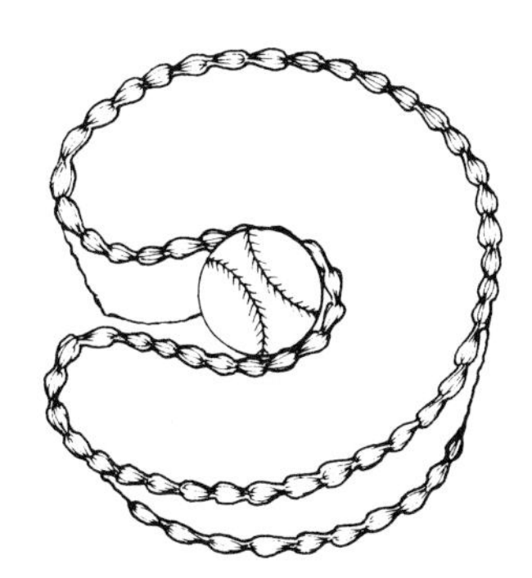

Million-Dollar Pound Cake (see page 42)
or any 10″ tube cake
1 cupcake, home-baked (see Index) or store-bought
3 c. decorating icing (see Index):
tint 2 c. golden brown;
tint 2 tblsp. red;
tint ¾ c. dark brown
decorating tubes: round #2; star #17

1. Cut away a small section from the cake, all the way to the center, rounding the edges as illustrated.
2. Enlarge the hole at the top of the cake enough to hold the cupcake as shown.
3. Frost top and sides of cake with golden brown decorating icing. Smooth icing, using a metal spatula.
4. Frost cupcake with white decorating icing and place in hole on top of cake.
5. Using red decorating icing and round tube #2, pipe 2 stitching lines on top of cupcake.
6. Using dark brown decorating icing and star tube #17, pipe a shell border around bottom and top edges of cake.

T-Shirt

(14 servings)

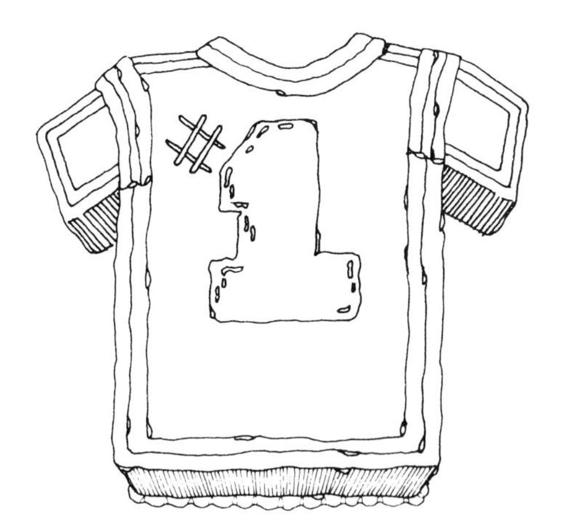

Carrot Cake (see page 36)
or any 13x9x2″ cake
4¼ c. decorating icing (see Index):
tint 1¼ c. brown;
tint 2 c. orange;
tint 1 c. yellow
decorating tubes: star #17; round #3

1. Cut cake as illustrated and join sections with some of the brown decorating icing.
2. Frost top and sides of shirt with brown decorating icing. Smooth icing, using a metal spatula.
3. Use a toothpick to draw "#1" in center of shirt as shown. Using some of the orange decorating icing and star tube #17, pipe stars evenly and close together to fill in the "1."
4. Continuing with the orange decorating icing, pipe a star border around bottom and top edges of shirt and at shoulder seams.

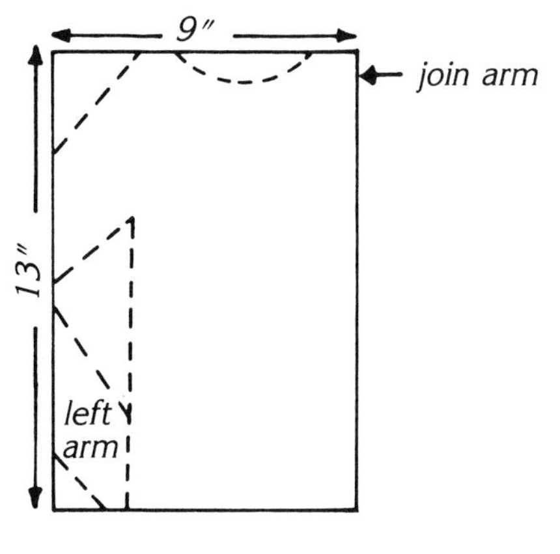

Cutting the cake

5. Using yellow decorating icing and star tube #17, pipe a star border inside the orange border on top of shirt as shown. Pipe a yellow star border on each side of the orange borders at shoulder seams.
6. Using orange decorating icing and round tube #3, pipe the number symbol beside "1."

Cowboy Boot

(12 servings)

One-Bowl Cocoa Cake (see page 20)
  or any 13x9x2″ cake
2¾ c. decorating icing (see Index):
  tint 2¼ c. medium brown;
  tint ¼ c. yellow;
  tint ¼ c. red
decorating tubes: rose #104; round #3
silver dragées
aluminum foil
2″ cardboard round

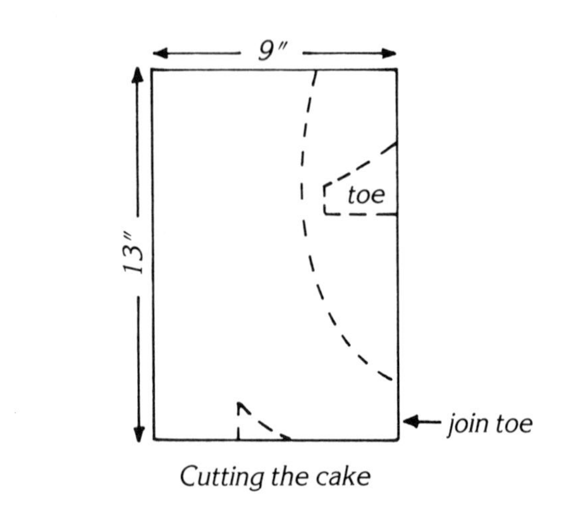

Cutting the cake

1. Cut cake as illustrated and join sections with some of the medium brown decorating icing.
2. Frost top and sides of boot with more of the medium brown decorating icing. Smooth icing, using a metal spatula. Add a little more brown paste food color to darken remaining brown icing.
3. Using dark brown decorating icing and rose tube #104, pipe bootstraps as shown. Use a toothpick to score heel.
4. Using yellow decorating icing and round tube #3, pipe design on boot as shown.
5. Using red decorating icing and round tube #3, embellish yellow design as shown.
6. Decorate boot with silver dragées as shown.
7. Glue foil to cardboard circle and cut into a 10-point spur. Glue one end of a toothpick to back of spur and insert other end into boot.

Clown

(16 servings)

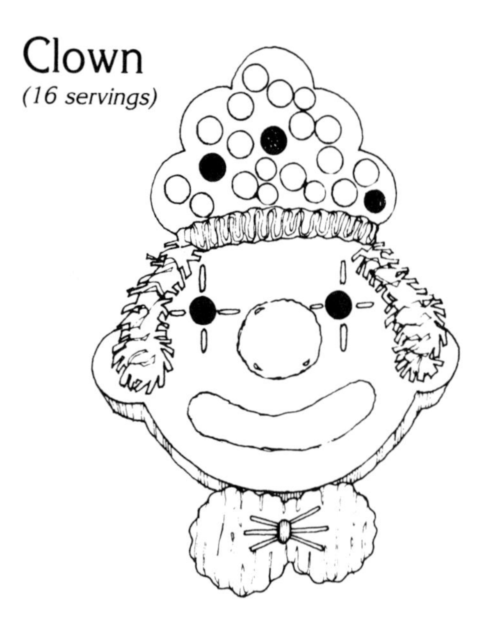

Fluffy Gold Cake (see page 8), baked into 1
  (9″) round cake layer and 10 cupcakes (or
  any 9″ round cake layer and cupcakes)
3¼ c. decorating icing (see Index):
  tint ¼ c. red;
  tint ¾ c. yellow;
  tint 2 tblsp. brown;
  tint 2 tblsp. blue
decorating tubes: star #16; round #2
½ c. flaked coconut, tinted red
gumdrop slices

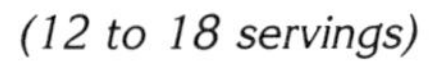

1. Assemble cake and cupcakes as illustrated. Frost hat, face and ears with about 2 c. of white decorating icing. Use a toothpick to draw eyes and mouth.
2. Using red decorating icing and star tube #16, pipe stars evenly and close together on nose and mouth.
3. Using yellow decorating icing and star tube #16, pipe a zigzag border for hatband. Then pipe elongated zigzags on sides and top of bow tie.
4. Using brown decorating icing and round tube #2, outline eyes.
5. Using blue decorating icing and round tube #2, pipe in detail on bow tie and eyes as shown.
6. Arrange coconut around face. Decorate hat with gumdrop slices.

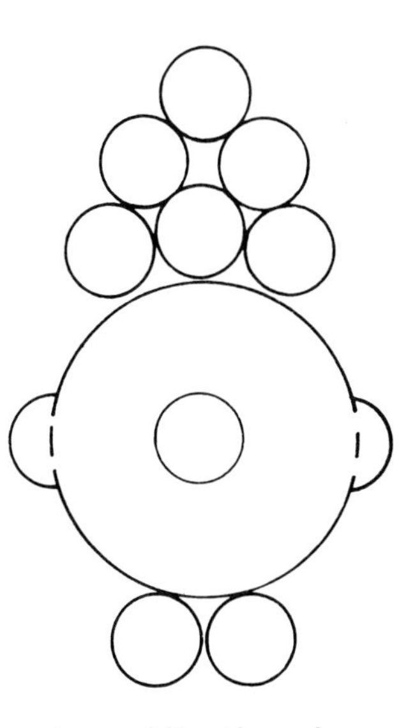

Assembling the cake

Drum

(12 to 18 servings)

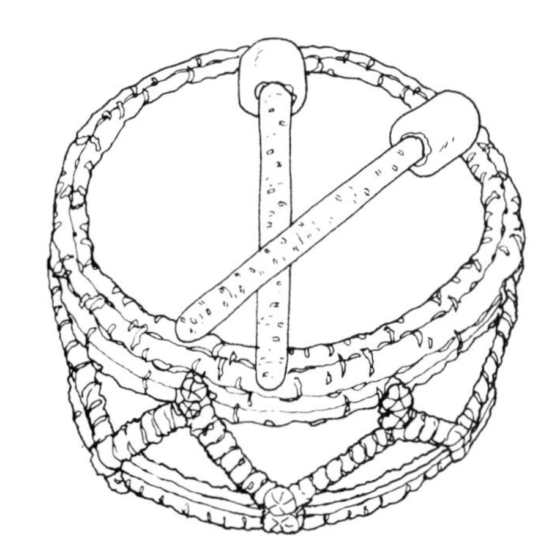

Italian Cream Cake (cake only; see page 8)
 or any 3 (9″) round cake layers
4 c. decorating icing (see Index):
 tint 1½ c. red;
 tint ¾ c. gold
decorating tubes: star #21, #17
2 pretzel rods (about 7″ long)
2 large marshmallows

1. Fill cake layers with some of the white decorating icing.
 Frost top and sides of drum with red decorating icing. Smooth icing, using a metal spatula.
2. Using some of the remaining white decorating icing and star tube #17, pipe 4 adjoining star borders around top of drum, starting with a border around top edge and adding another border inside and 2 more borders below the top edge.
 Then pipe 3 adjoining star borders around bottom edge of drum, starting at the bottom.
3. Use a toothpick to mark 8 points equally spaced just below the top border. Using gold decorating icing and star tube #21, pipe 2 stars, one above the other, on the white border above each mark. Repeat at bottom border, placing each pair of stars midway between upper stars as shown.
 Starting at top border, join upper and lower stars with a gold star border to form braid.
4. Insert pretzel rods in marshmallows. Cross drumsticks and join with a dab of icing. Arrange on top of drum.

Space Fantasy

(12 servings)

Walnut Cake (see page 12)
or any 2 (9″) round cake layers
3¼ c. decorating icing (see Index):
tint 1½ c. blue;
tint ¼ c. yellow;
tint ¾ c. green;
tint 2 tblsp. violet
decorating tubes: star #30, 17; round #11, #4
1 large marshmallow
2 (2″) round sugar cookies
2 (2″) star-shaped sugar cookies

1. Fill cake layers with white decorating icing.
Frost top and sides of cake with some of the blue decorating icing. Smooth icing, using a metal spatula.
2. Using more of the blue decorating icing and star tube #30, pipe shell border around bottom and top edges of cake.
3. Frost all cookies with yellow decorating icing.
4. Cut marshmallow in half and place one half in the center of each round cookie. Using remaining blue decorating icing and star tube #30, pipe stars on round cookies as illustrated. Change to round tube #4 and pipe faces on marshmallows.
5. Using green decorating icing and round tube #11, pipe concentric circles in the center of each star cookie.
Change to star tube #17 and pipe a star border around each star cookie.
6. Using green decorating icing and round tube #11, pipe space figures on top of cake. Apply maximum pressure and squeeze out 3 upright pear-shaped bodies, 1″ high. Pipe arms, legs and heads.
7. Using violet decorating icing and round tube #4, pipe faces on space figures and on green circles of star cookies.
8. Attach cookies to top of cake with a dab of icing.
9. Using yellow decorating icing and round tube #4, pipe *"Happy Birthday"* on side of cake.
Change to star tube #30 and randomly pipe stars on top of cake.

Turtle

(12 servings)

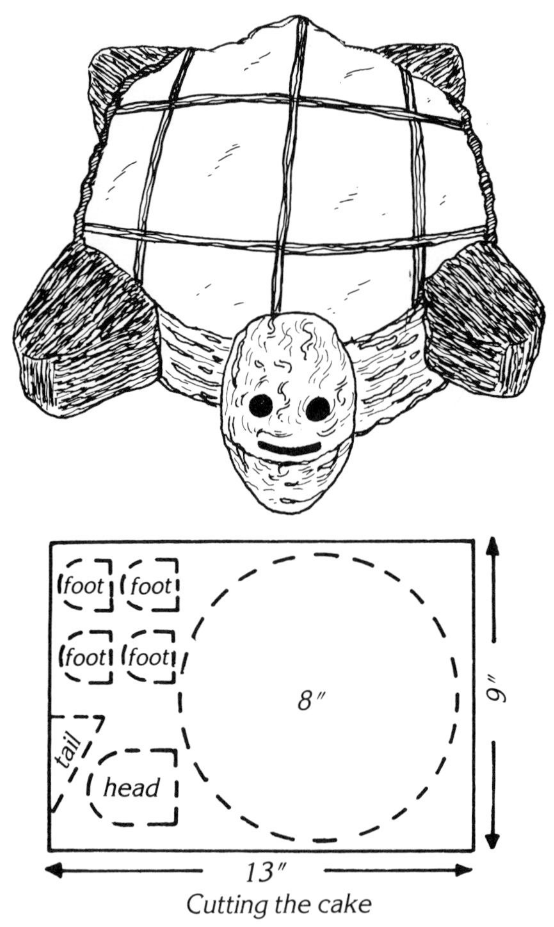

Cutting the cake

Gram's Chocolate Cake (see page 19)
or any 13x9x2″ cake
2¾ c. decorating icing (see Index), tinted green
2 c. Chocolate Butter Cream Icing (see page 61)
decorating tube: star #21
1 black jelly bean
2″ black shoestring licorice

1. Cut cake as illustrated and join sections with some of the green decorating icing.
2. Frost top and sides of turtle shell with more of the green decorating icing.
Using remaining green decorating icing and star tube #21, pipe a series of wavy lines along the sides of the body and over the head and tail as shown.
3. Using some of the Chocolate Butter Cream Icing and star tube #21, pipe a series of wavy lines over the sides and tops of the feet.
4. Using a toothpick, mark a series of vertical and horizontal grooves on the body as shown to resemble a turtle's shell. Using remaining Chocolate Butter Cream Icing and star tube #21, pipe a ribbed border over the grooves.
5. To make face, cut jelly bean in half and arrange jelly bean and licorice on head to form eyes and mouth.

Star Ship

(16 servings)

Never-Fail White Cake (see page 6)
or any 13x9x2″ cake
3¾ c. decorating icing (see Index):
tint ¼ c. blue;
tint ½ c. red
decorating tube: star #21

1. Cut cake as illustrated and join sections with some of the white decorating icing.
2. Frost top and sides of the ship with more of the white decorating icing. Smooth icing, using a metal spatula.
3. Use a toothpick to draw letters U, S and A and a rectangle for flag as shown.
4. Using blue decorating icing and star tube #21, pipe several rows of stars evenly and close together in upper left-hand corner of flag. Then pipe a star border around top edge of ship, making stars about 1½″ apart.
5. Using red decorating icing and star tube #21, pipe stripes on flag, leaving room for white stripes. Pipe letters U, S and A below flag as shown. Then pipe a red star next to each blue star on border.
6. Using more of the white decorating icing and star tube #21, pipe white stripes on flag between red ones. Then add a white star to top border between blue and red stars.
7. Continuing with remaining white decorating icing, pipe a zigzag border around the bottom edge of ship.

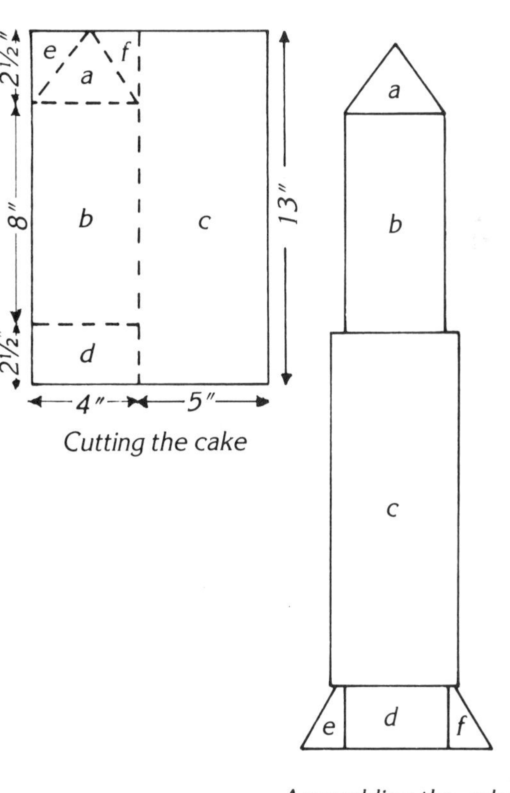

Cutting the cake

Assembling the cake

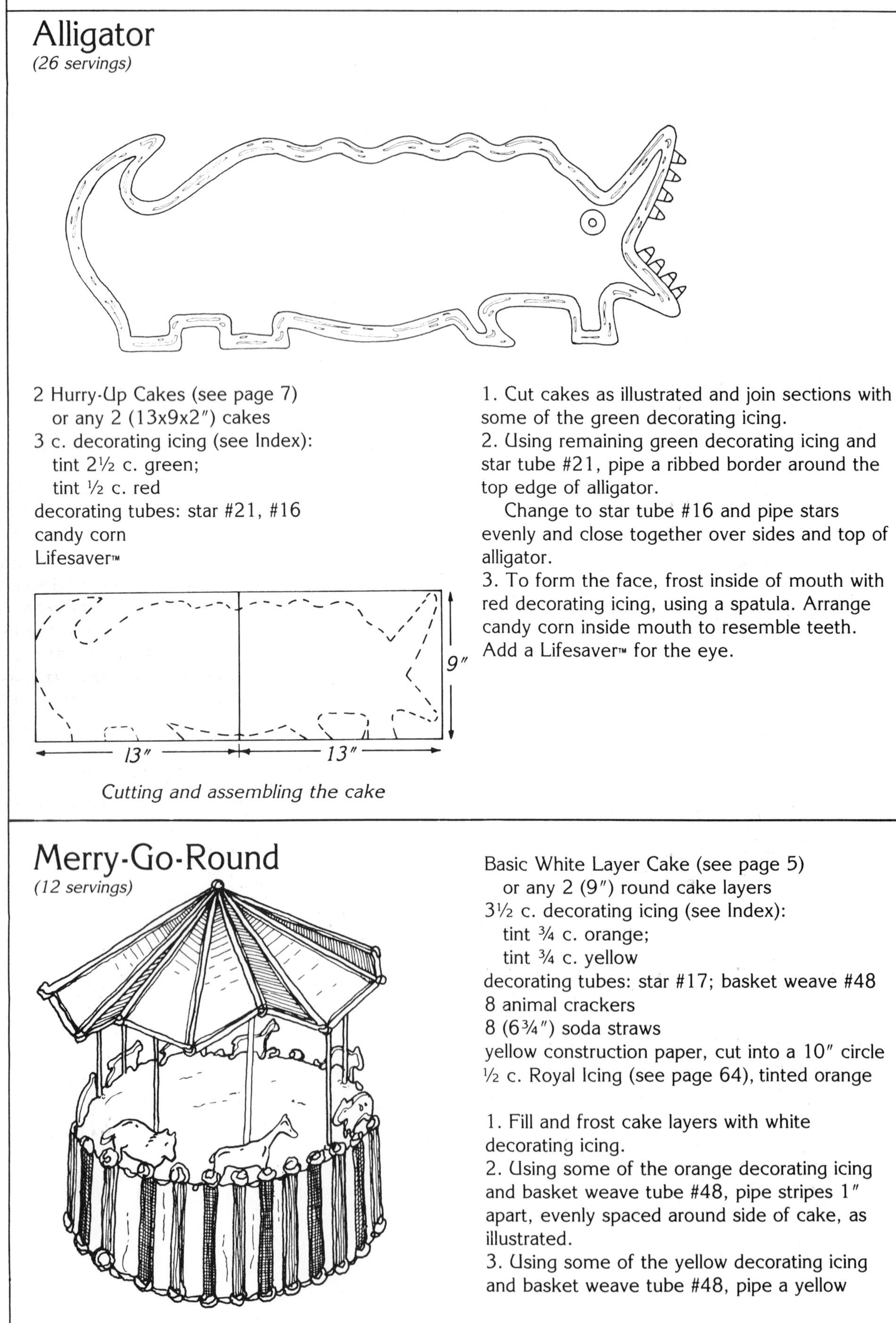

Alligator

(26 servings)

2 Hurry-Up Cakes (see page 7)
  or any 2 (13x9x2″) cakes
3 c. decorating icing (see Index):
  tint 2½ c. green;
  tint ½ c. red
decorating tubes: star #21, #16
candy corn
Lifesaver™

Cutting and assembling the cake

1. Cut cakes as illustrated and join sections with some of the green decorating icing.
2. Using remaining green decorating icing and star tube #21, pipe a ribbed border around the top edge of alligator.
   Change to star tube #16 and pipe stars evenly and close together over sides and top of alligator.
3. To form the face, frost inside of mouth with red decorating icing, using a spatula. Arrange candy corn inside mouth to resemble teeth. Add a Lifesaver™ for the eye.

Merry-Go-Round

(12 servings)

Basic White Layer Cake (see page 5)
  or any 2 (9″) round cake layers
3½ c. decorating icing (see Index):
  tint ¾ c. orange;
  tint ¾ c. yellow
decorating tubes: star #17; basket weave #48
8 animal crackers
8 (6¾″) soda straws
yellow construction paper, cut into a 10″ circle
½ c. Royal Icing (see page 64), tinted orange

1. Fill and frost cake layers with white decorating icing.
2. Using some of the orange decorating icing and basket weave tube #48, pipe stripes 1″ apart, evenly spaced around side of cake, as illustrated.
3. Using some of the yellow decorating icing and basket weave tube #48, pipe a yellow

To assemble this Easter Basket (page 149), begin with a pound cake baked in a 10″ tube pan and swirl it with Lemon Butter Cream frosting. The roses on the side of the cake are made in advance with Royal Icing, and the basket is filled with tiny chocolate-covered eggs—all homemade.

Chocolate cake in any form is hard to resist, and can be as simple or as elaborate as you like.

The Chocolate Mousse Cake above is a triple-layer combination of rich, brownie-like cake layers alternating with a chocolate mousse filling and topped with whipped cream and wedges of pure chocolate (page 112).

The Chocolate-Cherry Cake Roll at left is a no-fuss concoction of chocolate sponge cake and cherry pie filling (page 95).

Christmas cakes are cherished traditions among many American families, and two ideas for creating striking centerpieces are shown on the opposite page.

The Poinsettia Wreath at top starts with a cake baked in a fluted tube pan (page 155); the beautiful blossoms are made with Royal Icing.

The Himmel Torte (opposite, right) is a date-and-nut cake that tastes "heavenly" in any language; for the recipe, see page 105.

This merry Christmas Tree with Marzipan Fruit is made by cutting one 15½x10½" cake into three triangles and reassembling it as a single large triangle (see page 158). The sides of the cake are simply decorated with flaked coconut to point up the colors and shapes of the marzipan fruits.

stripe halfway between each orange stripe.
4. Change to star tube #17 and pipe a yellow rosette at the top and bottom of each orange stripe as shown.
5. Using remaining orange decorating icing and star tube #17, pipe an orange rosette at the top and bottom of each yellow stripe.
6. Stand animal crackers evenly spaced around top edge of cake.

Pleating the paper circle

7. Insert soda straws in cake, placing each one behind an animal cracker as shown.
8. To make the canopy, accordian-pleat the yellow paper circle as shown, making 16 folds.
Using orange Royal Icing and star tube #17, pipe a line over each fold and around the outer edge of the canopy. Then pipe a rosette at the bottom edge of each fold as shown. Pipe one more rosette on the center point.
9. Place canopy on top of straws.

Train

(12 servings)

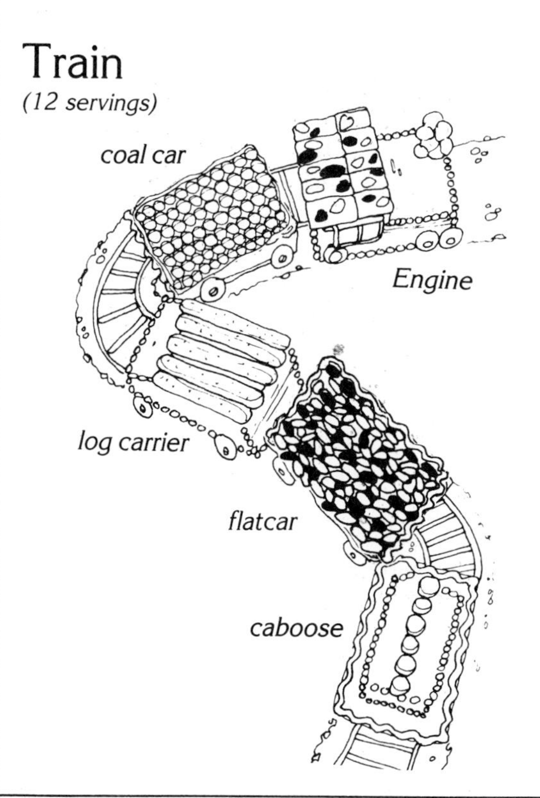

Luscious Banana Layer Cake (see page 36)
or any 2 (8″) square cake layers
2¼ c. decorating icing (see Index):
tint ½ c. black;
tint ¼ c. blue;
tint ¼ c. green;
tint ½ c. red;
tint ¼ c. yellow
2 lollipops
2 rolls Lifesavers™
2 oz. black shoestring licorice
1 large black gumdrop
⅓ c. miniature marshmallows
5 jelly nougats
decorating tube: round #2
¼ c. semisweet chocolate pieces
5 (3″) pretzel rods
¼ c. red cinnamon candies
½ c. graham cracker crumbs

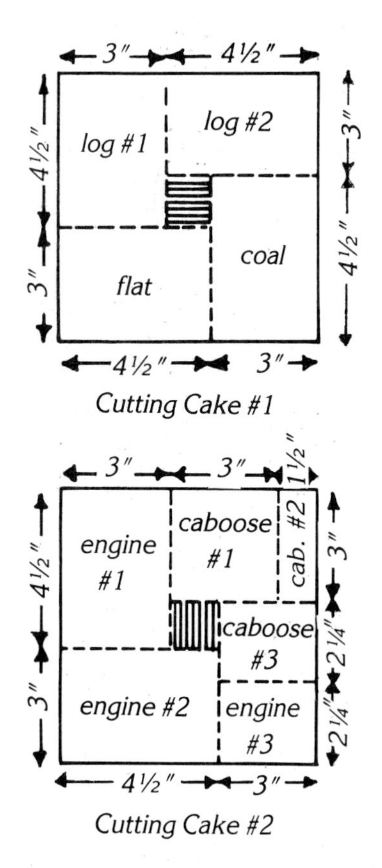

Cutting Cake #1

Cutting Cake #2

1. Cut cakes as illustrated. To make cars, join sections with white decorating icing as follows.
For engine: Stack engine #1 and #2. Place engine #3 crosswise on top as shown.
For coal car: Use coal section as is.
For log car: Trim away 1″ piece from 3″ side of log #1, cutting diagonally. Place on top of log #2.

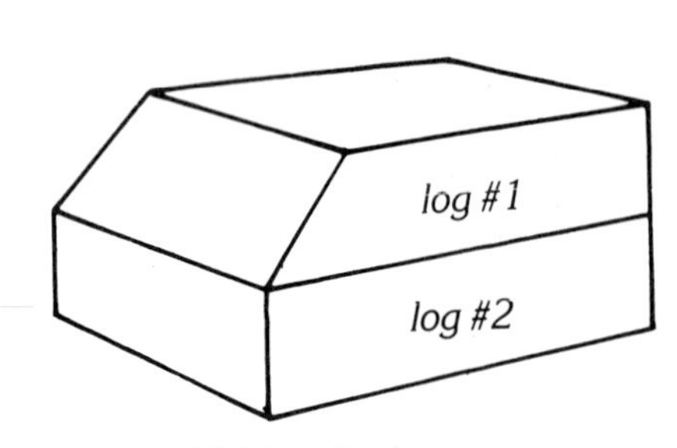

Making the log car

For flatcar: Use flatcar section as is.

For caboose: Center caboose #2 on top of caboose #1. Cut caboose #3 horizontally into 2 equal layers and place one layer on top of caboose #2. (Set aside remaining layer for snacking.)

2. Arrange cars as shown on a large tray or 22½x16″ sheet of sturdy cardboard covered with foil.
3. Frost the engine black, the coal car blue, the log car white, the flatcar green and the caboose red.
4. To decorate engine, remove sticks from lollipops and place a candy on each side for back wheels. To make front wheels, add two Lifesavers™ on each side.

Cut licorice into 1″ pieces for windows. Add several ½″ pieces to make cowcatcher at front.

Place gumdrop at front for smokestack. Attach marshmallows to top of gumdrop with white frosting. Cut nougats in half and place on roof.

5. To decorate coal car, using yellow decorating icing and round tube #2, pipe a zigzag border on top edges. Cover top with chocolate pieces.
6. To decorate log car, using red decorating icing and round tube #2, pipe a bead border on all edges of car. Cover top with pretzel rods.
7. To decorate flatcar, using white decorating icing and round tube #2, pipe a zigzag border on top edges. Cover top with cinnamon candies.
8. To decorate caboose, continue with white decorating icing and round tube #2 to pipe a zigzag border on top edge of car.

Using blue decorating icing and round tube #2, pipe a bead border on top edges of roof. Decorate roof with a row of marshmallows.

9. Place Lifesaver™ wheels on all cars.
10. Sprinkle graham cracker crumbs between the cars. Cut licorice into strips and arrange in the shape of tracks.

Ring-around-the-Rosy

(12 servings; see photo, page 81)

Blue Ribbon Yellow Cake (see page 6)
  or any 2 (9″) round cake layers
4 c. decorating icing (see Index):
  tint ½ c. pink;
  tint ½ c. yellow;
  tint ½ c. green
assorted paste food colors for facial features
small paintbrush
6 (1″) round white chocolate mints
6 (1″) round flat lollipops
6 (1¾″) paper muffin-pan liners in pastel colors
decorating tubes: rose #104; star #17
12 small gumdrops, cut in half
6 birthday candles
6 candle holders

1. Fill and frost cake layers with 2¼ c. white decorating icing. Smooth icing, using a metal spatula.
2. Using paste food colors and brush, paint faces and hair on mints. Place a dab of icing on the back of each mint and attach mints to lollipops.

To form bonnets, cut away a ¾″-wide strip from the pleated side of each paper muffin-pan liner and discard. Attach each paper liner to the back of a lollipop with a dab of icing as shown (see photo, page 81). Insert lollipops around the cake, evenly spaced, facing center of cake.

3. Using pink decorating icing and rose tube #104, pipe several rows of ruffle border below one lollipop, starting at the bottom, to make doll's dress. Pipe the last two rows of the dress so they extend across the top edge of the cake to make arms as shown. (When all arms are extended the dolls will join hands in a circle.) Repeat to make a second pink dress on opposite side of cake.

Then make 2 yellow and 2 green dresses in the same manner, piping them so that colors alternate.

4. Add gumdrop halves for hands and feet. Arrange candle holders and candles above hands.
5. Using white decorating icing and star tube #17, pipe a star border around bottom edge of cake, between dolls.

Rag Dolls

(12 servings; see photo, page 81)

3½ c. Royal Icing (see page 64):
tint 2 c. blue;
tint ½ c. pink;
tint 1 tblsp. red;
tint ⅓ c. yellow
decorating tubes: large round #6; round #11, #1; star #21, #17; leaf #67
4 soda straws
8 birthday candles
Luscious Banana Layer Cake (see page 36) or any 2 (8″) square cake layers
3½ c. decorating icing (see Index):
tint 2½ c. pale yellow;
tint 1 c. medium yellow

Piping the rag dolls

In advance:

1. One day in advance, make 8 rag dolls as follows.

Using blue Royal Icing and large round tube #6, apply maximum pressure and squeeze out 8 upright pear-shaped bodies about 2″ high as illustrated. For support, push a soda straw down into each body. Cut straws ¼″ above bodies.

2. Using white Royal Icing and star tube #21, pipe bloomers at base of each body.

3. Using blue Royal Icing and leaf tube #67, pipe 2 rows of ruffles around each body as shown.

Continuing with blue Royal Icing, change to round tube #11 and pipe arms. Insert a birthday candle between each pair of arms.

4. Using white Royal Icing and star tube #21, pipe stars for hands.

Using pink Royal Icing and round tube #11, pipe legs extending from ends of bloomers.

Change to large round tube #6 and pipe a ball for head on top of each body as shown.

5. Using blue Royal Icing and round tube #11, pipe shoes.

Change to round tube #1 and pipe eyes.

Using red Royal Icing and round tube #1, pipe mouths.

Using yellow Royal Icing and star tube #17, pipe hair as shown.

Allow dolls to dry until completely hard.

To assemble:

1. Fill and frost top and sides of cake with pale yellow decorating icing. Smooth icing, using a metal spatula.
2. Using medium-yellow decorating icing and star tube #21, pipe a shell border around top and bottom edges and down each corner of cake.
3. Center 4 Royal Icing dolls on top of cake with 1 doll facing each corner.
4. Place a Royal Icing doll at each corner of cake base (see photo, page 81).

Classic Car

(16 servings; see photo, page 82)

Foolproof Chocolate Cake (see page 17) or any 13x9x2″ cake
5 c. decorating icing (see Index):
tint ½ c. black;
tint ¼ c. brown;
tint ¼ c. gray;
tint ½ c. red;
tint 2½ c. blue
decorating tubes: round #3; star #21
silver dragées

1. Reserve ¼ c. white decorating icing. With remaining white decorating icing, thinly frost top and sides of cake.
2. Trace pattern for car (see page 144) on a sheet of paper. Use a toothpick to transfer pattern to top of cake.
3. Using black decorating icing and round tube #3, pipe an outline of car.

Change to star tube #21 and pipe stars evenly and close together to fill areas indicated, following the color chart (or see photo on page 82).

4. Continuing with star tube #21, fill in remaining areas with brown, gray, white and red in the same way, following the color chart.
5. Using blue decorating icing and star tube #21, pipe stars evenly and close together to fill sides and top of cake.
6. Using reserved white decorating icing and star tube #21, pipe a star border around top of cake.
7. Decorate horn and hub caps with silver dragées.

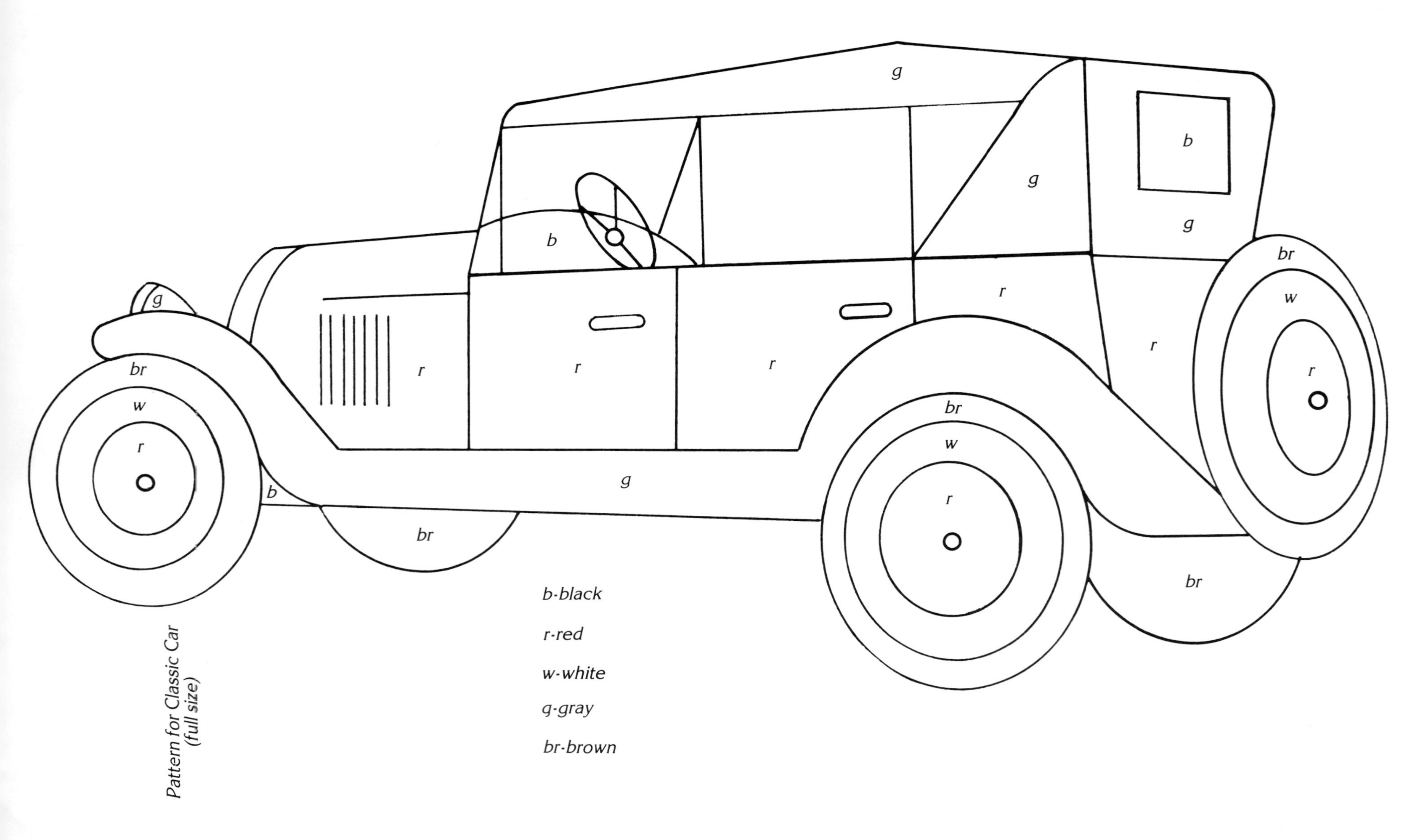

Pattern for Classic Car
(full size)

6

Cakes for Holidays and Seasons

No matter what the season, a decorated cake adds something special to any celebration.

Kick off the New Year with a sheet cake marked off into a football field, and your armchair quarterbacks will cheer. With a little creative magic, you can change a round and a square cake layer into a super-sized valentine like the one pictured on page 84. Or celebrate Presidents' Day with a patriotic 4-layer stovepipe hat piped with a star tube in red, white and blue (see page 82)—a good choice for your Fourth of July celebration, too!

A lattice shamrock tops our St. Patrick's Day cake. Follow an Irish tradition and bake a foil-wrapped coin inside the cake; legend tells us that the person who finds the coin will have good luck for the rest of the year.

Instead of buying Easter candy this year, make Easter Egg cakelets. Each is made by joining two cupcakes with a little icing, then frosting with chocolate or pastel frosting and decorating with garlands of tiny flowers.

If you're ambitious, you can make your own Easter baskets complete with chocolate eggs. A Pennsylvania man sent us his recipe for the spectacular Easter Basket cake pictured on page 137. It starts with a pound cake baked in a 10″ tube pan and frosted with Lemon Butter Cream; then it's filled with miniature chocolate Easter eggs. As you'd expect, this cook is well known for his creation, and several of his lucky friends and neighbors look forward to receiving one of these baskets every Easter.

For Mother's Day, most any of the pretty cakes in this book would tell Mom you love her, and in this chapter you'll also find a more challenging creation, an ultra-feminine Candy Box filled with real chocolates and topped with Royal Icing flowers (see page 103).

Of course, holiday cakes needn't be elaborate. You won't need a decorating tube to say "Hats off!" to a graduate by baking a batch of Graduation Cap Cupcakes—they're made by joining cupcakes and graham crackers to form miniature mortarboards.

Our Watermelon cake is a novel idea for a picnic basket; it's an angel food cake baked in a big bowl, then simply decorated with stripes of butter cream frosting in contrasting shades of green.

Autumn signals the start of a busy season, and you'll find an idea for easing your children back into the classroom with a Back-to-School Blackboard, plus some new tricks to turn cupcakes into Halloween treats.

Let a whimsical Tom Turkey cake enliven your Thanksgiving table after you carve the real turkey, and choose from a selection of cakes for the joyful celebrations of Christmas and Chanukah, including a Christmas tree with marzipan fruit.

For some extra-easy Christmas cakes, turn to our recipes for Individual Fruitcakes and Fruitcake Packages, page 98.

Football Field

(16 servings)

Chocolate Torte, cake only (see page 106) or any 15½x10½x1″ cake
3 c. decorating icing (see Index):
tint 1¾ c. green;
tint 2 tblsp. blue;
tint 2 tblsp. red;
tint ¼ c. gold
decorating tubes: star #21, #17; round #3

1. Frost top and sides of cake with green decorating icing. Smooth icing, using a metal spatula.
2. Using some of the white decorating icing and star tube #21, pipe a shell border around bottom edges of cake.
3. Use a toothpick to draw a 4″ circle on top of cake. Trace pattern for football helmet on a sheet of paper and cut out. Use a toothpick to trace pattern inside circle as illustrated.
4. Frost helmet with blue decorating icing, using a small spatula. Use more of the white decorating icing to frost remainder of circle.
5. Using red decorating icing and round tube #3, pipe chin guard. Using white decorating icing and round tube #3, pipe in the hinge on the chin guard.
6. Use a toothpick to mark 11 yard lines, 1″ apart, across the top of cake as shown, starting at the center. Mark the number for each line as shown. Then mark lines for goal posts at both ends of the field.

Using remaining white decorating icing and round tube #3, pipe the yard lines and numbers.
7. Using gold decorating icing and star tube #17, pipe in goal posts.

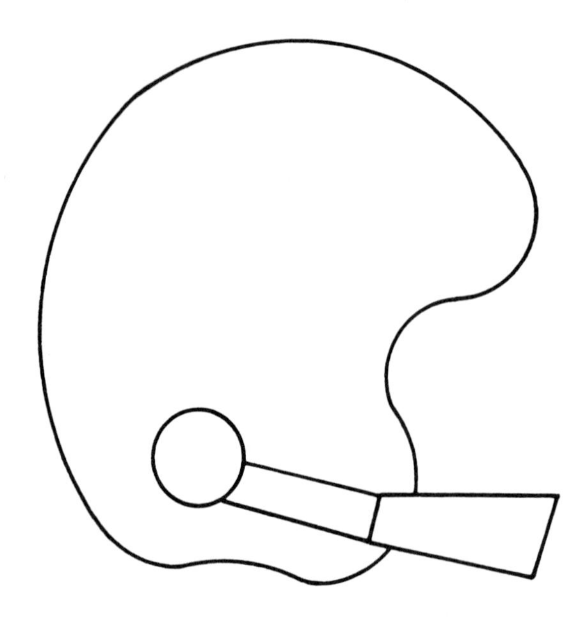

Pattern for football helmet (full size)

Sweetheart Cake

(12 servings; see photo, page 84)

Silver White Cake (see page 6), baked into 1 (8″) square and 1 (8″) round layer, or any 8″ square and round cake layers
4 c. decorating icing (see Index):
tint 2½ c. light pink;
tint ¼ c. dark pink;
tint 2 tblsp. green
decorating tubes: round #3; star #17; drop flower #225, #190; leaf #67

Assembling the cake

1. Cut round cake layer in half to form 2 semicircles. Use some of the light pink decorating icing to attach them to the square cake as illustrated to form a heart.
2. Frost top and sides of cake with more of the light pink decorating icing. Smooth icing, using a metal spatula.
3. Use a toothpick to draw a heart about 7½″ wide on top of cake as shown (see photo, page 84).
4. Using white decorating icing and round tube #3, pipe a lattice pattern inside the design lines of the heart.

Change to star tube #17 and pipe a shell border around the lattice heart and around top edge of cake. Then pipe a double shell border around bottom edge of cake.
5. Using dark pink decorating icing and drop flower tube #190, pipe 9 flowers on one side of lattice heart.
6. Using remaining light pink icing and drop flower tube #225, pipe flowers randomly between dark pink flowers.
7. Using green decorating icing and leaf tube #67, pipe leaves around flowers.

Uncle Sam's Hat

(24 servings; see photo, page 82)

2 recipes for Blue Ribbon Yellow Cake (see page 6) or any 4 (9″) round cake layers
5½ c. decorating icing (see Index):
tint ¾ c. blue;
tint ¾ c. red
1 (12″) cardboard round
decorating tubes: star #24, #21; round #2

1. Fill cake layers with some of the white decorating icing. Center cake on the cardboard round and place on a sturdy base.
2. Thinly frost top and sides of cake with more of the white decorating icing. Smooth icing, using a metal spatula.
3. Using blue decorating icing and star tube #21, pipe stars evenly and close together to make hatband 1½″ wide around the bottom of the cake as illustrated (see photo, page 82).
4. Using red decorating icing and star tube #21, pipe rows of stars 1″ wide to make stripes running from top of hatband to top of cake as shown, leaving 1″ spaces between stripes.
5. Using white decorating icing and star tube #21, pipe rows of stars to fill the areas between the red stripes.
6. Pipe a ring of stars evenly and close together all around the top edge of hat. Repeat with another ring of stars within the first one, and continue until top of hat is covered with stars. Then cover the cardboard round with stars in the same way to form the brim of the hat, starting at the edge of the hatband and working outward.
7. Change to round tube #2 and pipe an outline of a 5-pointed star on hatband directly under each red stripe.
Change to star tube #24 and pipe stars to fill the outlines of stars on the hatband.

Variation: To make this cake as a St. Patrick's Day Hat, tint 4 c. of the decorating icing green and 1½ c. yellow.
1. Fill cake layers with some of the green decorating icing and place on a 12″ cardboard round. Thinly frost top and sides of cake with more of the green decorating icing. Smooth icing, using a metal spatula.
2. Using yellow decorating icing and star tube #21, pipe stars evenly and close together to form a 1½″-wide hatband around bottom of cake.
3. Trace large shamrock pattern from Shamrock Cake (see page 148) on a sheet of paper and cut out. Trace pattern on top of cake, using a toothpick, and fill in shamrock with more yellow decorating icing and star tube #21. Then pipe a star border around the top edge of the hat and around the edge of the hat brim, using remaining yellow decorating icing and star tube #21.
4. Using green decorating icing and star tube #21, fill area around shamrock on top of the hat, area above the hatband on the sides of the hat and remaining area on the hat brim.

Shamrock

(12 servings)

Silver White Cake (see page 6) or any 2 (9″) round cake layers
3½ c. decorating icing (see Index):
tint 2¾ c. yellow;
tint ¾ c. green
decorating tubes: round #8, #2; star #21, #16

1. Fill and frost top and sides of cake, using some of the yellow decorating icing. Smooth icing, using a metal spatula.
2. Trace shamrock patterns on a sheet of paper

Pattern for small shamrocks (full size)

Pattern for large shamrock (full size)

and cut out. Use a toothpick to trace large shamrock pattern on top of cake as illustrated. Then trace 8 small shamrocks evenly spaced around the side of the cake as shown.
3. Using some of the green decorating icing and round tube #2, pipe a lattice pattern inside the design lines of the large shamrock.
Change to star tube #16 and outline the large shamrock with a shell border.
4. Change to round tube #8 and fill small shamrocks inside the design lines.
5. Using remaining yellow decorating icing and star tube #21, pipe a star border around the bottom and top edges of cake.

Easter Eggs

(12 servings)

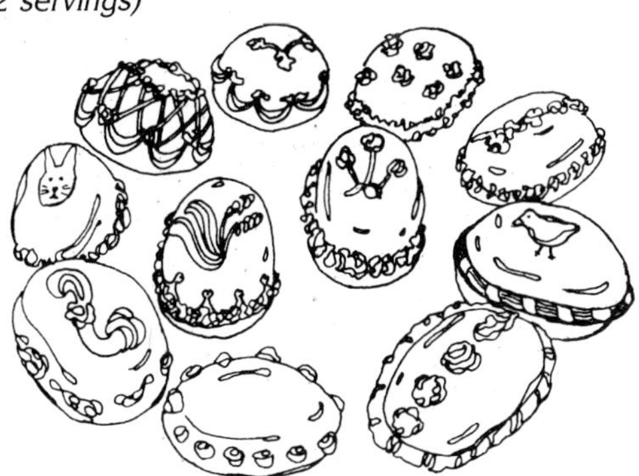

Light Chocolate Brownie Cupcakes (see page 21) or any 24 cupcakes
4 c. Chocolate Butter Cream Icing (see page 61)
2 c. decorating icing (see Index):
tint ⅓ c. pink;
tint ⅓ c. yellow;
tint ⅓ c. lavender;
tint ⅔ c. green
decorating tubes: round #8, #3; star #17; leaf #67, #65; rose tube #102; drop flower #225

1. To make one egg, arrange 2 cupcakes with tops together and join with some of the Chocolate Butter Cream Icing. (If necessary, trim the tops of the cupcakes to make them level.) Frost sides and top of egg with Chocolate Butter Cream Icing. Repeat with remaining cupcakes.
2. Using assorted colors of decorating icing and decorating tubes of your choice, pipe decorations on eggs.
To make dots, lattice work, flower stems and animal figures such as bunnies and chicks, use round tube #8 and #3.
To make star borders, shell borders and rosette flowers, use star tube #17.
To make leaves and ruffled borders, use leaf tubes #67 and #65.
To make rosebuds and scalloped ribbon borders, use rose tube #102.
To make flowers, use drop flower tube #225.
Variation: To frost these eggs pink or another pastel color, omit Chocolate Butter Cream Icing and use 6 c. decorating icing. Set aside ⅓ c. of the icing for white accents. Tint 4 c. of the icing pink or the color of your choice, and tint the remainder in assorted pastel colors.

Easter Basket

(12 servings; see photo, page 137)

4 c. Royal Icing (see page 64):
tint ½ c. light green;
tint 1½ c. light yellow;
tint 1½ c. light pink;
tint ½ c. light blue
decorating tubes: drop flower #225; round #2; rose large #125; leaf #67
Chocolate Easter Eggs (recipe follows)
Coconut Pound Cake (see page 44) or any pound cake baked in a 10″ tube pan
Lemon Butter Cream (recipe follows)
½ c. coconut, tinted green
corrugated cardboard
6′ ribbon, ¾″ wide
1 ribbon bow

In advance:

1. Cover and refrigerate light green Royal Icing for later use.
2. Using ½ c. of the light yellow Royal Icing and drop flower tube #225, pipe 28 yellow drop flowers. Repeat, using ½ c. of the light pink and ½ c. of the light blue Royal Icing, for a total of 84 flowers.
Change to round tube #2 and pipe centers on flowers, using assorted contrasting colors of Royal Icing.
3. Using remaining light yellow Royal Icing and rose tube large #125, pipe 5 roses. Repeat with remaining light pink Royal Icing and pipe 5 more roses.
4. Allow flowers to dry about 8 hours.
5. Prepare Chocolate Easter Eggs.

Chocolate Easter Eggs

3 oz. cream cheese, softened
½ c. butter, softened
4 c. sifted confectioners' sugar
1½ tsp. vanilla
1 (12-oz.) pkg. semisweet chocolate pieces
2 oz. paraffin wax

Cream together cream cheese and butter in a bowl, using an electric mixer at medium speed. Gradually add confectioners' sugar and vanilla; beat well.

Roll mixture into 84 miniature eggs, using about 1 tsp. for each egg. Place eggs on a waxed paper-lined baking sheet.

Refrigerate 30 minutes.

Melt chocolate pieces and paraffin in top of double boiler over hot (not boiling) water. Remove from heat but keep mixture over hot water.

Dip each egg into chocolate mixture and lift it out with a spoon. Gently shake spoon until chocolate is smooth. Place chocolate egg on a cooling rack set over waxed paper. Immediately place a Royal Icing drop flower on chocolate egg, before the chocolate is set.

Repeat until 84 eggs are decorated.

Beat reserved light green Royal Icing until stiff glossy peaks form. Using some of the light green Royal Icing and leaf tube #67, pipe a leaf beside each flower. Refrigerate remaining green icing.

To assemble:

1. Frost top and sides of cake with Lemon Butter Cream. Swirl frosting, using a metal spatula.
2. Sprinkle coconut around the hole in the center of cake, and around bottom edge of cake as shown (see photo, page 137).

Fill the hole with chocolate eggs and arrange some of the remaining eggs on top of cake over hole and coconut as illustrated. Serve remaining eggs separately.

3. Arrange light yellow and light pink Royal Icing roses around the side of the cake in 2 semicircles as shown, alternating colors.

Using remaining light green Royal Icing and leaf tube #67, pipe leaves around roses.

4. To make the handle, cut a U-shaped strip of corrugated cardboard about 10½x½". Cover it with ribbon and attach bow. Insert a toothpick in each end of the handle and push the handle down into the cake.

Lemon Butter Cream

½ c. butter or regular margarine, softened
¼ c. fresh lemon juice
½ tsp. grated lemon rind
4½ c. sifted confectioners' sugar
1½ tsp. vanilla

Cream butter in bowl, using an electric mixer at high speed. Add lemon juice and lemon rind alternately with confectioners' sugar, using medium speed; blend in vanilla. Beat at medium speed until smooth. Makes 2¼ c.

Easter Bunny

(12 servings)

Lemon Chiffon Cake (see page 53)
  or any 10" tube cake
3½ c. 7-Minute Frosting (see page 62)
1⅓ c. flaked coconut
jelly beans: 2 red; 1 pink
1 (36") strand black shoestring licorice
2 sheets construction paper: 1 pink; 1 white

1. Cut cake as illustrated. Cut leg sections in half horizontally to form 2 hind legs and 2 front legs. Join sections with a little of the 7-Minute Frosting.
2. Frost top and sides of cake with remaining frosting. Sprinkle with coconut to cover.
3. Arrange red and pink jelly beans on head to form eyes and nose as illustrated.
4. Cut licorice into 6 (1½") lengths. Insert 3 lengths on each side of bunny's nose as shown to form whiskers.
5. Trace ear pattern on a sheet of paper, including design lines for inner ear, and cut out.

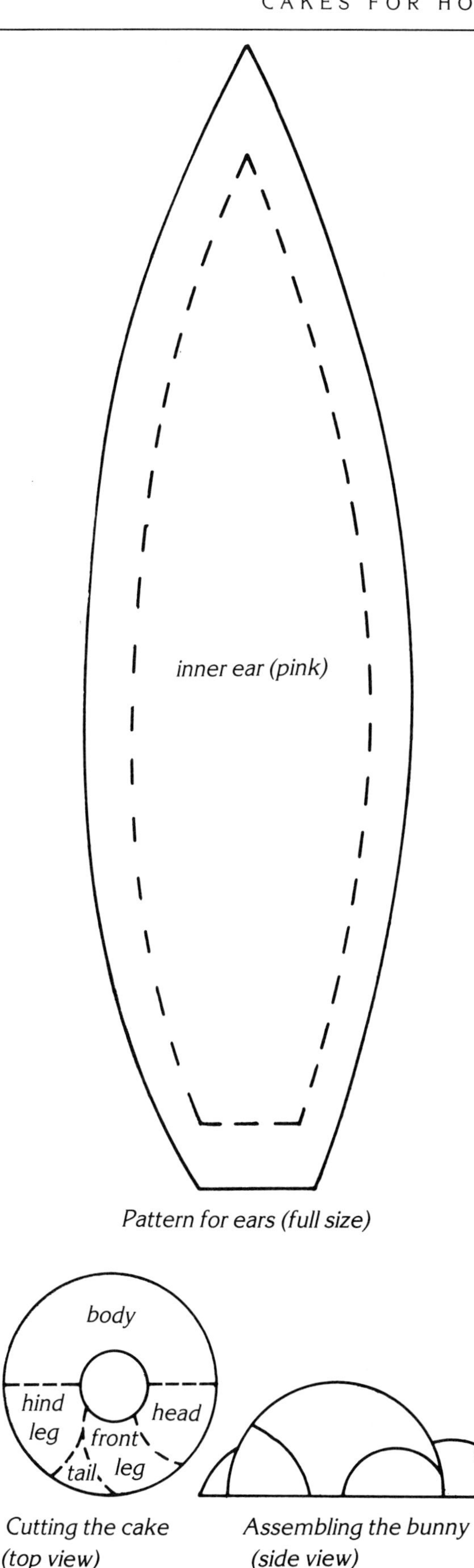

Pattern for ears (full size)

Cutting the cake (top view)

Assembling the bunny (side view)

Cut 2 complete ear patterns from white paper. Then cut away the outer ear from the original pattern and use the remaining pattern to cut 2 inner ears from pink paper.

Tape each pink inner ear to a white ear, fold the straight edge slightly, and insert in head.

Candy Box

(12 servings; see photo, page 103)

Run Sugar Icing (see page 64), tinted pink
3½ c. Royal Icing (see page 64):
  tint ¾ c. violet;
  tint ¼ c. yellow;
  tint ¼ c. green
violet paste food color
Mahogany Cake (see page 19), baked in 2 (9″) square cake pans, or any 2 (9″) square cake layers
3 c. decorating icing (see Index):
  tint 2½ c. pink
1 lb. assorted chocolate candies
decorating tubes: rose #104; round #4, #2; star #17; leaf #67

In advance:

(Preparation for this cake must begin 3 days in advance.)

1. Draw 1 (8¼″) square and 4 (8x¾″) rectangles on a sheet of waxed paper. Lightly grease the paper. Using some of the pink Run Sugar Icing before it is thinned and round tube #4, pipe over outlines of square and rectangles.
   Thin remaining pink Run Sugar Icing and fill in the square and rectangles.
2. Let dry 24 to 36 hours or until completely dry.
3. Set aside 1¼ c. white Royal Icing; cover and refrigerate. (This will be used later to assemble box lid.)
4. Using violet Royal Icing, remaining white Royal Icing and rose tube #104, pipe 18 pansies as follows on individual squares of waxed paper.
   Make some pansies all violet.
   Make some with the first set of back petals white, second set of back petals violet and lower petal white.
   Make some with the first set of back petals violet, second set of back petals white and lower petal violet.
   Make some with both sets of back petals violet and lower petal white.
5. Use yellow Royal Icing and round tube #2 to

pipe a center on each pansy.
6. Let Royal Icing pansies dry overnight.
7. Using violet food paste color and a small paintbrush, paint violet streaks on lower petals of all pansies.
8. To assemble the lid of the box, carefully peel the waxed paper off the Run Sugar square and rectangles and turn the square bottom side up. Using reserved white Royal Icing and star tube #17, pipe a strip of icing around each edge of the square. (If Royal Icing has softened, beat again until stiff, using an electric mixer.)

Stand a rectangle beside each edge of the square, using some of the reserved white Royal Icing to join the corners of the lid.
9. Allow lid to dry overnight.
10. Turn lid right side up on a sheet of waxed paper. Using more of the white Royal Icing and star tube #17, pipe a shell border around bottom edges of lid and down the corners.

Pipe a reverse shell border around top edges of box lid.
11. Attach pansies to top of lid as shown (see photo, page 103), using remaining white Royal Icing.
12. Using green Royal Icing and leaf tube #67, pipe leaves between pansies. Allow to dry overnight.

To assemble:
1. Fill and frost top and sides of cake, using pink decorating icing. Smooth icing, using a metal spatula.
2. Using white decorating icing and star tube #17, pipe a shell border around bottom edges of cake.

Then pipe a reverse shell border around top edges of cake.
3. Arrange chocolates on top of cake. Prop candy box lid on one side of cake.

Father's Day Cake
(12 servings)

Devil's Food Cake (see page 15)
or any 2 (8″) square cake layers
Super-Smooth Chocolate Frosting (see page 15)
Chocolate Icing (see page 61)
decorating tubes: star #32; round #2

1. Fill and frost top and sides of cake with Super-Smooth Chocolate Frosting. Swirl frosting, using a metal spatula.
2. Using some of the Chocolate Icing and star tube #32, pipe a border of tight S-shaped scrolls at top and bottom edges of cake as illustrated.

Use a toothpick to draw a large diamond on top of cake. Then pipe another series of scrolls on top of design lines.
3. Pipe a fleur-de-lis in the center of each side of the cake. Then pipe a fleur-de-lis in each corner on top of the cake.
4. Using remaining Chocolate Icing and round tube #2, pipe an inscription of your choice in the center of the diamond.

Graduation Cap Cupcakes
(12 servings)

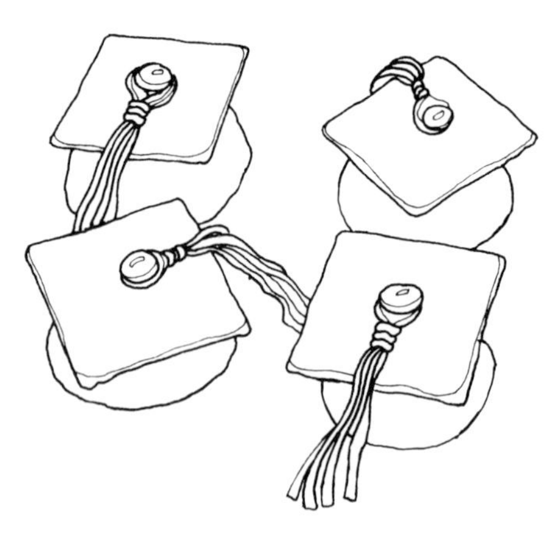

batter for Feather-light Yellow Cake (see page 7), baked into 12 cupcakes, or any 12 cupcakes
1¼ c. Chocolate Butter Cream Icing (see page 61)
12 squares chocolate-covered graham crackers
4⅔ yd. white yarn
12 dark brown candy-coated chocolates

1. To make each cap, place a cupcake upside-down and frost sides and top with Chocolate Butter Cream Icing, reserving 2 tblsp.
   Place a graham cracker square on top of each cupcake.
2. To make tassels, cut the yarn into 24 (7″) lengths. Holding 2 lengths together, fold them in half and tie a knot about ½″ from the fold to form a loop. Repeat with remaining yarn to form 12 tassels.
3. Place a little Chocolate Butter Cream Icing in the center of each graham cracker. Center the loop of a tassel on top of each cupcake and lightly press a candy-coated chocolate over each tassel to secure it.

Watermelon

(12 servings)

batter for Super Angel Food Cake (see page 45), or batter for any 10″ angel food cake
red food coloring
⅓ c. semisweet chocolate pieces
green food coloring
1½ c. butter cream frosting (see Index):
   tint ¾ c. dark green;
   tint ¾ c. medium green

1. Prepare batter as directed. Divide batter in half.
   Tint half the batter bright pink; then fold in chocolate pieces. Tint remaining batter green.
2. Spread green batter evenly in bottom and up sides of ungreased, 4-qt. oven-safe bowl.
3. Spoon pink batter into center of green batter.
4. Bake in 375° oven 35 minutes, or until top springs back when touched.
5. Invert cake in bowl on rack and cool. Remove cake from bowl.
6. Frost cake, round side up, alternating dark green with medium green butter cream frosting in vertical stripes to resemble watermelon rind.

Back-to-School Blackboard

(16 servings)

Carrot Cake (see page 36)
   or any 13x9x2″ cake
2½ c. decorating icing (see Index):
   tint ½ c. light gray;
   tint ½ c. yellow;
   tint ¼ c. red;
   tint ¼ c. green;
   tint ¾ c. charcoal gray
decorating tubes: basket weave #47; star #17; round #8, #2

1. Frost sides of cake with some of the light gray decorating icing. Smooth icing, using a metal spatula.
   Using remaining light gray icing and basket weave tube #47, hold tube flat side up and pipe a band across the top edge of the cake as illustrated. Then pipe a band down both sides of the cake, from top to bottom. Pipe another band across the cake, 1½″ below the top band.
   Turn tube tooth edge up and pipe a band across the bottom of the cake. Then pipe another band just above it to form a double band.
2. Using yellow decorating icing and star tube #17, pipe stars evenly and close together to fill the area between the two bands at the top of the cake.
3. Using red decorating icing and round tube #2, pipe an apple on each side of the yellow band.
4. Using green decorating icing and round tube #2, pipe the words *Welcome Back!* over the yellow band.
5. Using some of the charcoal gray decorating icing, frost remaining area on top of cake to form the blackboard. Smooth icing, using a metal spatula.

Using remaining charcoal gray decorating icing and round tube #2, pipe stems on apples.

Change to round tube #8 and pipe a bead border around bottom edges of blackboard.

6. Using white decorating icing and round tube #2, pipe *2 + 2 = 4* on blackboard. Then pipe a 2½″ strip over the light gray band at the bottom to resemble chalk.

Jack-o'-Lantern

(24 servings)

2 recipes for Pumpkin Pound Cake (see page 44) baked into 2 (10″) fluted tube pans, or any 2 (10″) fluted tube pan cakes
4¾ c. decorating icing (see Index):
tint 4 c. orange;
tint ¾ c. green
2½″ cardboard round
decorating tubes: star #17, large #4; round #2; leaf #67

1. If necessary, trim the tops of the cakes to make them level.
2. Spread some of the orange decorating icing on flat side of 1 cake with a spatula. Place the second cake on top, rounded side up, being careful to match the ridges on the sides of cakes.
3. Place the cardboard round over the hole in top of the cake. Frost top and sides of cake with remaining orange decorating icing.
4. Using green decorating icing and large star tube #4, pipe stem on top of cake as illustrated.

Change to round tube #2 and pipe tendrils around bottom of cake.

Change to leaf tube #67 and pipe leaves around bottom of cake.

Use a toothpick to mark eyes, nose and mouth. Change to star tube #17 and pipe face.

Jack-o'-Lantern Cupcakes

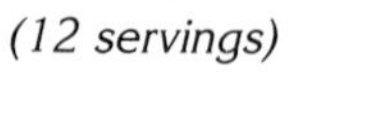

(12 servings)

Light Chocolate Brownie Cupcakes (see page 21) or any 24 cupcakes
4⅔ c. decorating icing (see Index):
tint 4 c. orange;
tint ⅔ c. green
decorating tubes: star #21; round #2; leaf #67

1. If necessary, trim the tops of the cupcakes to make them level.
2. To make each pumpkin, join 2 cupcakes with tops together, using some of the orange decorating icing. Frost top and sides of pumpkin. Repeat with remaining cupcakes.
3. Using green decorating icing and star tube #21, pipe stem on top of each pumpkin as illustrated.

Change to round tube #2 and pipe tendrils on top of pumpkins; then pipe faces.

Change to leaf tube #67 and pipe leaves on top of each pumpkin.

Thanksgiving Turkey

(16 servings)

1⅔ c. Royal Icing (see page 64):
- tint ⅓ c. gold;
- tint ⅓ c. orange;
- tint ⅓ c. yellow;
- tint ½ c. red

batter for Silver White Cake (see page 6), baked in a 13x9x2″ baking pan and 1 (10-oz.) custard cup
1½ c. butter cream frosting (see Index)
1 c. Chocolate Butter Cream Icing (see page 61)
decorating tubes: star #21, #17; round #2; leaf #67

In advance:

1. Trace patterns for turkey's tail feathers (see page 156) and head and neck on a sheet of paper. Place a sheet of waxed paper over patterns.
2. Using gold Royal Icing and star tube #21, outline 4 feathers on top of waxed paper, following the color chart. Then outline orange, yellow and red feathers in the same way. (You should have some yellow and red icing left over.)
3. Continuing with some of the red Royal Icing and star tube #21, outline each side of head and neck and fill in outlines. Cover remaining red icing tightly and refrigerate.
4. Using some of the remaining yellow Royal Icing and round tube #2, pipe an eye on each half of the head. Cover remaining yellow icing tightly and refrigerate.
5. Allow Royal Icing decorations to dry overnight.

To assemble:

1. Peel waxed paper off decorations.
2. Join head and neck sections, flat sides together, using a little red Royal Icing.
3. Frost top and sides of 13x9x2″ cake with white butter cream frosting.
4. Place Royal Icing tail feathers on top of cake. Place the large cupcake on top of lower part of feathers to form the body. Using some of the Chocolate Butter Cream Icing and leaf tube #67, pipe feathers over body.
5. Insert head and neck in top of body as shown.
6. Using remaining yellow Royal Icing and leaf tube #67, pipe beak on head.
7. Using remaining Chocolate Butter Cream Icing and star tube #17, pipe a rosette border around bottom edges of cake.

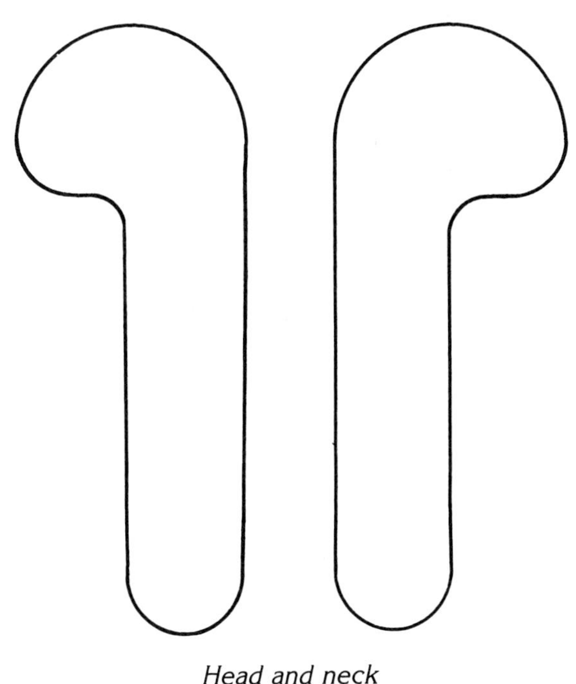

Head and neck patterns for Thanksgiving Turkey (full size)

Poinsettia Wreath

(12 servings; see photo, page 139)

2 cardboard tubes from rolls of waxed paper or aluminum foil
1½ c. Royal Icing (see page 64):
- tint 1 c. red;
- tint ⅓ c. green;
- tint 2 tblsp. yellow

2¼ c. decorating icing (see Index), tinted green
Heirloom Pound Cake (see page 42) or any (10″) fluted tube cake
decorating tubes: round #9, #2; leaf #67
3 strands red shoestring licorice

In advance:

1. To make 4 forms for poinsettia leaves, cut each cardboard tube in half lengthwise.
2. Trace the pattern for the poinsettia leaves 12 times on the same sheet of paper, leaving ¼″ between each leaf. Tape this 12-leaf pattern to countertop.

   Cut 4 (12x2″) strips of waxed paper.

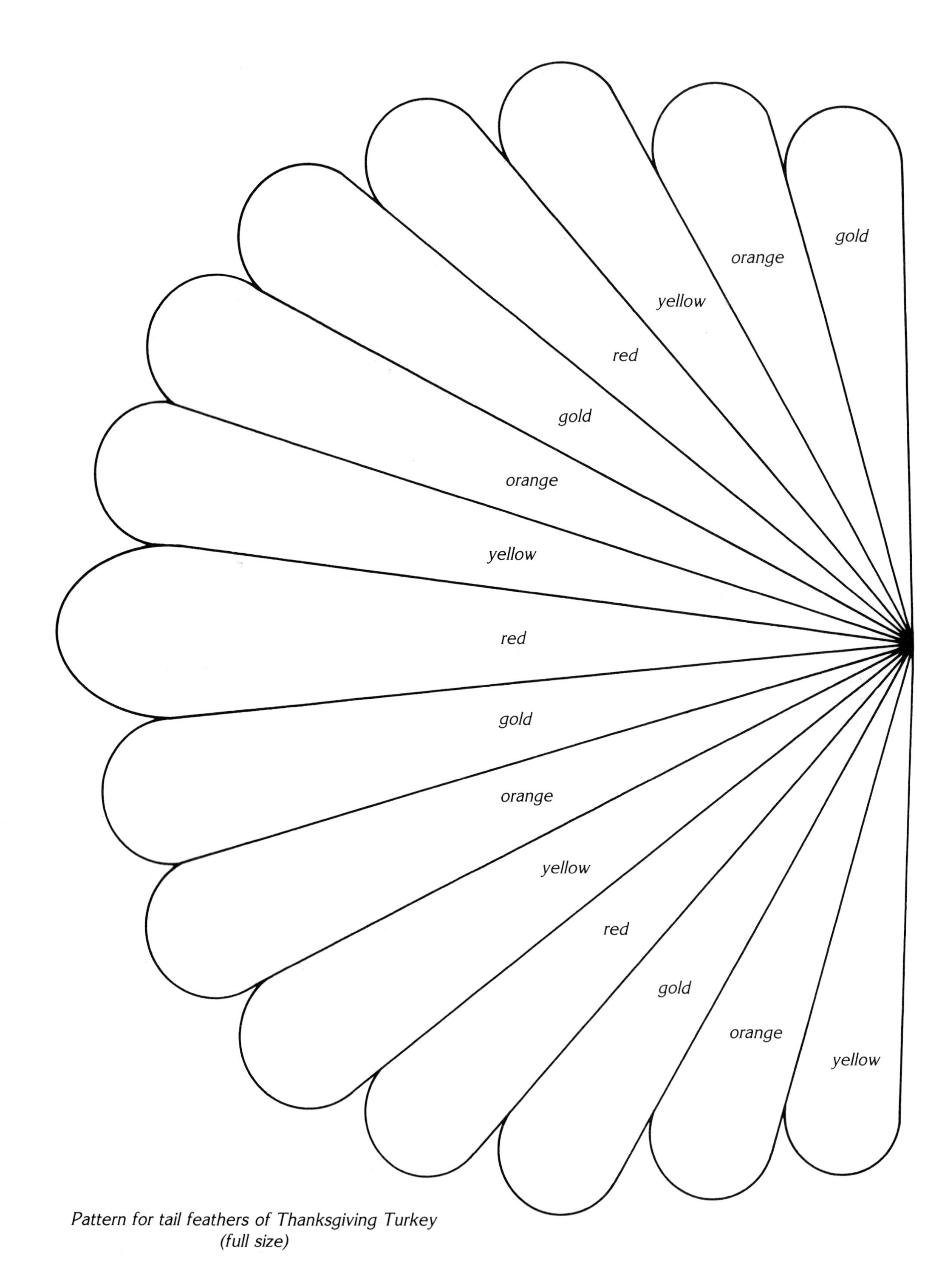

Pattern for tail feathers of Thanksgiving Turkey
(full size)

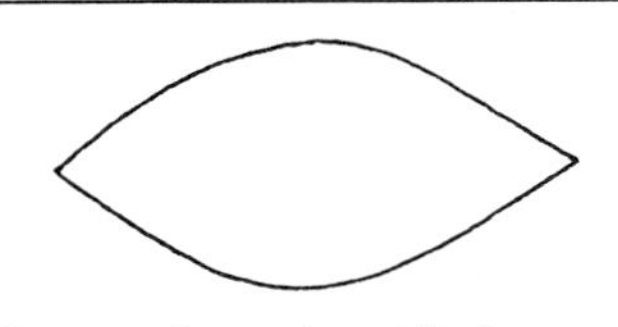

Pattern for poinsettia leaves (full size)

3. Place 1 of the strips over leaf patterns and attach with a dab of Royal Icing.
4. Thin ½ c. of the red Royal Icing (see Run Sugar Icing, page 64).
5. Using remaining red Royal Icing and round tube #2, pipe an outline of each leaf on the waxed paper. Using thinned red Royal Icing and round tube #2, immediately fill in the design lines of each leaf.
6. Immediately lift the waxed paper strips, with leaves, and place them on the outside of one of the cardboard forms to dry.
7. Repeat Steps 3, 5 and 6 to make 12 more leaves; let them dry on the outside of another cardboard form.

Repeat twice more to make 24 more leaves, but let these leaves dry on the insides of the remaining cardboard forms, so that 24 leaves will curve downward and 24 will curve upward.

8. Allow leaves to dry overnight.

To assemble poinsettias:

1. Using green Royal Icing and round tube #9, pipe a mound about ½″ in diameter on a sheet of waxed paper. Insert the pointed ends of 8 leaves into mound, evenly spaced, alternating up-curved and down-curved leaves.
2. Using green Royal Icing and round tube #2, pipe a cluster of green dots in the center of each poinsettia.
3. Using yellow Royal Icing and round tube #2, top each green dot with a yellow dot.

Repeat with remaining leaves to form 6 poinsettias. Let dry overnight.

To assemble wreath:

1. Using green decorating icing and leaf tube #67, pipe concentric rows of green leaves around the cake, starting at the bottom and working up to the top.
2. Arrange the poinsettias on top of the wreath as illustrated (see photo, page 139).
3. Holding 3 strands of licorice together, make a large bow. Place bow at the bottom edge of wreath; press gently to hold in place.

Variation: The poinsettias of this wreath are just the right size to top cupcakes.

Christmas Stocking

(14 servings)

Fluffy Gold Cake (see page 8) or any 13x9x2″ cake
2 c. decorating icing (see Index):
  tint 1½ c. red;
  tint 2 tblsp. green
decorating tubes: rose #104; round #8, #2; leaf #65
6 red cinnamon candies

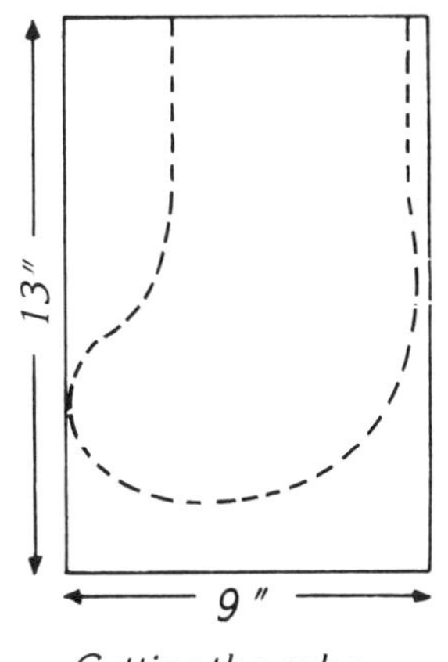

Cutting the cake

1. Cut cake as illustrated.
2. To outline the band at the top of the stocking, use a toothpick to mark a line across the cake, 3″ from the top. Frost the top and sides of the band with some of the white decorating icing. Smooth icing, using a metal spatula.

3. Frost remaining top and sides of stocking with some of the red decorating icing. Smooth icing.
4. Using remaining white decorating icing and rose tube #104, pipe a ruffled edge at bottom of white band.
5. Using more of the red decorating icing and round tube #2, pipe the words *Merry Christmas* on the white band.
6. Using green decorating icing and leaf tube #65, pipe a few leaves so that they touch at the top right corner of the stocking and at the toe.

Center 3 cinnamon candies on each cluster of leaves.
7. Using remaining red decorating icing and round tube #8, pipe a bead border around bottom and top edges of the red portion of the stocking.

Christmas Tree with Marzipan Fruit

(16 servings; see photo, page 140)

1¾ lb. Marzipan (recipe follows)
paste food colors: yellow, red, green, purple and orange
confectioners' sugar
1 egg white, slightly beaten
4½ doz. whole cloves
½ c. corn syrup
2 tblsp. water
Party Baked Alaska (cake only; see page 23) or any 15½x10½x1" cake
1½ recipes for 7-Minute Frosting (see page 62)
1⅓ c. flaked coconut

In advance:

1. Divide marzipan into 5 equal portions. Keep each portion covered when not in use.

Knead a different food paste color into each portion, a bit at a time, kneading until blended. Use just enough orange color to create a peach color.
2. Dust work surface with confectioners' sugar. To shape fruits uniformly, roll a tinted portion of marzipan in the palms of your hands into a cylinder ¾" thick.

Cut the cylinder into ¾" pieces. Then roll each piece into a ball.
3. Form marzipan fruits as follows.

Lemons: Using 2 balls of yellow marzipan, elongate each ball into an oval; then roll it over a grater to roughen texture. Makes 2 lemons.

Pears: Shape the remaining yellow marzipan into 7 balls. Elongate each ball into an oval, then pinch and roll one end. Touch a damp cloth to red paste food color and rub it on pears to give them a blush. Makes 7 yellow pears.

Repeat, using some of the green marzipan, to make 6 green pears.

Apples: Shape red marzipan into 9 balls. Makes 9 apples.

Grapes: Using remaining green marzipan, pinch off a little marzipan, form it into a leaf shape about 1x2" with your hands and curve it over your finger. (This will form a base for a bunch of grapes.)

Break off tiny pieces of marzipan and roll them into balls. Attach to leaf shape by dipping into egg white and pressing to leaf, starting at the pointed tip. Repeat to make 3 more bunches of green grapes.

Repeat with some of the purple marzipan to make 2 bunches of purple grapes.

Plums: Shape remaining purple marzipan into 3 balls. With the dull side of a knife, cut a groove into each plum. Makes 3 plums.

Peaches: Shape some of the peach marzipan into 5 balls. With the dull side of a knife, cut a groove into each peach. Touch a damp cloth to red paste food color and rub it on peaches to give them a blush. Makes 5 peaches.

Oranges: Darken remaining peach marzipan to make it a deeper orange. Shape orange marzipan into 4 balls; then roll them over a grater to ro' ·hen texture. Makes 4 oranges.
4. To make stems, insert a clove, stem end out, into each pear, apple and bunch of grapes. Insert a clove, stem end in, into each plum, peach and orange and into the bottom of each pear.
5. Place fruits on a sheet of waxed paper.
6. To prepare glaze for fruits, combine corn syrup with water in a small saucepan and cook over high heat until it comes to a boil. Remove from heat.

Brush each fruit with glaze and let dry.

To assemble:

1. Cut cake into 3 triangles as illustrated.
2. Arrange the 2 smaller triangles to form a large triangle, joining the sections with some of the 7-Minute Frosting. Spread top of joined triangles with more of the 7-Minute Frosting.

Place the large triangle on top to form a 2-layer triangle.
3. Frost top and sides of triangle with remaining 7-Minute Frosting.
4. Press flaked coconut into sides of cake.
5. Arrange marzipan fruit in rows on top of cake as follows. (See photo, page 140.)

Place 5 bunches of green and purple grapes across the bottom of the cake, starting with green and alternating colors. Then center another bunch of green grapes at the base of the tree.

Place a row of 7 yellow pears above the row of grapes.

Add a row of 6 apples above the pears.

Place a row of 5 peaches above the apples.

Add a row of 5 green pears above the peaches.

Place 4 oranges above the pears.

Add 3 more apples above the oranges.

Place 3 plums above the apples. Then add 2 lemons above the plums.

Top the tree with another green pear.

Marzipan

8 oz. almond paste
2 egg whites
6 c. sifted confectioners' sugar

Knead almond paste by hand in bowl. Add egg whites; knead until well mixed.

Continuing to knead, add confectioners' sugar, 1 c. at a time, until marzipan feels like heavy pie dough.

Cover with plastic wrap and refrigerate in airtight container until ready for use.

Before using, allow to stand at room temperature until soft enough to shape. Makes 1¾ lb.

15½″

10½″

Cutting the cake

Chanukah Menorah

(16 servings)

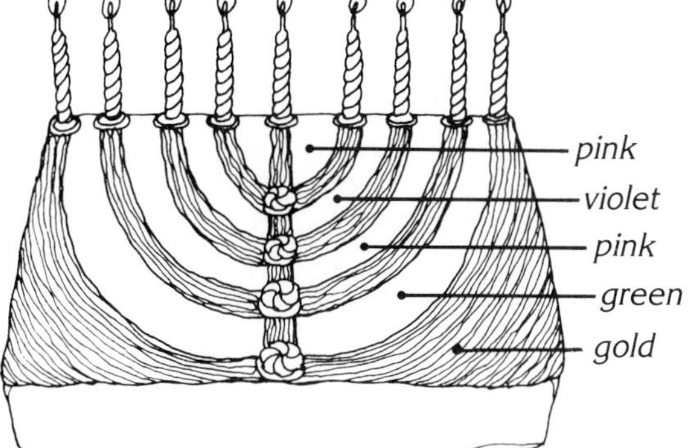

Blue Ribbon Yellow Cake (see page 6)
or any 13x9x2″ cake
3 c. decorating icing (see Index):
tint 1 c. gold;
tint 1 c. violet;
tint ½ c. pink;
tint ½ c. green
decorating tube: star #17
9 Chanukah candles

1. Frost sides of cake with violet decorating icing. Smooth icing, using a metal spatula.
2. Use a toothpick to draw a menorah on top of cake as illustrated.
3. Using some of the gold decorating icing and star tube #17, pipe a stripe over design lines.
4. Using pink decorating icing and star tube #17, pipe stars evenly and close together to fill areas inside the design lines, following the color chart.
5. Using violet decorating icing and star tube #17, pipe stars to fill areas inside the design lines, following the color chart.
6. Using gold decorating icing and star tube #17, pipe stars to fill areas inside the design lines, following the color chart.
7. Using green decorating icing and star tube #17, pipe stars to fill areas inside the design lines, following the color chart.
8. To form candle holders, use remaining gold decorating icing and star tube #17 to pipe a rosette at the end of each design line at the top of the cake as shown.

Pipe 4 rosettes down the center of the cake as shown, centering each one on a gold line.
9. Insert candles in candle holders.

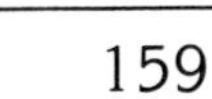

7

Cakes for Engagements, Weddings and Anniversaries

Have you ever wished you could make a wedding cake, but thought you'd never have the time or ability to create a cake worthy of the occasion? With forethought and advance preparation, you can do it—and the love that goes into the baking will add a special leavening to the celebration.

In this chapter are six cakes to get you started; the number of servings they provide ranges from 24 to 150. By changing the colors, borders and other decorations, you can create countless variations on these basic themes.

Our delicately tinted Pink Wedding Cake is just the thing to grace the head table at a springtime nuptial or bridal shower. Trimmed with contrasting white shell borders, each tier is embellished with outlines of hearts piped in white and filled with tiny pink flowers. The crowning touch is a ring of Royal Icing Hearts.

To make any cake elegant, add a spray of crystallized flowers. The technique is simple—just dip thin-petaled blossoms into egg white and dust with sugar. These graceful decorations, together with borders of delicate stringwork, are used in our Wedding Cake with Crystallized Flowers (see page 104), a majestic cake that amply serves 150 well-wishers.

Square and round cake layers combine in the Wedding Cake with Silk Flowers pictured on page 101. For a lovely harmonizing effect, match the color of the silk flowers to the bridesmaids' dresses.

And don't forget the bridegroom! A small informal gathering will be well served by the double-layer chocolate Bridegroom's Cake. Spread with coffee frosting and simply piped with white scrolls, this cake has clean lines that are set off by Royal Icing butterflies.

If time is at a premium, our Anniversary Cake is the solution. Pre-iced frozen cakes, available at your supermarket, let you skip the baking and get right down to decorating. Accented with deep red roses and trimmed with rosette borders, this two-tiered beauty will graciously serve 80 guests.

Whichever cake you decide to make, it will come together smoothly if you plan. Cake layers can be baked up to 3 months in advance and stored in your freezer, and the layers can even be iced before freezing so that you need only thaw them before assembling the tiers and decorating. Royal Icing flowers and decorations can be made several weeks before the big day. Decorating icings can be made days in advance and refrigerated in airtight containers.

To give yourself plenty of time, plan to decorate your wedding cake the day before; the butter cream borders will hold up fine. Refrigeration isn't necessary, but you'll want to set the cake in a cool place, out of direct sunlight.

With much of the preparation finished, you'll find that decorating even the largest wedding cake will be a challenge you meet with pride.

Pink Wedding Cake

(64 servings)

1 c. Royal Icing (see page 64):
  tint 2 tblsp. medium pink;
  tint 2 tblsp. light green
decorating tubes: star #21, #17; drop flower #225; leaf #67
4 recipes for Fluffy Gold Cake (see page 8), baked into 2 (12″) round cake layers, 2 (9″) round cake layers and 2 (6″) round cake layers (You may have some excess batter.)
1½ c. strawberry preserves
10⅔ c. decorating icing (see Index):
  7 c. tinted light pink;
  ⅓ c. tinted medium pink;
  ⅓ c. tinted light green
11 (¼″) wooden dowels, 6″ long
8″ cardboard round
5″ cardboard round
7″ circle of waxed paper
4″ circle of waxed paper

In advance:

1. To form the hearts that will decorate the top of the cake, trace the heart pattern onto a sheet of paper. Place a sheet of waxed paper over the pattern.

Using white Royal Icing and star tube #17, pipe a shell border over the pattern. Repeat to form 2 more hearts.

At the base of each heart pipe 2 horizontal shells, end to end, to make a stand. Then pipe stars to fill the bottom of each heart .

2. Using pink Royal Icing and drop flower tube #225, pipe 3 drop flowers on top of stars at the bottom of each heart.

Using green Royal Icing and leaf tube #67, pipe leaves between flowers, covering the white stars.

3. Cover remaining Royal Icing tightly and refrigerate for later use.

4. Allow hearts to dry overnight.

To assemble:

1. Fill each pair of cake layers with strawberry preserves to form a 12″ bottom tier, a 9″ middle tier and a 6″ top tier.

Place bottom tier on a sturdy base. Place the middle tier on the 8″ cardboard round, and the top tier on the 5″ cardboard round.

2. Frost top and sides of each tier with light pink decorating icing. Smooth icing, using a metal spatula.

3. Center the 7″ circle of waxed paper on top of the bottom tier. Use a toothpick to draw a 7″ circle on top of the tier, using the waxed paper as a pattern.

Remove the waxed paper and insert 1 dowel in the center of the tier and 6 dowels evenly spaced just inside the marked circle. Push each dowel all the way down through the bottom tier; then lift the dowels slightly and use pruning shears to trim them to the same height as the tier. Push the dowels down again, level with the top of the tier.

4. Center the 4″ circle of waxed paper on top of the middle tier. Use a toothpick to draw a 4″ circle on top of the tier, using the waxed paper as a pattern.

Remove the waxed paper and insert 1 dowel

Pattern for heart (full size)

in the center of the tier and 3 dowels evenly spaced just inside the marked circle. Push each dowel all the way down through the middle tier; then trim the dowels level with the tier in the same way as for the bottom tier and push them down again, level with the top of the tier.
5. Center the middle tier, including its cardboard base, on top of the bottom tier. Then center the top tier, including its cardboard base, on the middle tier.
6. Trace the heart pattern on a sheet of paper and cut it out. Using the pattern and a toothpick, trace 6 hearts evenly spaced around the bottom tier. Then mark 4 hearts evenly spaced around the middle tier. Mark 3 more hearts evenly spaced around the top tier.

Using white decorating icing and star tube #17, pipe shells over the outline of each heart.
7. Continuing with white decorating icing and star tube #17, pipe a shell border around the top edge of the bottom tier and around both the bottom and top edges of the other two tiers.

Change to star tube #21 and pipe a shell border around the bottom of the bottom tier.
8. Using medium pink decorating icing and drop flower tube #225, pipe 3 drop flowers in the center of each heart.

Using green decorating icing and leaf tube #67, pipe leaves between flowers.
9. Remove the 3 Royal Icing hearts from waxed paper and stand them upright. To join them in a circle, pipe a dab of white Royal Icing on the back of each heart at its widest edges and join hearts.

Carefully pipe a little Royal Icing on the top tier of the cake where the base of each heart will rest. Place the circle of hearts atop the cake.

Yellow Rose Wedding Cake

(24 servings)

3 c. Royal Icing (see page 64):
  tint 2 ½ c. yellow;
  tint ½ c. green
decorating tubes: rose #104, #102; leaf #67, #65; star #21, #17
2 recipes for Applesauce Layer Cake (see page 27), baked into 2 (9″) round cake layers, 2 (7¼″) round cake layers and 2 (5½″) round cake layers
6½ c. decorating icing (see Index):
  tint ½ c. light green
6¼″ cardboard round
4½″ cardboard round
8 (¼″) wooden dowels, 6″ long
wedding ornament of your choice

In advance:

1. Using some of the yellow Royal Icing and rose tube #104, pipe 16 yellow roses.

Change to rose tube #102 and pipe 68 yellow rosebuds.
2. Using green Royal Icing and leaf tube #65, pipe a leaf on each rosebud.
3. Allow roses and rosebuds to dry overnight.

To assemble:

1. Fill each pair of cake layers with some of the white decorating icing to form a 9″ bottom tier, a 7¼″ middle tier and a 5½″ top tier.

Place the bottom tier on a sturdy base. Place the middle tier on the 6¼″ cardboard round and the top tier on the 4½″ cardboard round.
2. Frost top and sides of each tier with more of the white decorating icing. Smooth icing, using

a metal spatula.
3. Insert 4 of the dowels, evenly spaced, 2¼″ from edge of bottom tier. Then insert remaining 4 dowels, evenly spaced, 2″ from edge of middle tier. (Dowels will extend about 1½″ above tiers to form pillars.)
4. Using some of the green decorating icing and leaf tube #67, pipe leaves over all 8 dowels, covering each dowel completely.
5. Place a Royal Icing rose at the base of each leaf-covered pillar, facing outward as illustrated. Using more of the green decorating icing and leaf tube #67, pipe leaves on 2 sides of each rose.

Add a Royal Icing rosebud on 2 sides of each rose on top of the bottom tier.
6. Using more of the white decorating icing and star tube #21, pipe a rosette border around the bottom edge of the bottom tier.

Continuing with white icing, change to star tube #17 and pipe a rosette border around the bottom edges of both remaining tiers.
7. Use a toothpick to mark 24 points, equally spaced, around the side of the bottom tier, just below the top.

In the same way, mark 20 points around the side of the middle tier and 16 points around the side of the top tier.
8. Continuing with white decorating icing and star tube #17, start at one marked point on the bottom tier and pipe a scallop edging all around the side, joining the points as shown. Repeat to form a scallop edging at the tops of the middle and top tiers.

Place a Royal Icing rosebud above each point of the scallop edging on all 3 tiers.
9. Use a toothpick to mark 4 points equally spaced around the side of the bottom tier, centering each point between two of the roses on the top of the tier. Arrange 2 Royal Icing roses at each point.

Using remaining green decorating icing and leaf tube #67, pipe several leaves around each pair of roses.
10. Center the middle tier, including its cardboard base, on the pillars of the bottom tier, arranging the middle tier so that its roses alternate with the ones below.

Then center the top tier, including its cardboard base, on the pillars of the middle tier. Center the wedding ornament on the top tier.

Bridegroom's Cake

(32 servings)

1 c. Royal Icing (see page 64)
decorating tubes: round #3; star #24, #17
2 recipes for Foolproof Chocolate Cake (see page 17) or any 2 (13x9x2″) cake layers
4 c. Coffee Frosting (see page 60)
1¼ c. decorating icing (see Index)

In advance:

1. To make 5 pairs of butterfly wings to decorate this cake, trace the full-sized pattern below on a sheet of paper.

Place a sheet of waxed paper over the

Pattern for butterfly (full size)

pattern. Using some of the white Royal Icing and round tube #3, pipe over the pattern, starting at the tip of the butterfly's antenna and piping each wing in one continuous motion. Use the same pattern to make 4 more pairs of wings.
2. Cover remaining Royal Icing tightly and refrigerate for later use.
3. Allow wings to dry overnight.
4. Carefully peel waxed paper off wings. Using a dab of Royal Icing, join 2 wings at a right angle. Repeat with remaining wings.
Line a 13x9x2" cake pan with waxed paper and place each butterfly inside so that one wing rests against the side of the pan, to help set the wings at a right angle.
5. Let dry.

To assemble:

1. Fill and frost top and sides of cake layers with Coffee Frosting. Smooth frosting, using a metal spatula.
2. Use a toothpick to mark a continuous scroll pattern on sides of cake, marking 3 scrolls on both long sides as shown and 2 scrolls on each short side. Then mark a rectangle on top of the cake, 1½" inside all edges.
3. Using some of the white decorating icing and star tube #24, pipe a shell pattern over the scrolls.
4. Change to star tube #17 and pipe a garland border around the bottom edges of cake.
Pipe a reverse shell border on the top edges of the cake. Then pipe a reverse shell border over the rectangle on top of the cake.
5. Arrange a Royal Icing butterfly at each corner and place one in the center of the rectangle on top, using a little white decorating icing to attach them.

Anniversary Cake

(80 servings)

2½ c. Royal Icing (see page 64):
  tint 2 c. red;
  tint ½ c. green
yellow food coloring
decorating tubes: rose large #125, #104; leaf #67; round #4; star #17
10 store-bought frozen white layer cakes, each 6" square, 2 layers high, and frosted with white icing
5 c. decorating icing (see Index)

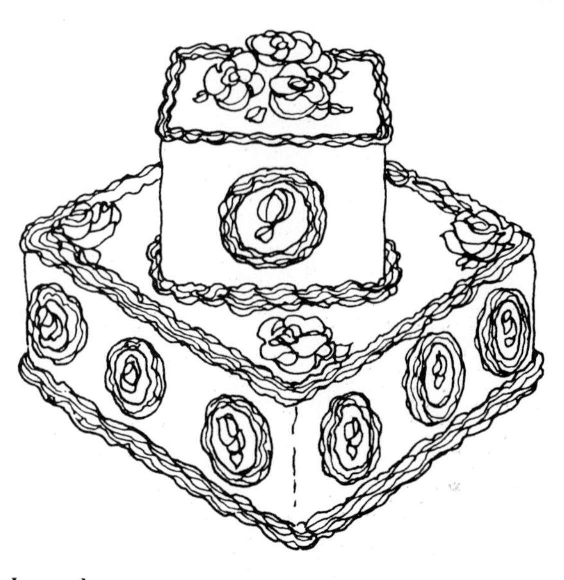

In advance:

1. Using red Royal Icing and rose tube #125, pipe 9 roses.
Change to rose tube #104 and pipe 16 rosebuds.
2. Using green Royal Icing and round tube #4, pipe stems on rosebuds. Cover remaining Royal Icing tightly and refrigerate for later use.
3. Allow roses to dry overnight.

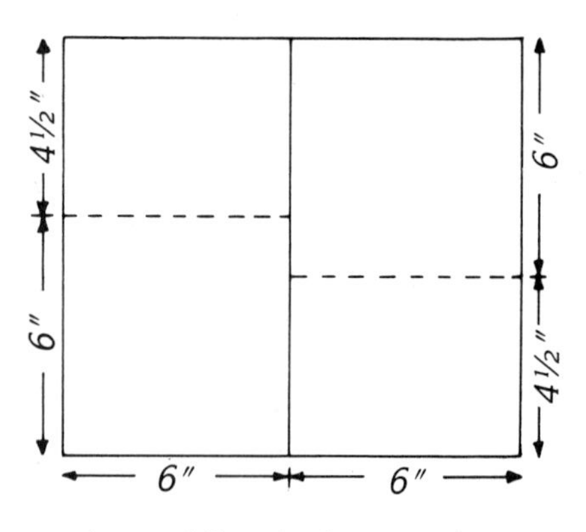

Assembling the bottom tier

To assemble:

1. Trim 1½" from one side of 4 of the cake layers. Arrange 2 of the trimmed layers and 2 of the untrimmed layers on a 16" platter or sturdy base as illustrated, placing cut sides inward. Repeat, stacking 4 more cakes on top.
2. Stack the 2 remaining cakes to form the top tier. Place this tier on the bottom tier, arranging it as shown so that each corner points toward the center of one side of the bottom tier.

3. Allow frosting on frozen cakes to thaw slightly. Smooth frosting and seal seams of both tiers, using a metal spatula. (If extra frosting is needed, add a drop or two of yellow food coloring to your homemade decorating icing until it blends with the color of the frosting on the purchased cakes.)
4. Use a 2″ round cookie cutter or a small glass to mark 3 circles evenly spaced on each side of the bottom tier. Then mark a circle in the center of each side of the top tier.
5. Using white decorating icing and star tube #17, pipe shells over each marked circle. Then pipe a rosette border around the top and bottom edges of both tiers.
6. Place a Royal Icing rosebud in the center of each circle. Place a Royal Icing rose in each corner on top of the bottom tier. Then center a cluster of 5 roses on the top tier.
7. Using reserved green Royal Icing and leaf tube #67, pipe leaves around roses. Refrigerate until ready to serve.

Wedding Cake with Silk Flowers

(80 servings; see photo, page 101)

6 recipes for Silver White Cake (see page 6) baked into 3 (13x9x2″) cake layers, 2 (10″) round cake layers and 2 (7″) round cake layers (You may have some excess batter.)
15½ c. decorating icing (see Index)
12 (¼″) wooden dowels, 6″ long
9″ cardboard round
6″ cardboard round
8″ circle of waxed paper
6″ circle of waxed paper
decorating tubes: round #2; star #21, #4B; drop flower #191; leaf #67
4 (5″) white ready-made pillars with 2 (6″) separator plates
silk flowers and leaves

1. To form the bottom tier, cut 1 (13x9x2″) cake in half lengthwise as illustrated. Place one of the remaining 13x9x2″ cakes on a sturdy base about 14″ square. Using some of the white decorating icing to join sections, place half of the cut cake on the base alongside the whole cake, long sides together, forming a square.

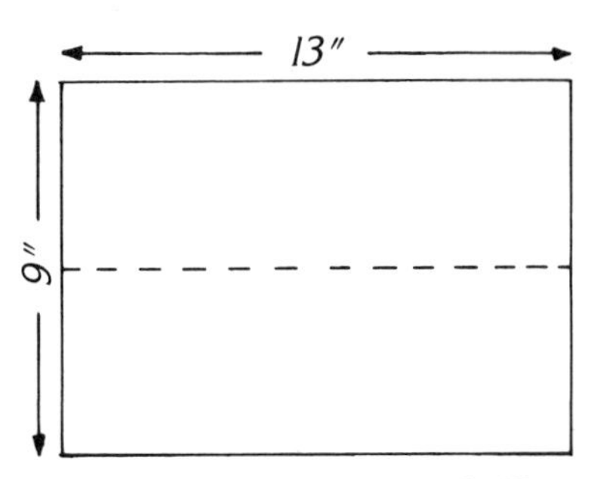

Cutting cake layer in half

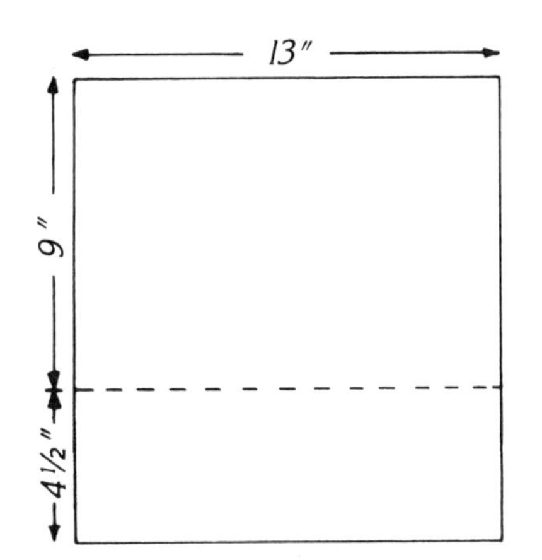

Assembling the bottom tier

Spread top of cake with some of the white decorating icing and top with remaining half of the cut cake and remaining 13x9x2″ cake. Trim edges to make an even square, about 12″.

Frost top and sides of bottom tier with white decorating icing. Smooth icing, using a metal spatula.
2. Fill remaining cake layers with more of the white decorating icing to form a 10″ middle tier and a 7″ top tier.

Place the middle tier on the 9″ cardboard round, and the top tier on the 6″ cardboard round. Frost top and sides of both tiers with more of the white decorating icing. Smooth icing, using a metal spatula.
3. Center the 8″ circle of waxed paper on top of the bottom tier. Use a toothpick to draw an 8″ circle on top of the tier, using the waxed paper as a pattern.

Remove the waxed paper and insert 1 dowel in the center of the tier and 6 dowels evenly spaced just inside the marked circle. Push each dowel all the way down through the bottom tier; then lift the dowels slightly and use

pruning shears to trim them to the same height as the tier. Push the dowels down again, level with the top of the tier.
4. Center the middle tier, including its cardboard base, on top of the bottom tier.
5. Use a toothpick to draw 2 large semicircles on each side of the bottom tier as shown (see photo, page 101).

Then mark 4 points at the bottom of the middle tier, marking a point just above the center of each side of the bottom tier. Draw 4 semicircles connecting these points, ending each at the point just above the end of a semicircle on the side of the bottom tier as shown.

Then draw 4 semicircles around the upper half of the side of the top tier and 4 semicircles on the lower half as shown.
6. Using more of the white decorating icing and round tube #2, pipe lace below semicircles on the bottom tier, above semicircles on the middle tier and between the semicircles on the top tier.
7. Center the 6″ circle of waxed paper on top of the 10″ middle tier. Use a toothpick to draw a 6″ circle on top of the tier, using the waxed paper as a pattern.

Remove the waxed paper and insert 1 dowel in the center of the tier and 4 dowels evenly spaced just inside the marked circle. Push each dowel all the way down through the middle tier; then trim the dowels level with the tier in the same way as for the bottom tier and push them down again.

Place pillars between separator plates and center them on top of the middle tier.

Center the top tier, including its cardboard base, on top of separator, arranging the top tier so that the ends of the semicircles on its side are directly above the ends of the semicircles on the middle tier.
8. Using white decorating icing and star tube #4B, pipe a shell border around bottom edge of bottom tier.

Change to star tube #21 and pipe a shell border over each semicircle on all 3 tiers. Then pipe a shell border around the separator plate at bottom of pillars. Continuing with white decorating icing and star tube #21, pipe a shell border around the top and bottom edges of the top tier.
9. Change to drop flower tube #191 and use remaining white decorating icing to pipe 1 drop flower in the center of each semicircle on the sides of the bottom tier. Change to leaf tube #67 and pipe 1 leaf on 2 sides of each flower.
10. Arrange several silk flowers on top of each corner of the bottom tier. Fill the centers of the middle and top tiers with remaining flowers.

Wedding Cake with Crystallized Flowers

(150 servings; see photo, page 104)

3 egg whites
17 or 18 thin-petaled fresh flowers with leaves (azaleas; alstroemeria or other small varieties of lilies; or small rosebuds)
1 c. sugar
12 recipes for Walnut Cake (see page 12) baked into 6 (10″) round cake layers, 2 (16″) round cake layers, 2 (12″) round cake layers and 2 (8″) round cake layers (You may have some excess batter.)
29 c. decorating icing (see Index)
4 (11″) cardboard rounds
8″ cardboard round
decorating tubes: star #21, #17; round #2
10″ circle of waxed paper
16 (¼″) wooden dowels, 6″ long
7″ circle of waxed paper
9″ cardboard round
1 (12″ or 14″) cake stand, 5″ high (or 6 Champagne glasses)
3 Champagne glasses

In advance:

Prepare crystallized flowers 3 days in advance.
1. Stir egg whites lightly with a fork; do not beat.
2. Dip fresh flowers and leaves, one at a time, into egg whites, covering all parts of flowers. Remove any excess egg white with a small paintbrush or your fingers.
3. Sift sugar over all parts of flowers to coat evenly. Gently shake off excess sugar. Place flowers on a sheet of waxed paper to dry.
4. Allow to dry in a cool place, 3 days.

To assemble:

1. Fill the 6 (10″) cake layers with some of the white decorating icing, using 2 layers for each cake, to form 3 "satellite" cakes.

Place each cake on an 11″ cardboard round. Frost tops and sides of cake layers. Smooth

icing, using a metal spatula. Set satellite cakes aside.
2. Fill remaining cake layers with more of the white decorating icing to form a 16″ bottom tier, a 12″ middle tier and an 8″ top tier.

Place the bottom tier on a sturdy base. Place the middle tier on the 11″ cardboard round, and the top tier on the 8″cardboard round.
3. Frost tops and sides of bottom, middle and top tiers with more of the white decorating icing.
4. Using more of the white decorating icing and star tube #17, pipe 2 rows of vertical shells around the bottom edge of the bottom tier. Then pipe a star on top of the tail of each shell in the top row as illustrated (see photo, page 104).

Change to round tube #2 and pipe a drop string border to join every other star. Repeat with alternate stars, overlapping the first string border as shown.
5. Change to star tube #21 and pipe a shell border around the top edge of each tier and all 3 satellite cakes.

Change to round tube #2 and pipe a drop string border on the side of each tier and all 3 satellite cakes just below the top, joining alternate shells as shown. Repeat to form an overlapping drop string border around the side of each tier and all 3 satellite cakes.
6. Center the 10″ circle of waxed paper on top of the bottom tier. Use a toothpick to draw a 10″ circle on top of the tier, using the waxed paper as a pattern.

Remove the waxed paper and insert 6 dowels evenly spaced just inside the marked circle. Then insert 3 more dowels evenly spaced, each 2″ from the center. Push each dowel all the way down through the bottom tier; then lift the dowels slightly and use pruning shears to trim them to the same height as the tier. Push the dowels down again, level with the top of the tier.

Place the middle tier on top of the bottom tier.
7. Using more of the white decorating icing and star tube #21, pipe a shell border around the bottom edge of the middle tier. Then pipe a shell border around the bottoms of all 3 satellite cakes.

Change to star tube #17 and pipe a second shell border just above the bottom borders of the middle tier and the 3 satellite cakes.
8. Continuing with white decorating icing and star tube #17, pipe a vertical shell border around the bottom edge of the top tier. Pipe a star on top of the tail of each shell.

Then pipe a scallop border below the shell border to fill any uncovered areas.

Finally, pipe a drop string border at the bottom edge of top tier, joining alternate stars. Repeat to form an overlapping drop string border as shown.
9. Center the 7″ circle of waxed paper on top of the middle tier. Use a toothpick to draw a 7″ circle on top of the middle tier, using the waxed paper as a pattern.

Remove the waxed paper and insert 1 dowel in the center of the tier and 6 dowels evenly spaced just inside the marked circle. Push each dowel all the way down through the middle tier; then lift the dowels slightly and use pruning shears to trim them to the same height as the tier. Push the dowels down again, level with the top of the tier.
10. Frost the 9″ cardboard round with more of the decorating icing and center it on top of the middle tier. Using white decorating icing and star tube #21, pipe a shell border around the cardboard round.

Change to star tube #17 and pipe a second shell border on top of the first.
11. Place the bottom tiers on cake stand, or balance them on 6 inverted Champagne glasses arranged in a circle.
12. Place 3 inverted Champagne glasses evenly spaced on top of the frosted 9″ cardboard round. (These will support the top tier.) Lift the glasses and center a small crystallized flower with leaves in the circle left by the rim of each glass.

Replace the glasses and place a dab of icing on the base of each glass. Place the top tier, including its cardboard base, on top of the glasses.
13. Arrange a spray of 4 or 5 crystallized flowers with leaves on the center of the top tier. Arrange 4 more flowers with leaves equally spaced around the edge of the middle tier. Place remaining flowers with leaves in clusters at the top edge of each satellite tier as shown.
14. Arrange the 3 satellite tiers around the bottom tier as shown, sliding part of each one underneath the bottom tier.

Index

References to color photographs are in italics.

A

B

C

D